AN INVITATION TO GEOGRAPHY

McGRAW-HILL SERIES IN GEOGRAPHY
Edward J. Taaffe and John W. Webb, *Consulting Editors*

Broek and Webb   A Geography of Mankind
Carlson   Africa's Lands and Nations
Cressey   Asia's Lands and Peoples
Cressey   Land of the 500 Million: A Geography of China
Demko, Rose, and Schnell   Population Geography: A Reader
Detwyler   Man's Impact on Environment
Fryer   Emerging Southeast Asia: A Study in Growth and Stagnation
Fryer   World Economic Development
Lanegran and Palm   An Invitation to Geography
Murphy   The American City: A Urban Geography
Pounds   Europe and the Soviet Union
Pounds   Political Geography
Raisz   General Cartography
Raisz   Principles of Cartography
Starkey and Robinson   The Anglo-American Realm
Thoman, Conklin, and Yeates   The Geography of Economic Activity
Trewartha   An Introduction to Climate
Trewartha, Robinson, and Hammond   Elements of Geography:
    Physical and Cultural
Trewartha, Robinson, and Hammond   Physical Elements of Geography
    (A republication of Part I of the above)
Trewartha, Robinson, and Hammond   Fundamentals of Physical
    Geography
Van Riper   Man's Physical World
Watts   Prinsiples of Biogeography: An Introduction to the Functional
    Mechanisms of Ecosystems

AN INVITATION TO GEOGRAPHY

DAVID A. LANEGRAN
Macalester College

RISA PALM
University of California, Berkeley

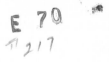

McGRAW-HILL BOOK COMPANY

New York   St. Louis   San Francisco   Düsseldorf
Johannesburg   Kuala Lumpur   London   Mexico
Montreal   New Delhi   Panama   Rio de Janeiro
Singapore   Sydney   Toronto

AN INVITATION TO GEOGRAPHY

1234567890 KPKP 79876543

This book was set in Theme by Creative Book Services,
division of McGregor & Werner, Inc. The editors were Janis
Yates and Susan Gamer; the designer was Rafael Hernandez; and the
production supervisor was Thomas J. Lo Pinto. The drawings were
done by Vantage Art, Inc.
The printer and binder was Kingsport Press, Inc.

Library of Congress Cataloging in Publication Data

Lanegran, David A
    An invitation to geography.

    (McGraw-Hill series in geography)
    Includes bibliographical references.
        1.   Human ecology—Addresses, essays, lectures.
2.   Geography—Text-books—1945-   3.   United
States—Social conditions—Addresses, essays, lectures.
I.   Palm, Risa, joint author.   II.   Title.
GE43.L36   910   72-10537
ISBN 0-07-036215-7

To: *Jan O. M. Broek
Teacher, Scholar,
and Friend*

CONTENTS

LIST OF MAPS AND GRAPHS

LIST OF CONTRIBUTORS

Ronald F. Abler
  Pennsylvania State University
John S. Adams
  University of Minnesota
Richard V. Francaviglia
  Antioch College
David A. Lanegran
  Macalester College
Vaughn Lueck
  University of Pittsburgh
Robert W. McColl
  University of Kansas
Risa Palm
  University of California, Berkeley
Roger Prestwich
  Cambridgeshire College of Art and Technology
Gerald F. Pyle
  University of Akron
John F. Rooney, Jr.
  Oklahoma State University
Richard Skaggs
  University of Minnesota

John G. Snowfield
Anoka-Hennepin School District
Yi-Fu Tuan
University of Minnesota

PREFACE

Geography is firmly anchored in the basic problems of human existence and in many of the experiences of daily life. When a young man asks where he should go to college, where he should seek work, where he should spend his vacation, or where he can find a date, he is asking questions which not only have importance and meaning to him but also are related to fundamental concepts of academic geography. When the fashion editor of a national women's magazine notes that hemlines and hairdos in certain cities lag behind the latest fashion trends in other cities, she is remarking on a process which is central to much research in geography. When government representatives debate means of alleviating metropolitan transportation problems by locating new routes for mass transit or discuss the integration of school systems by building new schools, when they discuss possible sites for a power plant or airport, or even when they reapportion their own legislative districts, they are dealing with questions with which geographers have been vitally concerned.

Geography's fundamental questions—"Where is it?" and "Why there?"—can thus be addressed to a seemingly endless variety of everyday situations. While the responses to these questions will vary with the purpose and the background of the inquirer, the questions themselves form the core of a discipline which incorporates a wealth of subject matter.

It is unfortunate that American geographers writing for the beginning student or for the general public have often ignored the everyday concerns and ordinary curiosity about place on which a conceptual geographic structure could be built.

An inventory of the anthologies presently available for introductory geography courses reveals a general absence of material written on subjects familiar to college students. Since the basic geographic concepts can usually be communicated in many ways, there is no reason why applications of geographic theory that are of interest to the student should not be utilized.

The purpose of this book is to direct beginning students toward an appreciation of the role which geographic questions play in the ordering of their environment and activities. It is hoped that such an appreciation may reopen communications between professional geographers and non-geographers at a time when exciting advances are being made in geographical research.

This book is not a sampler containing essays representative of all the subfields and opinions in geography. Anthologies attempting to provide a survey of geography are available, and reprint series allow readers to assemble a group of articles that fits their conception of the field. The goal of this book is, rather, to enable students to determine the significance of their location by asking basic geographic questions. The essays are not definitive statements but introductions to the geographic point of view; they have been selected to illustrate how the questions and concepts of geography can be applied to a wide range of situations.

The book begins with a discussion of geography. In the first essay we see that everyone actually uses geography in his or her daily activities, albeit in a very basic form.

In Part One, "Environmental Perception," the theme of personal geography is elaborated. The essay "Maps and the Perception of Space," in Part Two, focuses our attention on the manner in which we communicate some of our spatial information and values in a graphic form. This essay forms a bridge between the personal and group geography of Part One and the more disciplinary orientation of the readings in Part Three, "Spatial Organization." In Part Three, we turn from a discussion of how people organize space to a demonstration of how geographers use their concepts to explain events. In Part Four, geography is applied to the background of four contemporary problems in the United States. Although these essays are only introductions to the problems in question, they do illustrate how the geographic point of view can add to our interdisciplinary attempts to solve the pressing problems of society. In the final essay, "Monoculture or Miniculture?" in Part Five, we have a glimpse of the possible effects of a change in the nature of space through the geography of communications. In this selection, we see how the concepts of our discipline will have utility even in landscapes greatly altered by telecommunication.

Acknowledgments

A collection like this is the result of many minds, and we wish to thank all the essayists who contributed to our volume. Truly, without their help this book would not have been published. We appreciate the use of facilities at Normandale State Junior College during the early stages of manuscript preparation, and the encouragement of our colleagues there. In addition we wish to thank the patient geography students at Macalester College who read, discussed, and were questioned on the various early drafts of the essays, and whose comments and encouragement were greatly appreciated. Special thanks are due to John Berquist for constructing the maps in "Maps and the Perception of Space," to Sara Peterson for the maps in "Where Is Everybody?" and to James Peters for the map in "Families with Low Incomes in Rural America."

David A. Lanegran

Risa Palm

CHAPTER ONE

GEOGRAPHY IN EVERYDAY LIFE

DAVID A. LANEGRAN
RISA PALM

Where are you? Why are you reading this book in this particular place? How did you get to this place, and where will you go from here? Why will you go there? How are the various places you visit interconnected? These are simple questions, but their answers are likely to be very complicated. These questions illustrate the major theme of geography—the study of location. For centuries the question "Where am I?" has been foremost in men's minds.

The problem of knowing where you are has many variations. The child just learning about the world always keeps the location of his home, his place of security, well in mind. This preoccupation with a refuge is also characteristic of hunters in unfamiliar lands, as well as of tourists in strange cities who organize the city around their refuges—the airport and their hotel.

Knowing where you are also involves more complex information. Being "found" (locating yourself) means knowing the areas where you can best live according to your income, occupation, and social group. It means knowing which school is best for you. It means knowing where to go to meet a congenial member of the opposite sex. Being found also means knowing where an airport, an atomic reactor, a power plant, or a university should be located. To do any of these things with a degree of satisfaction, you must know in great detail where you are in relation to other features on the earth's surface.

To know where you are, you must know the location of other things and why they are there. You have to be able to answer questions like: "Where are Indian reservations located?" "Why are they located there?" "Where do people with an annual income in excess of $50,000 live?" "Why?" "Where is the urban population located at 10:00 A.M. on a weekday?" "And where are they at 10:00 P.M.?" "Why?" If you don't know the answers to these questions, you are "lost."

Knowing where you are means knowing how the surface of the earth varies and why. In order to ski we must know where snow falls. In order to take a spring vacation we must know where the weather is warm and sunny in April. We must be able to locate ourselves and other places in relation to the world circulation of energy and moisture. In addition, variations in the cultural landscape are important. Who could understand Belfast without a knowledge of the distribution of Catholics and Protestants? How many of Canada's problems are affected by the distribution of the French and English languages? Moreover, you must be able to place current events and political decisions in their spatial contexts. Why do hostilities in the Middle East have relevance for you? How does the relative location of South Vietnam, Laos, Cambodia, and Thailand affect your life? How does the location of a new airport change the growth patterns and land values of your city and thereby your property values and taxes?

The study of geography will help you to develop an understanding of the location of the elements of your environment. It is the geographer's task to analyze these elements and their interrelationships in detail, but in order for you to be found, you must do some evaluation on your own.

How do you and people in general keep from becoming lost? How do you keep track of where you are? These questions approach the complex question of the methods people use to organize space, that is, how we establish order in the space around us. By identifying elements of the system used to order space we will uncover the primitive or basic notions of geography.

GEOGRAPHICAL PRIMITIVES: DIRECTION AND DISTANCE

As you look around and think about the room you are now in, you are probably seeing it in relation to yourself. We are all self-centered in our view of space. At the core of the system of spatial organization is the concept of direction. Although we do not completely understand the process you use to relate to your environment, you learned at a very early age to divide the world into the visible and invisible (front and back). While in the womb, you developed a sense of gravity, and from that came concepts of up and down. Eventually you learned to divide the world according to the sides of your body, left and right. We can call these directions personal or egocentric because each individual determines them for himself. We all order our surroundings with these concepts, but when we try to convey understanding of our ordering systems to another person, for example when describing routes, we often encounter difficulties. Inanimate objects like trees, rocks, or tables seldom have a left or right, and how do we determine the front and back of a hole? What does the expression "just a little way *down* the road" really mean?

Because of these limitations of egocentric ordering systems, we have developed a "domicentric" system; that is, we substitute for ourselves a set of inanimate objects whose location in space, if not fixed, is at least predictable. We develop a set of angular relationships between points or landmarks, and we organize our spatial environment around them. We learn the location of new places in terms of the location of known places. For most of us, home or our present abode is the most constant, dominant feature in our system of landmarks, and for this reason we call these systems domicentric.

North, south, east, and west, the conventional directions, are based on a worldwide landmark, the rising and setting of the sun, augmented and refined by the use of the earth's magnetic field and the location of the earth in relationship to visible stars. The use of celestial landmarks has become common throughout the world because of the problems involved in communication with domicentric directions. The task of organizing geographic areas is so large that a system based on local landmarks becomes too complicated.

Although the importance of directions in navigation is well recognized, few realize that concepts of direction also affect us in other ways. Could you be reading this book if you were unable to differentiate the left side of the page from the right? Could you write your name if you could not distinguish the left side of your body from the right? What is the difference between dog and god? How important is the concept of left and right in the regulation of traffic?

We have also given values to our concepts of direction. The explanations of these values are complicated, and their effects are often difficult to assess. The religious aspects of direction, for example, while not entirely understood, are still widely recognized. The word "orientation" is based on the practice of putting "orient" at the top of the map. The medieval Christian map makers did this because they thought the Garden of Eden was located somewhere in Asia, and therefore, as a place important to God, it belonged at the top of the map. Today when we use the word "orientation," we no longer mean the placement of Asia at the top of the map, but rather we use it to convey the idea of goals. Most of us have a set of spatial goals, places of particular importance to us that we want to visit or be in. For example, the goal for a suburban housewife may be a shopping center or an especially fine restaurant. You are most likely oriented toward school and a number of recreational places. Religious people are oriented toward holy sites and places of pilgrimages. American outdoorsmen are oriented toward wild areas.

What do directions mean to you? Does north symbolize wilderness, freedom, and adventure? What images does east evoke in your mind? All cultures generally use directions in the same way, although the interpretations given to directions may vary considerably. However, directions are only part of our spatial ordering system; we also use distance.

DISTANCE

The role of distance in human interaction has been the topic of many heated discussions in the social and physical sciences. But before we can take part in these discussions, we must decide what distance means. Geographers recognize two major ways of evaluating distance: absolute and relative. The basic element in the concept of distance is contiguity, the property of nearness. Early in our lives we all develop the ability to distinguish objects as near or far, within or outside our reach. Like egocentric directions, such notions of contiguity or proximity are not precise enough for clear communication of location. We therefore soon learn to manipulate society's measures. Absolute distance on the surface of the earth refers to the space or the interval of the earth's surface between two points. We usually think of this distance in terms of standard or conventional units to which we compare the distance in question. Most of our early measurements were based on either references to the body such as walking paces, the spread of a hand, the length of a foot, or references to some familiar standard in the real or mythical environment such as the volume of a hog's head. These units were used in the various estimates of the size of Paul Bunyan and his ox. Bunyan was so big that 97 ax handles would just barely measure him from hip to hip. The estimate is a little misleading, however, as no one is sure whether the ordinary ax handle is meant or one of Paul's, which was seven or perhaps seventy times as long as the ordinary one. At any rate, it can be seen that he was no little fellow. The ox, on the other hand, was said to be 24 ax handles and a plug of tobacco between the eyes. Units such as these provide standards against which we can compare a given expanse of space, and may be used by geographers in discussions of absolute distance.

Important as these measures are, we are often more interested in the relative distance between places. The earth is not a billiard ball, and consequently its surface is not everywhere the same. You can appreciate the difference between 10 miles of freeway and 10 miles of bog. For a running halfback, even a foot through the defensive line of a pro-football team is much longer than 100 yards of suburban sidewalk. Most of us transform standard units of absolute distance. The modern city dweller typically organizes the urban landscape in terms of travel time. Home is 30 minutes from school or work, not 20 miles. The concept of relative distance may be called other names, such as "ecological distance," but its essence remains the same—the ease of communication and transportation between places.

Relative distance varies according to an individual's or a group's perception of the distance. For some of us, the space we can travel through on a crowded urban freeway in 30 minutes seems much smaller than the space we can traverse in 30 minutes on a rural highway. In addition, we function as though familiar places are closer to us than those that are unfamiliar. Have you ever noticed that it seems to take much longer going to a new place than it does to return?

Distance, like direction, has value imparted to it by our perception.

Space, personal
Some thirty inches from my nose
The frontier of my Person goes,
And all the untilled air between
Is private pagus *or demesne.*
Stranger, unless with bedroom eyes
I beckon you to fraternize,
Beware of rudely crossing it:
I have no gun but I can spit. [1]

The images of ourselves we see in photographs show only a part of us—our physical bodies. Photographs do not show the volume of space surrounding our bodies which we call our own, and into which we allow others only under unusual circumstances. This space is commonly referred to as our personal space. Although the extent of an individual's personal space varies according to his personality and circumstances, certain regularities can be observed.

Our attitude toward our personal space, or the distance we maintain between ourselves and others, is one aspect of our perception of the total environment. Human beings, like all animals, acquaint themselves with the environment around them through their senses. Therefore we use our sense organs to measure our personal space. We respond to sounds, smells, touches, and visual images with an appropriate reaction—welcoming, evasive, or defensive. Although a great deal is known about the ways our bodies and nervous systems perceive space, such questions lie more properly in the realms of psychology and physiology. Therefore let us instead concern ourselves with how the phenomenon of personal space affects our behavior.

By careful observations, Edward Hall, an American anthropologist, was able to develop a system of "action zones" based on distance. He calls these zones intimate, personal, social, and public. Each zone is further divided into a close and a far phase. The most restricted zone is, of course, the intimate distance. The close phase in this zone is for physical interactions like making love, soothing, defending, or fighting. We can smell, feel, and hear the person's body in such situations, although our view of it is incomplete and distorted. In the far phase, body contact is less likely although people can still maintain contact with their hands. Personal distance ranges from 1½ to 4 feet. At this distance we talk softly and can normally smell and hear the other person's body. It is a distance for friendly interaction. Social distance—close phase 4 to 7 feet, far phase 7 to 12 feet—is the zone for formal business and social exchanges. Information and opinions are exchanged in a low voice. Public distance—close phase 12 to 25

[1] W. H. Auden, *About the House*, Random House, New York, 1965, p. 4.

feet, far phase anything over 25 feet—is, as the name indicates, the distance for communications on an impersonal level. It is the zone for politicians, preachers, and lecturers. These distances are approximate and were determined by observing Americans living in the northern portions of the United States. As might be expected, these uses of space are culturally determined; that is, they are learned behavior and vary from people to people. Middle-class Americans generally keep their distance from each other. They arrange living room furniture along the walls so that they can converse in a loud voice. Their conversations are most comfortable when the speakers are at arm's distance from each other. They occasionally run into problems, however. When an American and an Englishman walk down a sidewalk together, a strange game is played. The American, seeking to maintain his distance, speaks rather loudly and edges away from his companion. The Englishman, also seeking to maintain the proper distance, speaks softly and pursues the fleeing American. This game continues until the American steps into the gutter or bumps the wall of a building, leaving the Englishman amazed at the loud American and his strange behavior.

Distance also affects our behavior in other ways. Consider the "Fisherman's Delight," a tavern in one of North America's beer-drinking interior regions. This tavern sells beer at 5 cents a gallon! Although a few of you may have drunk your fill of beer, most people (all people over thirty) have a capacity for beer that is finite. Therefore, there is a limit on the amount of liquid gold they can consume. In addition most people have placed a limit on the amount of money they will pay for beer. If the price of beer is close to this maximum, people will limit their drinking. Should the price ever rise above this maximum, they would stop drinking. Assuming that consumption of beer is related in some way to the price of beer, we can draw the graph shown in Figure 1-1.

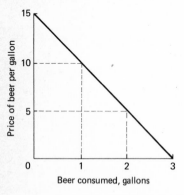

Figure 1-1 The relationship between the price of beer and the amount consumed. In this situation the greater the price, the less the amount of beer drunk.

According to this graph (demand curve), people will drink no beer priced at 15 cents a gallon, 1 gallon if priced at 10 cents, and if the beer is free, they will stop after consuming 3 gallons (theoretical maximum capacity). In this simple case, the amount of beer consumed is related directly to the cost of the beer.

Let us return to the Fisherman's Delight. Assume you live 5 miles from this palace of culture and it costs you 1 cent per mile to drive your car. Therefore, if you drive there to drink, the real cost of the beer is 5 cents per gallon plus the 5 cents travel cost, or 10 cents. A graph incorporating travel costs or distance in the demand curve would look like Figure 1-2.

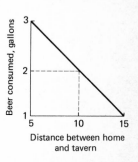

Figure 1-2 The relationship between the distance separating tavern and home and the amount of beer drunk. The addition of travel cost to the price of beer produces a situation where the closer a person is to the tavern, the greater the amount of beer he will drink.

The price at the establishment is fixed at 5 cents per gallon. Now the variable determining consumption is travel cost or distance. We can see from this simple graph that people who live far away can afford to drink less than people who live nearby. This is how the principle of "distance decay" operates. Interaction between two places decreases in frequency and intensity as the distance increases.

The world seldom conforms to our models, and so few behavior patterns fit our simple curve of distance decay. Nevertheless these regularities do exist. How many times a year do you visit or telephone people living in your immediate neighborhood? How often do you go more than one hundred miles to shop or for entertainment?

It should be remembered that geographers recognize both absolute and relative distance. Many times interactions between places are impeded by either physical or perceptual barriers, which have the effect of increasing the distance between places. Likewise, certain forms of transportation systems have the effect of reducing distance between places. If these transport systems are in the form of a network or set of paths (like the railroad or freeways), places on the system are brought closer together while places outside are farther removed. Thus we can see how these two basic elements in our spatial environment affect our behavior in space. Their influence has only recently come under study, and so you might like to conduct some experiments on your own.

GEOGRAPHIC PRIMITIVES: SHAPE AND SIZE

By combining distance and direction we can develop two additional fundamental aspects of geography, *shape* and *size*, or magnitude. "Shape" is defined as a spatial form with respect to a relatively constant periphery. Although the effects of a particular shape are important to the function of any phenomenon, to measure and describe a given shape is often difficult. We can compare the shape of an urban area to regular polygons, and we can measure the sides and angles, but unless the urban area happens to fit exactly, this method has limited value. We can also compare the urban area to an analogue, that is, to a well-known standard shape in our environment such as a doughnut, an oak leaf, or a pancake. This doesn't solve our problem, however, because the shapes of dough-nuts, leaves, and pancakes are not always constant. Some efforts have been made to describe shapes numerically, that is, to measure shape. As you might expect, this is not an easy task. To date, these attempts have not fulfilled the require-ments for description, for without some visual aid to be used as a standard of reference, the numbers do not convey a spatial image.

Size, or physical magnitude, does not present many problems to geography. The size of a phenomenon like a city may be expressed in relative terms, a size larger or smaller than another city, or it may be expressed in absolute terms, a population of n and an areal extent of so many square miles. It is hard for many people to visualize cities in terms of population or square miles, and consequent-ly much description is couched in comparative terms.

The shapes and sizes of phenomena are closely related and together they influence the functioning of a phenomenon. For example, the cost of delivering electricity to a lineal city 100 miles long and 3 miles wide is different from the cost of delivery to a circular city of equal area. The effect of size is equally obvious.

LOCATION: ABSOLUTE AND RELATIVE

The basic notions of geography, distance and direction, along with their derivatives, shape and size, are used by all people to organize space. The task of geographers is somewhat more specialized. We seek to understand the earth as the home of man. Therefore, the goal of geographers is to understand the loca-tion and character of places. As you might expect, the term "location" has meanings for the geographer which are not always used by the layman. The location of a place in relation to the earth grid is known as its mathematical location or its position. Position may be expressed on a global level by degrees of longitude and latitude, on a regional level by reference to survey systems such as township and range, and on an urban level by street names. At present, the positions of most places of interest to geographers are known, and thus we are no longer concerned with determining them. The knowledge of a place's position in the global or even the urban setting is not meaningful in itself. To prove this, tell your Aunt Maud that you live at 901 College Avenue, and carefully record her reaction. Then tell her something about the place, e.g., it is a coed dorm or a free love community, located next to the regional LSD distributors. Carefully record her reaction. Geographers concern themselves with the character of places and their locations in terms of other places.

Just as the relative distance between places is often more important than the absolute distance, the relative location of a place is most often more important than its absolute location, or latitude and longitude. Two aspects of location can be identified: *site* and *situation*. Site refers to those aspects of a place's location that have to do with local or internal forces or processes. It should be noted that site is thus more than simply a statement describing the actual ground on which phenomena occur. Situation, on the other hand, refers to external aspects of a place: its relationships with other places. Therefore, when geographers consider the situation of places, they focus primarily on how places are interconnected.

SCALE

Site and situation depend upon the scale of our inquiry, or the level of generalization at which we seek answers to our questions. If we are examining a school, the movement of students from room to room and the communication of ideas and information from teacher to student are site characteristics. The pattern of commuting from home to school by students is an external aspect of the school and is thus an aspect of the school's situation. If, however, we take the city in which the school is located as our place, the pattern of students commuting to school is an internal process of the city and becomes an aspect of the city's site.

The combination of site and situation within the framework of a particular scale of inquiry provides the basis for the description of a single place. We are usually more interested in a comparison of several places than in the description of a unique, single place. For example, in describing your hometown to a stranger, you might choose to verbally escort him to a single city block, but he would probably learn much more about the city if the character of several blocks from various parts of the city was compared.

REGIONALIZATION

We constantly engage in classifying and comparing places when we talk of "seaports," "farm villages," and "college towns," or when we talk of "downtown," "wealthy suburbs," and "ghettos." We may refer to this classification and comparison as "areal differentiation," the study of the variations of distributions in earth space, or of "regionalization," the study of areas which are "alike" or have unity according to the elements we have used to define them.

The problems involved in classifying and comparing places, and of defining meaningful regions are acute, not only to the academic geographer but also to citizens and interest groups who live in or are interested in the areas being defined. We are well aware of the problems which have at times been created by placing an international boundary in the midst of people who are of the same nationality, or of joining together people who have neither language nor religion nor customs in common. We are also beginning to realize that within our cities people have widely varied views about what constitutes a neighborhood or a community or whether the concepts of an areal neighborhood or place-bound community are even relevant to life in the 1970s. For example, are ghettos homogeneous, or alike, in all respects? Are all ghetto residents members of the same "interest community"? Will a single urban plan meet with unanimous approval or disapproval in the ghetto? Do ghetto residents have anything at all in common besides a house or apartment in an area which has been dubbed "ghetto"? Such questions concerning regionalization in the city are of obvious practical relevance and are also of interest to those who want to understand the geography of the city.

SUMMARY: THE GEOGRAPHIC PRIMITIVES

Although in our analysis we have separated concepts of distance, direction, shape, size, relative and absolute location, site and situation, scale and regionalization from one another, they are all interconnected, and to some degree they overlap each other. Distance and direction are the most fundamental and, as we have seen, are greatly influenced by an individual's interpretations of his surroundings. By combining the concepts of distance and direction we can develop shape and size. With these four primitive notions we can locate ourselves in space. First we order the world around our bodies. Gradually we expand our frame of reference until we are able to utilize our society's standards for measuring distance and direction. Once we can locate ourselves in space, we can then locate places in terms of other places (relative location) and eventually we can locate places in regard to something as abstract as our system of latitude and longitude. Having begun the fascinating study of places, we soon learn that we can divide the characteristics of places into internal aspects (site) and external aspects (situation). Site and situation are determined by the scale of our study— the size of the places in which we are interested. Scale, or level of generalization, is a concept found in all sciences, but geographers pay close attention to it because of its role in questions of site and situation.

Areal differentiation and regionalism are classifications based on the elements of site and situation at a particular scale. Now that we have these concepts mastered, we can go on to an examination of some that are more complex.

SPATIAL CIRCULATION SYSTEMS: THE NOTIONS OF CONNECTIVITY, HIERARCHY, AND SPATIAL ORGANIZATION

Back in the good old days, before the advent of the mini, midi, and maxi skirts, young ladies could tell the world how well "connected" they were by altering the length of their skirts. In those simpler times, the shorter the skirt, the more modern the girl. She was getting all the latest fashion news from Paris, London, and New York. While girl-watching is not necessarily a part of field work in geography, it does reveal some of geography's foundations, especially the concept of connectivity. "Connectivity" refers to the extent to which places are bound to each other by many and diverse linkages. Places may be interconnected by commuters going from their homes to shop and to work. Places may be bound by migrants seeking new homes or temporary places of employment. Places are also connected to each other by flows of money in the form of purchases, loans, and taxes. In addition, telephone calls, mail service, and the shipment of both raw materials and manufactured goods link places together. Nodal places thus exchange large numbers of goods, people, and ideas. Marginal locations, on the other hand, have few connections with other places and participate in few exchanges.

However we define and measure separation or connectivity, it seems that we can always locate ourselves in a circulation surface or network; that is to say, it is possible to transform or represent a multitude of dimensions in two- or sometimes three-dimensional space. On a communications surface, you can move in any direction with equal ease. In a network, however, circulation is possible only along certain paths. Obviously those places not on the network are isolated. In times past, when everyone walked, humans existed on a surface. However, transportation and communication technology developed a system of networks. Canals and wagon roads made it possible to carry large cargo faster than people walking, but only when the canals or roads went to the places they were interested in. The railroad linked the nation, but it so isolated the small-town trade centers it bypassed that many of them ceased to exist. The circulation system gained speed but sacrificed choice of direction. The grid pattern of city streets is a fairly close approximation of transportation surface; the freeway is a network. Distance, or separation, is the key to locating yourself in these networks. As Lueck indicates, separation is most often not measured by physical distance.

To return to our well-connected young lady, ideas about fashion are one of the many ways in which people and therefore places are bound together. If a girl lives in a place which is well connected to a fashion center like New York, she will know about all the latest style changes. On the other hand, if she is in a marginal location, one poorly connected, she will be less likely to learn of changes in style and will be content to wear yesterday's fashion.

It will come as no great surprise to you that geographers think that some locations in this interconnected system of places called the earth are more important than others. Local pride notwithstanding, in the context of the North American urban system, New York is more important than Cando, North Dakota. New York's importance results from its having more functions, connections, and people. We can order cities in these terms: function, connections, size. Such an ordering system is called a "hierarchy." Places with many people and functions, and with extensive connections, would occupy the higher levels. All places at the same level in the hierarchy would be similar in terms of types of functions and intensity of connections with other places.

THE RELATIONSHIP BETWEEN MAN AND LAND

Although spatial analysis is fundamental to geography, we must go beyond these questions to study the interaction between the physical elements of the environment and man and the cultural elements. Needless to say, the cultural and physical elements of the environment are closely intertwined. One deep breath of city air is enough to convince most skeptics of the important effect man has had on the environment. We are constantly exposed to the results of man's impact on the physical landscape. We drive on and through man-made landscapes and constantly use resources from one part of the landscape while littering another. Because contemporary problems in man and land relationships occur in specific places, they are open to geographic inquiry. One such problem has been the location of power generating plants.

Throughout the postwar period the need for electric energy in the United States has expanded. In response to these needs the power industry built large steam generating plants fired by either coal or nuclear fuels. These plants need a constant source of water for cooling, and when possible, they are supplied with coal by way of barge. Obviously, the places that meet this requirement are river valleys. However, the power plants return heated water to the rivers. This practice can cause the river temperature to rise and create an environment unfavorable for game fish. In addition, any barge traffic adds to the congestion in urban waterways, and causes consternation among the weekend commodores. The power plants' exhaust, or the flue gases, can also create problems of fly ash and the concentration of sulfur dioxide or nitrogen oxides. The problems of exhaust are compounded when atmospheric conditions conspire to either hold the gases near the surface of the earth under a temperature inversion, or deposit them on residential areas with strong winds. If a plant is located in a river valley and has chimneys that are level with the river bluffs, the residents living on the bluffs tend to join conservation groups. Obviously, we must be able to answer the "where" questions in terms of both the cultural and physical landscapes. Geography is the discipline equipped to do this.

THE ROLE OF ENVIRONMENTAL PERCEPTION AND ATTITUDES

People's opinions about what the world is, how it got that way, and what it should be like, are very diverse. Even basic things, like the shape of the earth, have been open to question. Every Italian knows that Columbus proved the earth is round—but *did* he? In a letter to his patrons, the king and queen of Spain, he wrote:

I have come to another conclusion respecting the earth, namely that it is not round as they describe, but of the form of a pear, which is very round except where the stalk grows, at which part it is most prominent; or like a round ball, upon one part of which is a prominence like a woman's nipple, this protrusion being the highest and nearest the sky, situated under the equinoctial line, and at the eastern extremity of this sea, —I call that the eastern extremity, where the land and the islands end. [2]

Columbus then goes on to present evidence that he felt substantiated his opinion and explains his reasons for believing that the Garden of Eden was located on this protrusion. Columbus's opinion is no longer accepted, but his statement does illustrate the possibility of different views of the spatial environment, views which vary with time and from culture to culture.

In recent years we have grown more sensitive to the implications of environment. Places sacred to some individuals are seen as sources for industrial raw materials by others. Unfortunately, in many cases people's perceptions of the environment do not merely differ; they conflict. Such conflicts are not easily resolved. Although geographic research on these questions has only begun, it holds the promise of greatly enhancing our understanding of the relationships between man and land.

GEOGRAPHY AND EVERYDAY LIFE

Geography's concern with places, spatial analysis, and the relationships between man and land gives it a unique and vital role among all other disciplines. It is a field in which the concerns of both the social and physical sciences converge in the study of specific places. It functions like a bridge between these two major branches of academic life. More important than this academic role is its viewpoint or approach to problems. Most problems become more understandable when seen in their spatial context and in terms of the relationships between man and land. Because their concern for the welfare of society is not confined to the academic community, geographers are able to communicate to the majority of the population on subjects of mutual concern. The geographers, however, always seek answers to the questions "Where?" and "Why here rather than somewhere else?"

[2] R. H. Major, *Christopher Columbus: Four Voyages to the New World*, Corinth Books, New York, 1961, p. 130.

PART ONE

ENVIRONMENTAL PERCEPTION AND BEHAVIOR

Where do you spend your vacations? Are you attracted to soft landscapes filled with rounded objects colored in light shades of green and brown? Are you enchanted with rolling hills dotted with clumps of hardwood trees seen through a mist? Do you like cosy and secluded nooks and crannies? Or do you prefer firm landscapes filled with straightedged objects of strongly hued colors? Does your enchanted forest consist of pointed evergreens standing boldly against a big, bright blue sky or standing dark against the brilliant snow? Are you attracted by the steep slopes, rocky crags, and deep V-like valleys of young mountain ranges? Do you like free and unencumbered spaces? The many different answers to these questions indicate that we all perceive or relate to our environment and act according to our interpretation of what we sense.

People interested in human behavior realize that we act in accordance to what we think the world is like. We can summarize this realization as follows: any spatial behavior is a result of resources, modified by people's perceptions of them and people's access, or ability to get to the resources. Thus, the likelihood of a person going to a particular place is a function of the attributes of the place (resources) modified by the person's knowledge of and attitudes toward those attributes (perception) and further qualified by the availability of access to the place (accessibility). For example, a person is likely to go to a public beach if a public beach exists, if he knows of the beach and likes to swim at public beaches, and if he can either take his car or another form of transportation to the beach in a reasonable period of time.

If we want to be able to explain spatial behavior, we must determine the significance of these three terms. For many years geographers and others have been engaged in the process of locating various resources such as precious minerals, human manufactures, and routes from one place to another. The locating process is complex but relatively well understood. We know much less about people's attitudes toward resources, and we know even less about the manner in which these attitudes develop in cultures or in individuals. In the past few decades scholars from a wide variety of disciplines have concerned themselves with this question and have produced some exciting findings. Psychologists have focused their research on laboratory experiments using either rats or human subjects. Their work is seminal, but the scale at which the psychologists conduct their study and the number of controls available to them make the results of their work difficult to utilize at the broader scale available to geographers. For example, Tolman has found that rats apparently have the ability to remember complex spatial relationships. This ability enables laboratory animals to manipulate mazes under a variety of controlled conditions. Geographers have taken this notion and have expanded it to hypothesize that humans have these cognitive maps, and these maps enable them to maneuver through their environment without losing their way. There are, however, considerable differences between a laboratory rat and the contemporary American city dweller. The most significant is that it is difficult to persuade people to become subjects for laboratory experiments. They have seen too many movies of the Frankenstein variety and are afraid of mad social scientists. Nonetheless, several geographers are attempting to unravel the elements of the human mental map.

The psychologists' work with human beings is extraordinarily interesting but largely focused on the mechanics of human perception. Their work on the manner in which we sense our environment is fundamental to the other behavioral sciences although, as in the case of the research performed on small animals, it is not directly applicable. Sociology, anthropology, and political science also contain a growing body of literature on the effect of people's attitudes on spatial behavior. This research reflects the viewpoint of the various disciplines but has wide implication in the behavioral sciences.

Because so many people are interested in the manner in which our knowledge and perceptions of the environment affect our behavior, there exists a babel of names for the field in which they work. As many as twenty-one different names have been used, ranging from "environmental psychology" to "psychological ecology" to "psychogeography."

Despite the wealth of terminology, it is possible to categorize the research on the effects of human environmental perception on human spatial behavior. There are studies that focus on people's *information* about the environment, and studies that focus on people's *attitudes* toward space and elements of the environment.

It is fairly obvious that spatial opportunities or places in the objective environment do not exist for people who are unaware of them. If you do not know of stores selling phonograph records at discount prices, you are doomed to pay list price. If you do not know where to find the latest style, you're destined to be "out of it." Some recent work in geography has examined the correlation between spatial activities of identifiable groups and their knowledge of environmental opportunities. These studies indicate that we tend to confine our activities to places we are familiar with, or at least places we have some knowledge of. This insight becomes valuable when we are confronted by people who are forced to live in inadequate housing because sound houses are not available in the area they are familiar with and they are unaware of better conditions elsewhere in the city. In such situations a third party may be useful in helping these people search for a better place to live.

Most of us believe that the area people confine the bulk of their activities to—their "action space"—is directly influenced by their "mental map," or their knowledge of the world they occupy. Likewise, we are convinced that spatial experience has a great effect on people's knowledge of and attitudes toward their environment. Mental maps affect action spaces and action spaces affect mental maps. We must determine the degree and kind of effect, and eventually we may be able to use this knowledge to alleviate some of the inequities produced by restricted action spaces and limited mental maps.

The second aspect of this two-part category is composed of those studies that deal with people's attitudes toward space and the influence these attitudes have in determining spatial behavior. There is a rich and varied literature on this subject, and much of it has great social significance. These studies include the work discussed in the first chapter on personal space. In addition Robert Ardrey would have us believe that the attitudes which lead us to surround ourselves with a bubble of personal space, and keep us at our proper distance for various forms of social behavior, are related directly to the instinctive territorial behavior in animals. He also contends that this territorial behavior in animals lies at the root of nationalism and international warfare. While acknowledging Ardrey's information on such behavior in animals, most other scholars are reluctant to make the connections between spatial attitudes of human beings and animals so explicit. These scholars argue that nationalism and other forms of aggressive behavior are learned.

No matter how they are derived, our attitudes toward places are strongly affected by notions of ownership or possession. Most cultures have regularized social rules for maintenance and exchange of property rights, but fluid situations often occur. Keiser reports a discussion among members of a black gang in Chicago, the Vice Lords, concerning plans for going to a movie at the Central Park. One gang member mentioned that the Lords used to "have" the show but it now "belonged" to the Roman Saints. Another member answered:

Yeah, man, we owned that Central Park show! Couldn't none of the Roman Saints come. They was afraid, Jack! They know we'd whup their ass.[1]

Differing attitudes and values have often caused conflict over space, but occasionally shared attitudes toward places unite people.

The most striking example of how attitudes toward space bind together people of diverse languages, races, and economic systems is in India. For three millennia the region inhabited by the people practicing Hinduism has been considered sacred by them and distinct from the nonsacred, non-Hindu world. This sacred region is India. Here the Hindu gods have established the arena of their activity, and here the land has been purified and made fit for Indo-Aryans to occupy. This attitude toward India as hallowed ground, the only area where the fire god had ritually purified the land, united the people culturally although they were never a part of one single political entity.

One of the forces that has fostered a unity in the midst of diversity is the pilgrimage. Each year millions of devout Hindus visit sacred places outside their immediate area. This movement takes them through areas where languages other than their own are spoken and where people live differently. The information pilgrims gain from their experiences is especially significant because in India's agricultural society people live in villages that are basically self-sufficient, and therefore they have few reasons to leave their home area. Were it not for the pilgrimages, the villages of India would languish in deep isolation.[2]

We, too, have our sacred places, such as historic sites and natural wonders where members of our society can commune with nature. However, our culture is still a good deal more immature than the Indian, and so our notions of sanctity in space do not have the power to draw us together in the same way that the pilgrimages in India unite the Hindus.

Antisacred places also exist in the United States. These are locales where people we do not like are forced to live. Our urban areas contain several such places. They are not all contiguous spaces easily defined in absolute terms, but they are nonetheless very real. Consider the space occupied by the group called "homeless men," "urban nomads," or "bums," according to the view of the describer. These people live in the streets, alleys, and old buildings fringing the central commercial core of cities. They sleep in safe places—under bridges, in parks, behind empty buildings, or in missions. The distance between these men and most Americans cannot be measured in miles. They are separated from you by a gulf in relative distance so great that you cannot see or feel across it. Our society has confined these men to valueless space, to areas we don't occupy. When they venture into public places such as warm libraries on cold winter nights, they are

[1] R. Lincoln Keiser, *The Vice Lord Warriors of the Streets*, Holt, New York, 1969, pp. 22-25.
[2] Surinder M. Bhardwaj, "The Religious Organization of Space," unpublished essay.

hurried out to make room for the legitimate patron. Like the Hindu pilgrims, they travel great distances. Unlike the pilgrims of India, they do not bind places together. As with the Hindu pilgrims, attitudes toward places deterimine their spatial behavior. Their behavior, unlike that of the pilgrims of India, is determined by the spatial attitudes of others, however.

These examples indicate that studies of the influence of environmental perception on spatial behavior have produced insights at a variety of scales. In addition, investigations have been conducted of people's behavior in rooms, on campuses, and in hospitals. Using the information on personal space, these studies show how the arrangement of chairs in a room can either break down or reinforce the barriers around the personal space of individuals. Other studies by Robert Sommer have focused on how perceptions of personal space influence the utilization of study areas, classrooms, and dormitories.

Under the leadership of the urban planner Kevin Lynch, several architects and social scientists have concerned themselves with environmental perception at another scale. Lynch's book, *The Image of the City*, is about the look of cities and the importance and the possibility of affecting the look. He structures his discussion of the image of the environment around the notion of legibility of cityscapes and their imageability. "Legibility" means apparent clarity or the degree to which elements of the city can be recognized and ordered into a pattern. Objects are imageable; that is, they have attributes which give them a high probability of evoking a strong image or are easily remembered by any person who sees them. Image building, according to Lynch, is a two-way interaction between the observer and the environment. The environment "suggests distinction," and the individual observer selects elements and identifies and orders the environment according to his experience and values.

Working with residents of Boston, Newark, and Los Angeles, Lynch gathered data about the image of cities held by local residents by asking them to describe routes through the city and to draw sketch maps of the city. He found that despite individual differences, people tend to organize their images around paths, areas, nodes, edges, and landmarks. Lynch would have planners design cities so they would be legible and would be recognizable by their residents, for he says: "A sense of place enhances every human activity that occurs there."[3]

Although a few geographers have focused on perceptions of regions and nations, most research has concentrated on specific elements in the environment. Geographers have studied people's attitudes toward such hazards in the environment as drought, floods, storms, air and water pollution. This work has been greatly aided by studies in psychology and is perhaps the most rigorous of all the analyses of environmental perception. Ian Burton, Robert Kates, and Gilbert White, along with their students, have found that variations in perception among

[3] Kevin Lynch, *The Image of the City*, M.I.T., Cambridge, 1960.

people living in areas where hazards occur can be explained by three general principles. First, people are very sensitive to hazards that are directly related to the resources which drew people into the area—for example, water pollution on a fishing lake. People are also sensitive to hazards that occur frequently and to those that affect them directly. Currently, under the auspices of UNESCO, attempts are underway to make cross-cultural studies of people's attitudes toward hazards. Research on environmental perception such as that outlined above will continue at a rapid rate. Like most exciting research topics, it includes experts from many disciplines as well as individual scholars.

The following essay, written by Yi-Fu Tuan, provides a synthesis of our knowledge on the manner in which people perceive their environment. He has divided the factors influencing our attitudes into three classes: the influences resulting from our being human, those resulting from our belonging to a certain culture, and those resulting from our individuality.

First, we see that the human species seems to share perceptions that are influenced by body size. We see only things larger than a minimum size and smaller than our field of vision. In addition, we all are inclined to see our environment as made up of discrete objects. Tuan argues that we tend to order these objects into opposite pairs and try to resolve these contrasting pairs with intermediate terms and symbols of harmony. As a group we share cultural norms, and subgroups often have different attitudes toward or information about the environment. Finally, we see how our perceptions are influenced by the physical variations among individuals.

CHAPTER TWO

PERCEIVING AND EVALUATING THE WORLD: THREE STANDPOINTS

YI-FU TUAN

The English poet John Donne (1572-1631) said: "No man is an island, entire of itself; every man is a piece of the continent, a part of the main." A person belongs to a group, which may be as small as the nuclear family and as large as the nation or the human species itself. His attitudes and behavior reflect his membership in these nested groups. On the other hand, a person is also an individual—a prisoner (so to say) within his own skin; and we have all known how difficult it is at times to establish common ground even with those closest to us. In a profound sense we live and die alone. To understand how a human being perceives and structures his environment, we need to consider him from three standpoints: (1) as a member of a biological species, (2) as a member of a group (cultural unit), and (3) as a uniquely endowed individual.

THE HUMAN SPECIES: COMMON TRAITS

By virtue of possessing similar sense organs, all human beings share common perceptions and so live in a common world. The uniqueness of the human perspective should be obvious if we reflect upon the well-known biological differences among the higher animals. Contrary to appearance, a person cannot enter imaginatively into the life of his dog: canine sense organs are too different from our own for us to leap into the dog's reality of smells, sounds, and sights. But with goodwill one person can at least stand within the portals of another's world, however much they may differ in age, temperament, and culture. Yet we are constantly tempted to ascribe human characteristics to the behavior of other species. Spectators of a bullfight like to believe that the bull sees "red," that it sees "blood," and is aroused to a pitch of excitement by the color of the matador's cape. But bulls are color blind, and the perception of one thing as the symbol of another (the color red stands for the fluid blood) is unique to human beings.

Human sense organs are admirable instruments: we have color and stereoscopic vision, dexterous and strong hands, fairly good hearing, and an adequate nose compared with other primates. But above all we are distinguished by our exceptionally well-developed brain, which enables us to acquire an abstract language of signs and symbols that is unique to the species. With language, human beings have been able to construct intricate mental worlds to mediate between themselves and external reality. The artificial environments they have built are an outcome of mental processes, no less than their myths, legends, taxonomies, and science. We may think of all these achievements as so many cocoons that the human animal has woven about himself to feel at home in nature. We are well aware that people perceive and structure their worlds very differently; the multiplicity of cultures is a persistent theme in geography. We shall take up the impact of culture on perception later. First, let us characterize the world we share as a species.

The objects we perceive are commensurate with the size of our body, the acuity and range of our perceptual apparatus, and our purposes. Although it is true that the size of perceived objects varies greatly from culture to culture, they (the objects) fall within a certain range. Neither the very small nor the very large come under our purview in the course of day-to-day living. People notice bushes, trees, and grass but rarely the individual leaves and blades; people see sand but not its individual grains. The emotional bond between man and animal seldom holds below a certain size—the size of the goldfish in the bowl and of small turtles that children play with. Bacteria and insects are beyond our normal perceptual range, and well beyond the human capacity to empathize. At the other end of the scale we can see stars, but only as specks of light in a ceiling of modest height. The mind can manipulate astronomical dimensions as abstract entities; we cannot, however, imagine concretely distances of a million miles, or even a hundred miles. No matter how often one has traversed the length of the United States, it is not possible to see it in one's mind's eye as other than a shape, a small-scale map.

Three-dimensional vision and dexterous hands enable human beings to perceive their environment as consisting of objects like bushes and trees, individual animals and people, boulders, mountain peaks, and stars. Human beings also recognize that nature is partly made up of continua like air, light, temperature, and space. They tend to segment nature's continua. For instance, the light spectrum visible to the human eye is perceived as discrete bands of color: violet, indigo, blue, green, yellow, orange, and red. In the middle latitudes temperature changes continually in the course of a year but people commonly divide it into four or five seasons, often with festivities marking the passage from one to the other. An infinite number of directions radiate from one point, but in many cultures four, five, or six directions are especially privileged. The earth's surface possesses certain sharp gradients: for instance, between land and water, mountain and plain, forest and savannah. But even where these don't exist, the human being makes an effort to differentiate his space-making distinctions between the sacred and the profane, the center and the periphery, the home estate and the common range.

The human mind tends not only to segment nature but also to arrange the segments in opposite pairs.[1] Thus we break the continuous color spectrum into discrete bands and then see "red" as the opposite of "green." Red is the signal for danger, and green is the signal for safety. Traffic lights use these colors for the readiness with which we perceive their messages. In cultures other than our own the colors may have somewhat different emotional associations, but the general point remains valid: humans show a propensity to pick pairs among segments perceived in nature's continuum and to assign opposed meanings to each pair. This tendency may reflect the structure of the human mind, but the emotional force of some bipolar antinomies, or contrary principles, suggests that the whole person, at all levels of experience, is involved. One may speculate on some of the fundamental opposites in human experience: life and death, male and female, "we" (or "I") and "they" are among the most important. These antinomies of experience are carried over to the enveloping external reality, which is polarized as light and darkness, heaven and earth, high and low, center and periphery in the cosmological schema, and as mountain and valley, land and water, north and south on the geographical plane. Not only do so-called primitive peoples categorize the world this way; thinking in polar opposites is also characteristic of modern man. For example, some social scientists persist in using the categories of urban and rural to designate contrasting life-styles when the distinctions between them are increasingly difficult to define.

Opposites are often mediated by a third term. Thus, to the polarized meanings of red and green we select the color "yellow" to represent caution, neither "stop" nor "go"; and in this case yellow happens to be the band of wavelength intermediate between red and green in the color spectrum and not just an arbitrarily selected color. In the cosmological schema, earth mediates between the forces of the upperworld and underworld. The idea of the center reconciles the bipolar tendencies of the cardinal directions.

---

[1] This section owes much to the ideas of Claude Lévi-Strauss. See his book *The Savage Mind*, Weidenfeld and Nicolson, London, 1966; and Edmund Leach's exposition of his ideas in the book *Claude Lévi-Strauss*, Viking, New York, 1966. The example of the human tendency to recognize discrete bands in the color spectrum comes from Leach, pp. 16-18. On the general human tendency to recognize discontinuities in nature, see Peter H. Raven, Brent Berlin, Dennis F. Breedlove, "The Origins of Taxonomy," *Science*, vol. 174, pp. 1210-1213, Dec. 17, 1971.

Life's fundamental antinomies are commonly resolved in myths and rituals, that is, in narration and formalized acts. A geometric figure may also serve to harmonize opposites, and of such figures the most important is the circle or the mandala. (*Mandala* is a Hindu term for "circle," although its meaning has been extended to include complex isometric shapes.) Apparently all members of the human species possess the circle as a symbol of wholeness and harmony. It is a recurrent motif in the arts of ancient Eastern civilizations, in the thinking of ancient Greece, in Christian art, in the alchemical practices of the Middle Ages, and in the healing rites of some illiterate peoples. Some psychoanalysts see the circle (or mandala) as an image of wholeness, common to mankind. Architecturally the mandala pattern is evident in the layout of certain Indian shrines and Chinese temples. Cities that were built to reflect the harmony of the cosmos often have a circular or square shape. The city, the temple, and indeed any dwelling of isometric figure such as a hut or the nomad's tent may be taken to be a symbol of psychic wholeness, a microcosmos capable of exercising beneficent influence on the person who enters the place or lives there.[2]

The human world view is richly symbolic. Different cultures have evolved symbolic systems that differ in content; thus, only within the European monarchical tradition would the scepter stand for royal power. On the other hand, certain phenomena transcend the interpretation of any particular group; their meanings are transcultural, if not universal. I have mentioned the circle. Fire and water are another: in widely different parts of the world they carry the meaning of "masculine" (activity and conscious striving) and "feminine" (passivity and the unconscious), respectively. The interpretation of the three colors "black," "white," and "red" appears to be similar worldwide.[3] They are probably among mankind's earliest symbols. Almost every known language has special words for black and white. Among terms for chromatic colors, red is usually one of the oldest in a given language, and as a rule it is a native word. According to Victor Turner, black, white, and red are important to mankind because they represent products of the human body whose emission, spilling, or production is associated with a heightening of emotion. The physiological events associated with the three colors are also experiences of social relationships; thus:[4]

> White = semen (tie between man and woman)
> = milk (tie between mother and child)

[2] Aniela Jaffé, "Symbolism in the Visual Arts," in Carl G. Jung (ed.), *Man and His Symbols*, Dell, New York, 1968, pp. 266-285.

[3] Brent Berlin and Paul Kay, *Basic Color Terms: Their Universality and Evolution*, Berkeley, University of California Press, 1969.

[4] V. W. Turner, "Colour Classification in Ndembu Ritual," in Michael Banton, A.S.A. (ed.), *Anthropological Approaches to the Study of Religion*, monographs 3, London, 1966, pp. 47-84.

Red = bloodshed (war, feud, social discontinuities)

  = obtaining and preparing of animal food (male productive role; sexual role of work)

  = transmission of blood from generation to generation (index of membership in the corporate group)

Black = excreta (bodily dissolution; change from one status to another—mystical death)

THE GROUP: CULTURAL DIFFERENTIATION

Infants have neither geography nor culture: no matter where they live, their environments and worlds are pretty much alike. To survive, a newborn child needs a constant environment close to his delicate body and the constant reassurance of the human touch and warmth. The infant may live in the Arctic or in the rain forest, in a hovel or in a mansion, but the physical condition necessary to his well-being remains roughly the same. Moreover, the perceived world of each infant differs little from one to the other since it is confined to his immediate vicinity. As the human child grows, he acquires the values and enjoys the dimensions of the adult's world. His environment is now the savannah, the rain forest, or the city, and what he perceives in these settings will reflect the cultural norms he has acquired in order to play an effective role in society. That cultural norms exert a general influence on the perceptual world of individuals requires no elaborate proof. A few examples suffice to show its reality, and should we wish, we need only look about us to find further instances. Begin with two simple examples, comparing the attitudes of man and woman, visitor and native, in the same environment. A more complex case is that in which two groups of people (for example, the Zuni Indians and Texan farmers) have evolved different environmental values in the same part of New Mexico.

In cultures where sex roles and spatial experiences are strongly differentiated, men and women will perceive different worlds. For example, the mental maps of male and female Eskimos on Southampton Island, Hudson Bay, diverge greatly. When the male hunter is asked to draw a map, he shows in detail and accuracy the island's outline as well as the harbors and inlets of the neighboring coast of Hudson Bay. But a woman does not express her knowledge by outlines: the shape of harbors has little value for her. A woman's map is made of points, each of which marks the location of a settlement or trading post. These locations too are admirably accurate as to direction and relative distance, although distances become increasingly distorted away from the home base on the island.[5]

In Western society the mental map of a housewife with small children is likely to differ from that of her husband. Every workday the circulation routes of the married couple rarely parallel each other except (perhaps) in the homestretch.

[5] E. Carpenter, F. Varley, R. Flaherty, *Eskimo*, University of Toronto Press, 1959 (pages unnumbered).

On a shopping trip the man and woman will want to look into different stores. They may walk arm in arm, but they do not necessarily see and hear the same things. Occasionally one is jolted out of his own perceptual world to make a courtesy call on that of the other, as, for example, when the husband asks his wife to admire some golf clubs in the shop window. Think of a street that you frequent and try to recall the shops along it: certain stores will stand out vividly while others dissolve in a dreamlike haze.[6] Among middle- and working-class adults in Western society, sex will account for much of the difference in patterns perceived and recalled. Comic misunderstandings between man and wife who live in the same house but in different perceptual worlds are a major theme of the popular cartoon strip "Blondie." Sex roles are not sharply drawn among members of the cosmopolitan upper class, and may be quite blurred in specialized communities such as "street people" and scientists working in research centers; their differences in perception are minimally based on sex.

Contrasts in viewpoint are striking when we compare what a visitor sees with what a native sees. Generally speaking, only the visitor has a viewpoint; his perception is often a matter of using his eyes to compose pictures. The native has a complex attitude derived from his immersion in the totality of his environment. The visitor's viewpoint, being simple, is easily stated. He may also feel a greater urge to express himself since he faces novelty. The complex attitude of the native, on the other hand, can be expressed by him only with difficulty and indirectly through behavior, local traditions, lore, and myth.

The contrasting perspectives of visitor and native were noted by the eminent philosopher and psychologist William James (1842-1910) following his journey through the back country of North Carolina. His first impression of the back-woods farms was one of unmitigated squalor. Boorish pioneers were desecrating the natural beauties of the landscape. In James's words, "The settler had in every case cut down the manageable trees, and left their charred stumps standing. He had then built a log cabin and had set up a tall zigzag rail fence around the scene of his havoc to keep the pigs and cattle out. Finally, he had irregularly planted the intervals between the stumps and trees with Indian corn, which grew among the chips. . . . " The philosopher, with his romantic image of what nature and the countryside should offer, was much disillusioned. Turning to the moun-taineer who was driving him, James asked, "What sort of people are they who have to make these new clearings?" The reply was, "All of us. Why we ain't happy here unless we are getting one of these coves under cultivation." Instantly James realized that he had interpreted the landscape as an outsider and had therefore missed "the inward significance of the situation." He explained: "Be-cause to me the clearings spoke of naught but denudation, I thought that to those whose sturdy arms and obedient axes had made them they could tell no

---

[6] See the fascinating story by C. S. Lewis, "The Shoddy Lands," in Walter Hooper (ed.), *Of Other Worlds,* Harcourt, Brace & World, New York, 1966, pp. 96-106.

other story. But when *they* looked on the hideous stumps, what they thought of was personal victory. The chips, the girdled trees, and the vile split rails spoke of honest sweat, persistent toil and final reward. The cabin was a warrant of safety for self and wife and babes. In short, the clearing, which to me was a mere ugly picture on the retina, was to them a symbol redolent with moral memories and sang a very paean of duty, struggle, and success."[7]

The visitor's evaluation of environment is essentially aesthetic. He judges by appearance, often by some formal canon of beauty learned in another socio-economic sphere. The outsider has to make a special effort to empathize with the lives and values of the local people. We may wonder why a generous and enlightened person like William James should at first take such a jaundiced view of the pioneer settlers and their farms since it is easy for us now to appreciate a rural scene of log cabins and split-rail fences. But are we so innocent of bias? In our time the pioneer scene is not the crude farmstead; it is the crude commercial strip—the endless chain of gas stations, motels, "Dairy Queens," and hamburger stands—that offends our eyes as we drive into a rapidly growing city; it is also the suburban sprawl. In judging them harshly, have we missed what James called "the inward significance of the situation"? Isn't it possible that the operator of an "eat" stand is as proud of his business—of his modest role in the community —as the backwoods farmer of an earlier era in his untidy corn patch? Moreover, may not a time come when we shall view hamburger joints and car-dealer lots as quaint and picturesque rather than as visual blight? These remarks are not offered as arguments; they serve simply to remind us that our judgments reflect our personal experiences, that they are culture-bound and are subject to change.

Consider now how outlook between resident and outsider may differ in an urban setting. Turn to the experience and findings of the sociologist Herbert Gans, who studied Boston's working-class district, known as the West End, before it was torn down in the interest of urban renewal.[8] When Gans first saw West End, he was struck by its opposing aesthetic qualities. On the one hand, there was the appeal of its European character. The high buildings set on narrow curving streets, the Italian and Jewish stores and restaurants, and the crowds of people on the sidewalks in good weather all gave the district an exotic flavor. On the other hand, Gans noticed the many vacant shops, the abandoned tenements, and the alleys choked with garbage. After he had lived in the West End for a few weeks, his perception altered. He became selective, turning a blind eye to the empty and dilapidated quarters for those that were actually used by people; and these transpired to be far more livable inside than their exteriors proclaimed.

[7] William James, "On a Certain Blindness in Human Beings," in *Talks to Teachers on Psychology: And to Students on Some of Life's Ideals* (1899), Norton, New York, 1958, pp. 150-152. See David Lowenthal, "Not Every Prospect Pleases: What is Our Criterion for Scenic Beauty?" *Landscape*, vol. 12, no. 2, pp. 19-23, Winter 1962-1963.
[8] Herbert J. Gans, *The Urban Villagers: Group and Class in the Life of Italian Americans*, The Free Press, New York, 1962, pp. 11-12, 150.

Gans also discovered that the outsider's view, even when it was sympathetic and generous, depicted a world alien to the native resident. For example, a settlement house memorandum for the training of new staff described the West End warmly as a multicultural residential area which, despite the poor housing, held "a charm and security for its residents"; and that what served to draw the people together were such pleasurable aspects of life as the stability of long-time residence, the nearness of the river, its parks and pools, and the richness in the variety of cultures. Actually, residents were not interested in ethnic variety. Although they used the riverbank and swimming pool, they did not see them as part of the neighborhood. And no native resident would think of applying the word "charm" to the West End district.

As has been seen, sharply differentiated sex role and socioeconomic class bring about distinctive patterns of environmental perception and value. Resident and visitor, with their contrasting experiences and purposes, cannot be expected to have the same view of a physical setting. Examples of this can be multiplied readily and analyzed with any degree of finesse. What they do not tell us are the contradictions, paradoxes, and ironies that become evident when we focus on culture as a whole, that is, when we take environmental values as part of a system of harmonizing and counterpoised values. Consider the environmental attitudes and world views of two groups, Zuni and Texan, in northwestern New Mexico where the environment is semi-arid.[9] First of all, note that both groups are highly ethnocentric, a common trait that serves to divide rather than unify. The Zuni Indians think of themselves as *ashiwi* (the "flesh" or "cooked ones"); their legends tell them that they occupy the Middle Place. The Texans take themselves to be not only "white man," a status they have to share with their Mormon neighbors, but "real Americans"; their settlement is the Pinto Bean Capital of the World. The Zuni believe that impersonal forces, including man, dominate the universe. The cosmos holds together and works in harmony as an integrated, mechanistic system. Rituals performed by the priesthood with the support of the community are the means for maintaining the harmonious cosmic system and for setting right what may have gone wrong temporarily. Their attitude to nature is one of adaptation, adjustment, and reverence. Food-gathering activities, for example, are linked not only to their economic life but also profoundly to their ceremonial life. Despite the Zuni emphasis on harmony in the natural and social orders, natural calamities and social dysfunctions occur; and given their idealized world view the Indians lack the mechanism to cope adequately with disorder and conflict. If there is no rain, for example, rumors may spread to the effect that the priests have broken taboos. A smallpox epidemic may create witchcraft hysteria. In short, bitter factionalism is perfectly compatible with the sincere belief in harmonious order.

[9] Evon Z. Vogt and Ethel M. Albert, eds., *People of Rimrock: A Study of Value in Five Cultures*, Harvard, Cambridge, Mass., 1966.

Unlike the Zuni Indians, the Texan pinto-bean farmers of New Mexico believe that man has the right and the power to dominate nature. Protestant Christianity and faith in technology buttress the Texan ego vis-à-vis his natural environment. Man can take the initiative and order his world rationally. This is the ideal, but in fact the Texan farmer combines pragmatism with irrationality, a sense of superiority with insecurity, and superstition with faith in the rational procedures of science. Though the economy is geared to material success (with no nonsense about reverence for the cosmos), excessive individualism among the settlers encourages wasteful duplication in the businesses of the very small town. There is the common boast of manhood, but virility cannot be accepted in quiet confidence: it has to be proved repeatedly through the manly sport of hunting, killing deer and lugging the game home to the womenfolk. Big machines, far more powerful than necessary, are used to till the bean fields. Reasonable hope in technology's ability to generate rain appears side by side with blind confidence in the powers of the water diviner. The attitudes of the Texan farmer are very mixed and contradictory.[10] We may attribute the inconsistencies to the fact that the Texans moved into New Mexico during the dust-bowl and depression years and have not had time to adjust. On the other hand, the Zuni world view is far from being fully compatible with the Zuni reality, and the Indians have lived in northwestern New Mexico for at least five hundred years.

THE INDIVIDUAL: UNIQUE PERSPECTIVES

Although as members of the human species and of culture groups we share certain common attitudes toward the environment, important individual differences exist. Human beings come in a variety of shapes and sizes; we are highly polymorphic. Outward physical variations among individuals are striking, but they are minor when compared with the internal differences. We are not exactly "brothers under the skin," if this expression is taken to assert the similarity of internal organs as distinct from outward differences in, say, pigmentation.[11] Attitudes to life and environment are clearly influenced by individual variations in biochemistry and physiology. A color-blind person's world is somewhat less polychromatic than that of someone with normal vision; and, in fact, everyone has his weaknesses and strengths in discriminating among fine color shades. Sensitivity to sound differs markedly among individuals with no recognized hearing defects. There are enormous variations in the sense of touch. Some rare individuals appear to lack pain receptors. "Hot" and "cold" are subjective responses that vary greatly among people. This is a fact we readily observe: how, for instance, one person goes to open a window at a time when another is about to put on a coat; how, in a hurry to catch the plane, one person is obliged to sip his coffee while another gulps it down. But differences in the brain are perhaps

[10] Evon Z. Vogt, *Modern Homesteaders*, Harvard, Cambridge, Mass., 1955, pp. 63-92.
[11] Roger J. Williams, *You Are Extraordinary*, Random House, New York, 1967.

the most surprising of all. The brain is extremely variable from person to person in every trait that has been observed and measured. People may be presumed to possess highly distinctive minds.

Polymorphism among human beings implies temperamental diversity. Cultural norms are frequently transcended by the wayward nature of individuals, which is related to physique. The association is commonplace in literary works. It is hard to envisage such immortal creatures of the imagination as Falstaff and Mr. Micawber, Sherlock Holmes and Mr. Murdstone, without calling to mind their physiques. Body type and personality seem all of a piece; it is as difficult to imagine a lean Micawber as a rotund Holmes. In everyday life people frequently infer character and talent from physical appearance without being fully conscious of the process: it comes so naturally. Science, however, has hesitated to make the association or even to give it much thought despite its obvious importance to the understanding of attitudes and behavior. In the 1930s and 1940s, William Sheldon made a bold attempt to relate somatotype to temperament.[12] His work was criticized for its taxonomic naïveté: body type, for instance, resists simple classification since the chief criteria of bone, fat, and muscle may vary independently. On the other hand, recent studies tend to support his general conclusions.[13] Sheldon classified people on three scales that measure visceral (endomorphic), muscular-skeletal (mesomorphic), and skin-and-nervous (ectomorphic) development.

Each body type is associated with a cluster of temperamental traits which in turn may affect environmental attitudes.

Body Type	Temperamental Traits and Attitudes to Nature
Ectomorph	Detached, thoughtful, shy, introspective, serious (contemplates nature and environment; interprets nature to reflect his own moods)
Mesomorph	Dominant, cheerful, adventurous, optimistic, argumentative (enjoys dominating nature: for example, hunters, civil engineers)
Endomorph	Relaxed, cooperative, affectionate, social (enjoys nature sensually; enjoys nature with others)

Although we may find fault with his method and argue with his conclusions, his work serves the useful purpose of drawing attention to the polymorphism of the human species. Polymorphism and biochemical individuality together account significantly for the uniqueness of personal worlds.

Differences in age and sex extend the range of human perspectives. These are

[12] William H. Sheldon, *The Varieties of Temperament*, New York, Harper, New York, 1942.
[13] Juan B. Cortes and Florence M. Gatti, "Physique and Propensity," *Psychology Today*, vol. 4, no. 5, pp. 42-44, 82-84, 1970.

the biological bases for individuality; in addition each person has his own history—sequences of experiences that are not duplicated elsewhere. It is hardly surprising, therefore, that culture—the shared ideals of the group—explains only a part of the range of attitudes among its members. As a homely illustration of the way individuality can transcend the cultural forces that make for consensus, think of the family on a weekend outing. This is not always the smooth and happy affair that advertisements for the camp stove would have us believe. At the planning stage the members of a family may haggle over where to go, and once the party reaches its destination, further disagreement may surface about where to camp, when to stop for supper, or which scenic places to visit. Differences in age, sex, temperament, and personal history often override the social demand for harmony and togetherness. Two final points should be noted: First, there is difficulty in isolating the biological basis for individuality from the contribution of unique events and experiences; and second, observation of public behavior tends to make one stress culturally induced conformity at the expense of the uniqueness of individual perspectives. Novelists, more than any other group of people, have shown how personal worlds can differ widely within the context of an objectively defined culture.

CODA

A person's world view is compounded of elements unique to himself, of elements which he shares with his group, and of elements that are characteristic of the species. As a human being he has the need and the ability to create symbolic structures of the world in which, for example, nature's continua tend to be perceived as segments, and experiences are dichotomized and reconciled. As a member of a socioeconomic class he prefers, let us say, suburban living to its perceived antithesis, the life style of the inner city. Elements unique to himself may be expressed by his eccentric work habits and taste in furniture. The unique elements, considered in isolation, are often trivial. But the personal world is not, for it is compounded of all three levels. We are "islands"; yet deep below sea level we are also "part of the main."

PART TWO

INTRODUCTION TO MAPS AND PERCEPTION OF SPACE

Because our sense organism limits our ability to perceive the environment, we have established a system of signs to mediate between reality and our minds. As Yi-Fu Tuan pointed out, these signs may be of several types. Some are colors and geometric figures. Others may be place names like "Yukon," or descriptive terms such as "college town." Some signs are used to designate, for example, woman or bird. Others are used to appraise or connote—good or beautiful, for example. Others are prescriptive, for example, should or should not. These signs provoke our behavior.

One picture equals a thousand words, so we are told, but we hardly take this hoary piece of advice very seriously. Instead we concentrate our efforts to communicate on the written or oral form, and ignore the numerical and graphic forms. Naturally, signs are fundamental to all forms of communication. Although we often encounter signs such as numbers or maps, our ability to communicate by using them is limited. Of the four types of communication skills, our ability to manipulate graphics is usually the least developed. Consequently, we have difficulty exchanging locational information by utilizing maps.

The average reader of news magazines is constantly confronted with a variety of maps, all designed to convey spatial information and to influence his opinion of an event. For centuries maps have been used for locating places and conditioning people's perceptions of the world. While we are accustomed to using maps as tools of locational analysis, we too frequently overlook this influence on our perception of the environment. This is a cause for concern, because when maps are used as a stimulus, in travel literature for example, people may respond not according to their perception of the map itself. That is, they may know nothing about a place like Arizona, but may vacation there because of a map pleasantly colored in warm tones and covered with alluring place names.

Because so many spatial decisions and their resulting behavior are influenced by maps, we must attempt to develop some appreciation of the potentialities and limitations of cartography. Reading the following essay will not enable you to make maps, but it will enable you to avoid some of the more obvious pitfalls encountered when reading and interpreting maps.

CHAPTER THREE

MAPS AND THE PERCEPTION OF SPACE*

ROGER PRESTWICH

On the average, most Americans probably see at least one map every day. Such maps may vary from those picked up at gas stations to "visual aids" presented on television, in magazines, or in newspapers. Relatively few people, however, realize just what is involved in the process of mapmaking; rather, the average individual frequently views a map as the precise portrayal of reality. In fact, a map is a symbolic representation of the whole or a part of the earth's surface, and as such is subject to both misrepresentation and misinterpretation. Hence, the way in which we perceive and interpret the reality of our environmental space has a very substantial influence on the way we map that space, and, in turn, the cartographic representation of phenomena has an impact on our spatial perception. The apparent "chicken and egg" controversy here is misleading; maps are attempts by man to represent, usually as objectively as possible, his environment as he sees it.

MAP HISTORY IN BRIEF

The media of cartography have run the gamut from rock carvings and clay tablets to computer maps and earth-satellite photographs. The earliest known map is carved in a rock overlooking the former site of a neolithic village in a central Italian valley and dates from approximately the year 5000 B.C. The

*Acknowledgment: Thanks are especially due to John Berquist, who assisted in the compilation and drafting of the maps in this essay.

ancient civilizations of China, India, Mesopotamia, and Persia also had their mapmakers, and judging by some of the remnants, the art of cartography was relatively well advanced, especially in China. Many of these remnants, however, show real estate and building arrangements, so that they should more strictly be referred to as "plans" rather than maps. Some of the best maps that vividly illustrate spatial perception are to be found among hunters, nomads, and seafaring peoples, such as the Innuit and the Polynesians, who had considerable spatial mobility. The former constructed scale models of territory using carved pieces of driftwood (for islands) pasted on sealskin, and the latter using seashells (islands) fastened to a wooden framework with strings showing waves and currents. Further, many "primitive" tribes have the ability to define spatial relationships accurately within their own sphere simply by scratching out a map with a stick on the ground.

One might assume from such advances in the ability to perceive and symbolically represent space that modern cartography evolved as a logical sequence of events. . . . Not so. Certainly, considerable development took place throughout the Greek and Roman periods, as deduced from the writings of Strabo in A.D. 25, and culminated with Ptolemy's map of the known world circa A.D. 150. Unfortunately, it was not Ptolemy's remarkable achievement which became the model for the medieval cartographers in Europe, but rather the simplistic disc-shaped "Orbis Terrarum" of the Romans. The mapmakers of the Middle Ages were concerned more with the perfection of God's world than with its physical reality, and irregularity was irreconcilable with harmony, so that the *T* in *O* maps were conceived (Figure 3-1). The Roman original centered on the eastern

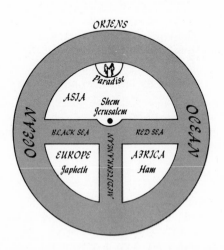

Figure 3-1   Medieval *T* in *O* map. The Black Sea here includes the Aegean— sometimes together called Tanais.

Mediterranean, the European derivative on Jerusalem, and an Arabic version on Mecca. Other maps were rectangular in an attempt to accommodate the Biblical reference to the "four corners of the earth," a phrase still heard even though somewhat misleading.

The breakthrough into a cartographic renaissance came with the Portolan charts in the late thirteenth century. These charts were accurately surveyed by compass, probably by the Genoese admiralty, and served as the basis of navigation charts for three centuries. The renewal of interest in the Greek and Roman culture during the sixteenth century led to a revival of the Ptolemy maps, although many of the Ptolemy derivations also copied the mistakes of the originals. Most maps of this period, especially those of Dutch and Flemish cartographers, were richly decorated with marginal superfluities and oceanic monsters where precise information was unavailable. Later, the discoveries of the New World necessitated totally new maps, as man's spatial mobility increased over larger areas.

As the seventeenth century moved into the Age of Reason, the decorative aspects of maps decreased, largely on account of the achievements of the Cassini family of France in the development of triangulation and topographic mapping. Nevertheless, some utilitarian versions of the decorated Dutch and Flemish maps remain, particularly that of Mercator (1569), which is probably the single most easily recognized projection today (Figure 3-2). The artistic quality of eighteenth-century mapping was less inspired than that of its predecessors. Accuracy, however, was much improved during the rational topographic surveys of the ninteenth century, which were largely initiated and conducted by the army, just as navigation charts had been by the admiralty. In addition to topographic or relief mapping, this period also saw increasing use of new techniques and a broader range of map types, particularly the thematic or topical maps dealing, for example, with geology, climate, transportation, and economics.

While surveying had to be done on foot or by carriage, the process of mapping was relatively slow,[1] but the impact of air photography and, more recently, earth-satellite photography has increased the speed and accuracy of mapping tremendously. There is probably no area of the surface of the globe which has not now been photographed by satellites, although it is doubtful that maps have been made from all the photos. In most advanced countries the basic maps are primarily surveyed initially on the ground and then periodically updated by air photography.

We are now into the era of computer cartography, with coastline and boundary plots, for example, of any world projection and at any scale contained within the memory of the magnetic tape, and with automatic print-outs of statistical data on any unit basis, as shown in Figure 3-3.

[1] As an example, the British Ordnance Survey started in 1823 and only finished the first national edition in 1851, with the mapping of Ireland occupying the years 1825 to 1840.

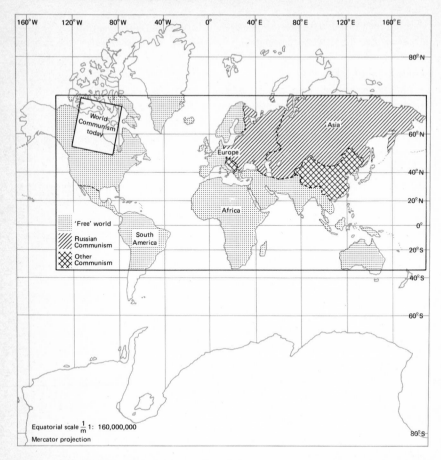

Figure 3-2 Mercator projection. Parallel spacing increases with latitude; hence so does areal distortion. Useful for navigation purposes since all compass directions from any point are straight lines, but not appropriate for showing areal distribution—least of all that of a political ideology.

There are other kinds of computer mapping which can show areal densities of phenomena from any cardinal point, at a variety of angles, and with an array of vertical exaggeration.[2] Computers are now also being used for color printing of maps to show land utilization, but the major difficulty is the necessity for adequately detailed statistical information (available in few countries) and for organizing these data into unit areas which can then be represented by one of

[2] George F. Jenks, "Generalization in Statistical Mapping," *Annals of the Association of American Geographers*, vol. 53, pp. 15-26, 1963.

the symbols available to the computer.[3] The level of aggregation means that such maps are very useful on a smaller scale, but at large scales the need to put data in uniform areas becomes a serious hindrance—the regularization of environmental perception in the geometric township and range survey of the United States was one thing, but the organization of space in 1- or 5-acre square blocks is perhaps a bit too artificial!

MAPS—VALUES AND LIMITATIONS

To the average user, a map is something which tells him directions and distances between places. Beyond this, it is a store of other information—an oversimplified, selective representation of reality. It has these attributes for the geographer as well, but to him it is also an analytical tool for the understanding of spatial forms and relationships. It is a means of communication, and as such, its positive and negative attributes must be understood if the message is not to be garbled.

Scale is a crucial aspect of maps. Any inquiry into spatial relations involves a certain amount of generalization: the smaller the scale per unit area, the greater the area covered and the more generalized the aggregated data; the larger the scale, the smaller the area and the more specific the data can be. The most familiar maps to the layman are probably the world maps, which in an atlas are usually at scales of 1:140,000,000 (single 8½ x 11 inch page) to 1:80,000,000 (across two pages), where 1 inch on the map represents respectively 140 million or 80 million inches on the actual surface of the earth. Continental maps vary in scale depending on the size of the continent, but on a one-page basis, a map of North America would be 1:32,000,000 and a map of the United States 1:20,000,000. The British Isles, by comparison, would be at 1:4,000,000 on a single-page basis.

A map of an individual state would show much more detail than the national map ever could on one page, and is on an average at a scale of 1:2,000,000 or so, depending on the area of the state (obviously Texas and Rhode Island might need different scales to get them onto a standard page). Finally, still using the same page basis, a map of a metropolitan area might be at about 1:400,000, that of a city at 1:200,000. The usual gas station street map of a city is at a scale of 1:50,000 (about 1 inch to ¾ mile). The next step is the neighborhood, the block, and the individual house, but by this time we are entering the realm of plans rather than maps, although precisely where the boundary between these two forms of surface representation lies is not well defined. The amount of detail which can be included on a map depends on the scale (the larger the scale,

---

[3] For example, a 40-acre unit area is being used by the Minnesota State Land Management System and a square kilometer by a similar New York State system in the preparation of a statewide natural resource inventory.

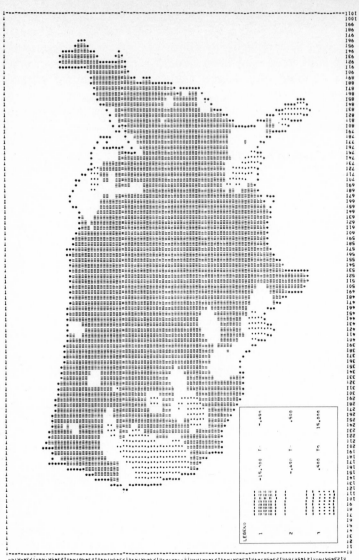

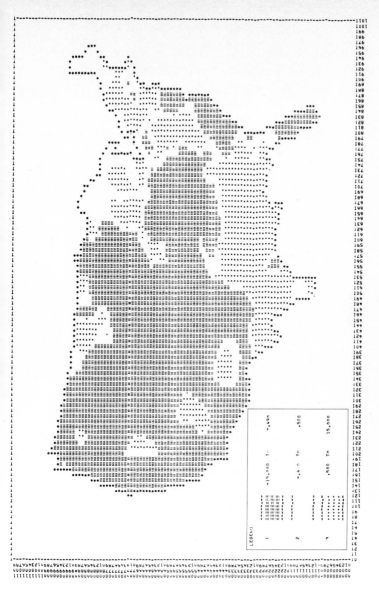

Figure 3-3 Computer mapping. The United States meteorological drought indices are shown here for summer and winter. Data are plotted according to a unit area based on latitude and longitude grid coordinates. Simply by punching new cards for those areas having a monthly change, a new map can be produced in seconds. These two maps are part of a monthly series running from 1931 to 1969.

41

the more detail) so that certain limits are set on data representation. Hence, a standard symbol such as a ¼-inch circle covers a far greater area on a world map than it does on a national or state map.

Care must also be exercised by the cartographer in the choice of projections that he makes for world, continental, or national areas. Once we move into areas which can be comfortably mapped in the thousands of units per inch, the projection has relatively little effect, but at a scale in the millions of units per inch, it is vitally important. Why? Simply because a map is drawn on a sheet of flat paper to represent a curved surface (the earth), and the only place where a flat surface can maintain contact (and accuracy) with a curved one is along the tangent. Away from that line of tangency the linear and areal distortions gradually increase.

All good atlases, as well as cartography and physical geography textbooks, give detailed descriptions of the derivation and construction of map projections.[4] Our concern as geographers is with the values and limitations of these projections in the representation of spatial phenomena, and so we might summarize the main characteristics of the most commonly used projections as follows:

Cylindrical

A cylinder is wrapped around the globe tangential to the equator, and latitude and longitude are projected as straight and equally spaced lines. Accuracy decreases away from the equator so that areal distortion amounts to a 250 percent exaggeration north and south of the 40° parallel, and the poles cannot be shown since they are straight lines running the entire width of the map. Mercator (Figure 3-2) and Miller (Figure 3-14) are two cylindrical projections— the latter modified at high latitudes in order to counteract excessive distortion found in the former.

Conical

A cone is placed over the globe so that tangency is achieved: if over the Northern Hemisphere, this will usually be somewhere between 40° and 60° North, depending on the angle of the side of the cone, and this line of tangency is referred to as the "standard parallel." Meridians are straight lines radiating from the cone apex, and parallels are curved lines. Scale error is very small, but does increase away from the standard parallel. With two standard parallels, where the cone in effect cuts the globe and effectively exhibits tangency in two planes, this projection is frequently used for maps of the United States, the Soviet Union, and Europe.

---

[4] See Erwin Raisz, *Principles of Cartography*, McGraw-Hill, New York, 1962; Arthur H. Robinson, and Randall D. Sale, *Elements of Cartography*, 3d ed., Wiley, New York, 1969.

Azimuthal

This is also known as "plane projections," where a part of the globe is projected onto a flat sheet which is tangential at only one point. These projections can be used in all positions: equatorial, polar, and oblique. Lines of longitude are straight in the polar case, curved in the others, and parallels are curved in all cases—see Figure 3-4, which is a stereographic version of an azimuthal projection. Scale error increases away from the point of tangency.

Each subtype of projection in these three very broad groupings has different characteristics, and the size and shape distortions of high latitudes can be seen in Figure 3-5, where Greenland is shown as it appears on seven types of projections. One of them is derived from an interrupted projection (Goode's homolosine, Figure 3-6), where the intention is to make each section more accurate than is possible for the entire world on a continuous sheet. Nevertheless, the oceans are frequently split, and even omitted, so that misconceptions can arise as to the relationships between land masses.

Every projection is designed to represent data of some kind, and in the case of geography these are frequently distributions and densities of phenomena. If correct shape is desired, correct areal size must be sacrificed, and vice versa, and if distances are shown correctly, then shape and size will be distorted. Projections which have the quality of equal area are termed "homolographic," those which have correct shapes "orthomorphic" (conformal), and those with correct directions from a central point "azimuthal." Since the earth graticule has lines of latitude and longitude which cross at right angles, the amount of distortion on a world map can be fairly accurately measured by this yardstick. Choice of the particular projection which shows data accurately in as many ways as possible is of great importance. Poor choices can result in very misleading maps, as we will see shortly.

The most familiar type of world map is probably the political one, with each country prettily colored in pastels. This is a useful way of identifying territories of jurisdiction in this century, but one must be very careful when coloring such areas on maps of the medieval and ancient worlds. The implication of such continuous coloring is spatial control by a centralized government equivalent to that of a modern nation-state. Frequently such maps also have line boundaries around the color, when in fact demarcation of territorial extent on a national basis did not become meaningful until the eighteenth and nineteenth centuries. One reason for this was that the available maps were inadequate for accurate boundary delimitations. Political boundary lines thus may be misleading, for we are really talking about transition zones between areas governed from one center and those governed from another.

The same boundary problem exists for maps showing distributions of natural vegetation, climatic types, and economic activity, and also maps of densities, particularly where strong shading is used to differentiate the areas, giving a steplike progression even when some kind of gradation is in evidence (e.g.,

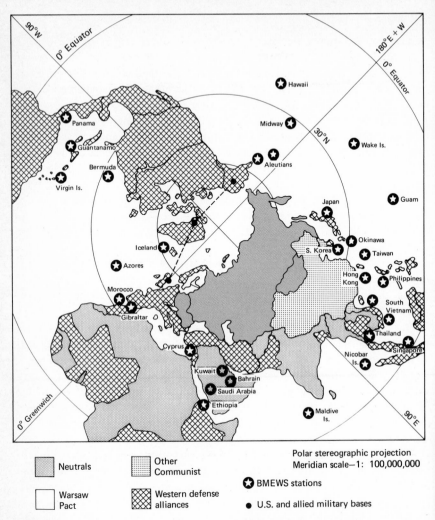

Figure 3-4 A view from the "other side." Use of an "air-age" polar projection, appropriate shading patterns, selection and labeling of bases, and lines of latitude emphasize the Russian view of encirclement and constriction by "Western" alliances. Change the shading, color Communist countries red, and the map becomes one of containment of "Communist expansion." (Cf. Figure 3-2)

population densities). It is very difficult to show a transition zone on a map, but to draw boundary lines is especially misleading. Hence, more use should be made of graded sequences, which are often used to show relief.

Color or black-and-white shading may carry to the viewer implications which can be used or abused—for example, on relief maps green is associated with low

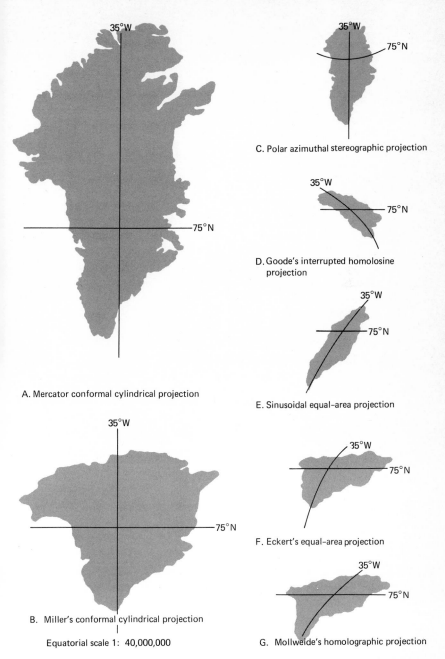

Figure 3-5   Variations on a theme. The shape and size of Greenland according to seven different projections, all with the same equatorial scale. The most accurate is *c*. (Compare with Figures 3-2, 3-4, 3-6, and 3-10.)

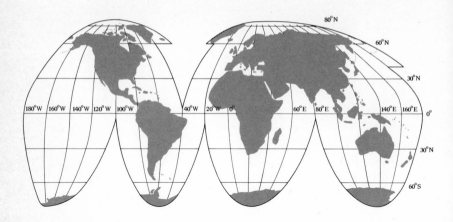

Figure 3-6   An interrupted projection. Goode's homolosine is an equal area projection employing Mollweide's homolographic poleward of 40° with Sanson-Flamsteed's sinusoidal. Better shapes result from the interruption which allows each continent in turn the advantage of being in the center of the projection. Useful for showing areal distributions.

and brown with high elevations; on temperature maps blue is cold and red is hot, while green is cool and yellow/brown is warm. Shading has a certain onomato-poeic quality about it, which has been used to effect by many cartographers, as, for example, the stipple used in the "Icy Sea" of Mackinder's map (Figure 3-7).

MAPS AS SHORTHAND

You can say on a map what may take several pages to write; giving someone the directions to reach your house is far easier (and less confusing) if it is done by drawing a sketch map. The shorthand symbols used in cartography vary from one map to another, but there are some which are very basic, as shown in Figure 3-8. These symbols are always proportionately larger than life, in the sense that if you measured the width of a standard railroad line symbol on a map at the "1 inch to 1 mile" scale (1:62,500), and calculated what this indicates as an actual width on the ground, you would have railroad tracks 50 to 60 feet wide! Simi-larly, boundary lines on a map might indicate a zone over 100 feet wide on the ground, when in reality the width of a boundary is nonmeasurable.

Symbolism in mapping can take a variety of forms such as lines, patterns, shapes, textures, letters, and colors. The wise cartographer chooses his symbols very carefully, since his decision will influence the way in which the map is perceived by the viewer. Indeed, the psychology of certain shapes and forms is vital to the message. Dots not only indicate location but also imply a potential for expansion or contraction, and when dots are plotted together, they create "energy" which affects the space between them and implies interrelationships

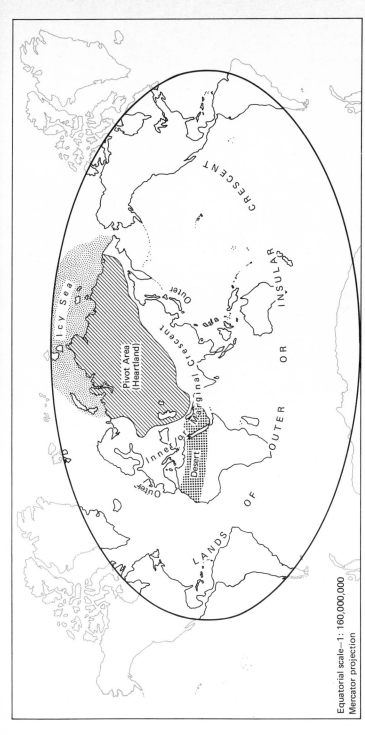

Equatorial scale—1: 160,000,000
Mercator projection

Figure 3-7 Mackinder's global perspective. The inner ellipse contains the naval view of the world—a Heartland inaccessible to the navies of the Inner or Outer Marginal Crescents controlled by a land power will have command of the world. The centrality of the Pivot Area is attained by repeating the Americas on each side of Eurasia—the size of this latter area is exaggerated by use of the Mercator projection. (Notice how the areal distortion of the Canadian archipelago and Greenland is simply avoided by omission.)

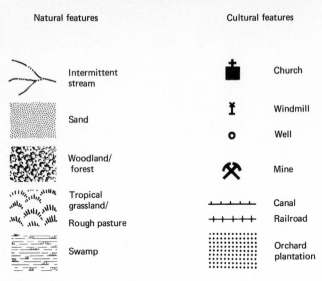

Figure 3-8 Symbols. These are some of the more commonly used symbols which appear on topographic maps—obviously rather generalized.

and movement.[5] A line indicates position and direction, and energy travels along its length—put an arrow on one end and the energy moves in that direction. Smooth, sweeping lines which enclose large areas tend to imply homogeneity within the boundaries, and this kind of functional geographic subdivision condemns the viewer to a loss of perspective, as in the case of U.S. State Department allocations of foreign relations to broad "regions" such as the Near East or Far East. Thick lines express strength and boldness, thin lines weakness; straight lines imply stability, wavy lines instability. Varieties of such lines are frequently used either as boundaries or as direction indicators in propaganda mapping (Figure 3-9).

The square, the triangle, and the circle are the most fundamental planal symbols, but once on a map their message varies. For example, if we change the interrelationships of easily recognizable shapes by changing the optical field, the visual unit itself will appear to possess different qualities. Hence, in Figure 3-10 the dark square in the center of the bounded light background appears to be larger than the light on dark, and a standard square symbol turned into a diamond seems to take on larger size and different energy. (Compare these shades with their effects in Figures 3-2 and 3-4.) We tend to group units on the basis of proximity or similarity, so that even though they may be dissimilar when

[5] "Energy" is used here in the psychological perception sense of dots and lines having the ability to change their size and significance relative to one another and to move in certain directions with variable speed and power.

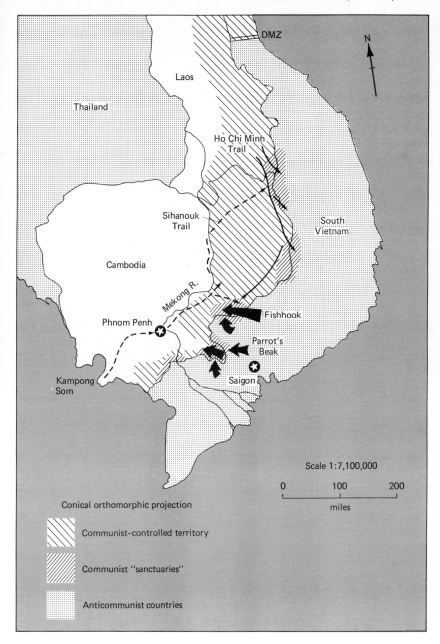

Figure 3-9 Contemporary propaganda mapping. A combination of shading patterns and intensities, arrows, and lettering point to the obvious strategic necessity for an invasion of Cambodia.

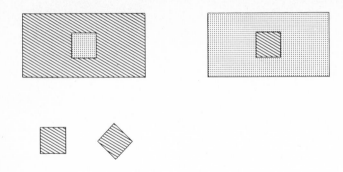

Figure 3-10 Misperception. A familiar optical illusion from introductory psychology. Note how the dark square on a light background appears to be larger than the same-sized light square on a dark background. Also, the same-sized square turned into a diamond appears to take on larger area.

close together, the fact that the background is totally different perceptually encourages grouping of the familiar. The gestalt phenomenon is similar: a circular shape is perceived as a complete circle even though there may be gaps, a feature illustrated to some extent by Figure 3-11. Where a polar projection is used, as in Figure 3-4, the artificial drawing of concentric circles to achieve the gestalt effect is not needed, since the lines of latitude are circles around the North Pole.

The kinds of symbols and shading used in mapping depend on what the cartographer wants to show, and there are a variety of ways in which this can be accomplished.[6] First of all, to put it bluntly, there is both good and bad shading. Look at Figure 3-12. Map 3-12a is an example of a poor choice of shading patterns—both increasing and decreasing values use lines, and the varieties of direction and density are confusing. This difficulty is remedied simply by choosing gradational patterns of different bases, depending on which aspect one wishes to emphasize: in Map 3-12b, dots are used for increasing and lines for decreasing population, with the intensity of shading indicating the rate of change.

Where shading is applied according to a value for a bounded area (in this case counties), it is referred to as "choropleth" mapping. This technique is also used in Map 3-13a of the Figure 3-13 sequence, where the same data are used for all four maps of New England but are plotted in different ways. Map 3-13b uses a modified "isopleth" technique, where each isoline joins points of the same value; in this case decennial percentage population change rates. The relief map is the most common isoline map, where the isolines are contours joining points of equal elevation above sea level. Map 3-13c uses proportional circles to show the

[6] See Francis J. Monkhouse and Henry R. Wilkinson, *Maps and Diagrams*, 2d ed., Methuen, London, 1963.

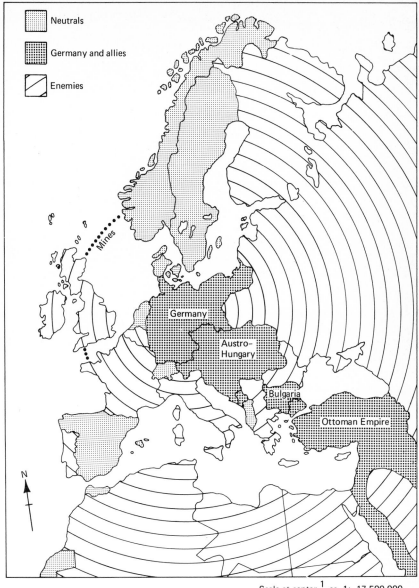

Scale at center $\frac{1}{m}$ ca. 1: 17,500,000

Figure 3-11   Gestalt perception in action. The use of concentric circles to indicate the constriction of Germany during the Great War by its enemies is obvious, but very effective. The projection used exaggerates area away from the center of the map. The occupation of Norway, Denmark, the Netherlands, Belgium, and France and the alliance with Italy in the Second War substantially reduced the amount of encirclement.

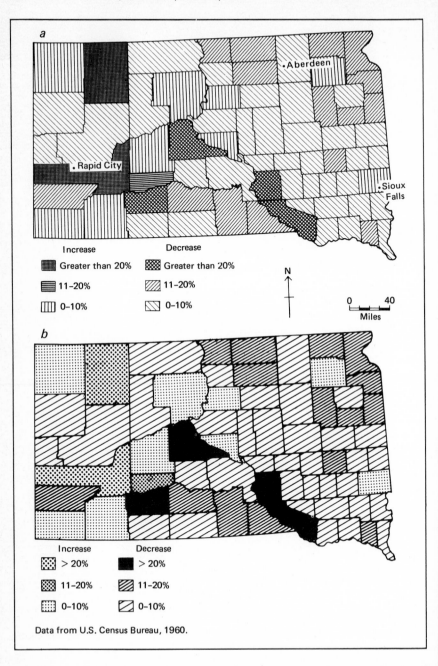

Figure 3-12 Shading makes a difference. The line shading for both increases and decreases in South Dakota's rural population in *a* is disturbing to the eye. The line and dot shading of *b* achieves the objectives much more satisfactorily.

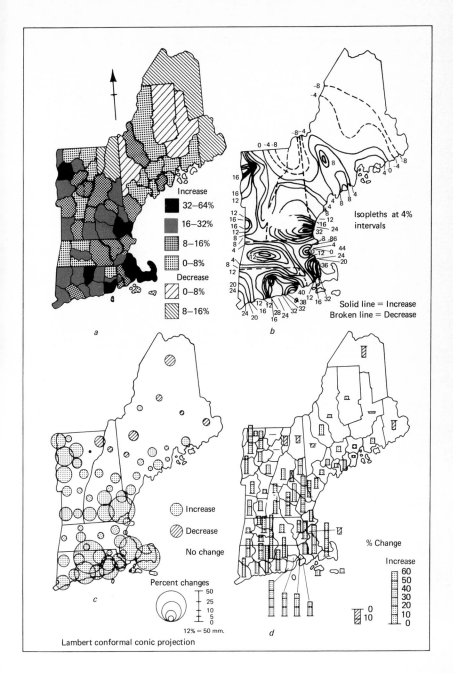

Figure 3-13 Same data: different presentation. These four maps of New England plot the 1960-70 population change on a county unit basis by different methods; (a) choropleth, (b) isopleth, (c) proportional circles, (d) bar graphs.

data, and Map 3-13d uses simple columnar diagrams or bar graphs. For this kind of mapping, the choropleth and proportional circle techniques are perfectly adequate to indicate the message: the isopleth adds little and the bar graphs give a cluttered appearance.

MAPS AND INFORMATION

The intention of a map is to present data to the viewer through various symbolic means. Even at the world scale, one's perception of the earth is very much influenced by the way in which the projection is presented. Figure 3-14 is a comparison of two maps of precisely the same projection (Miller cylindrical), but with the world divided from the point of view of the American (Map 3-14a), with the Americas centered, and of the European (Map 3-14b), with Europe centered. This simple exercise illustrates a rather striking difference in the perception of the world by the respective citizens. Both viewpoints can give rise to misconceptions, particularly regarding the spatial relationships of land masses. This map should be compared with the Mercator projection (Figure 3-2) and Goode's (Figure 3-6), which will illustrate the different qualities of area, shape, and direction.

The use of particular kinds of symbolization influences the way in which the viewer perceives spatial relationships. Like statistics, maps can "prove" just about any spatial relationship which the particular cartographer would like, and as such, can be a vehicle for misinformation.[7] An excellent example of a seemingly innocent presentation of "the facts" can be seen in Figure 3-2. Previously this figure was cited as an illustration of the amount of areal distortion which occurs in the Mercator projection; we might now note how this distortion can be put to a specific use.

The outer boundary of Figure 3-2 encloses the total Mercator projection, but the inner border indicates a selection process at work. The inner border conveniently stops short of Antarctica, since this continent is greatly distorted and irrelevant to the subject. It also cuts off at $75°$ North latitude, because virtually all the Soviet Union is included south of this parallel, but it excludes much of Greenland which, if included, would make the exaggeration too obvious (it appears larger than South America, when in fact it is only one-eighth the size). Similarly, Alaska is excluded, since it would appear half the size of the United States, and much of Canada is covered by a label, so that its distortion is not too noticeable. To complete the picture, shade the non-Communist world with a light-gray innocent-looking screen, and the exaggerated area of the Communist countries with a heavy diagonal grid (if color is to be used, red is very effective). The impact is precisely what the map maker intended—the obvious threat of Communism to the world, and as the map shows, any fool can see it! Notice also

[7] S. W. Boggs, "Cartohypnosis," *The Scientific Monthly*, June 1947.

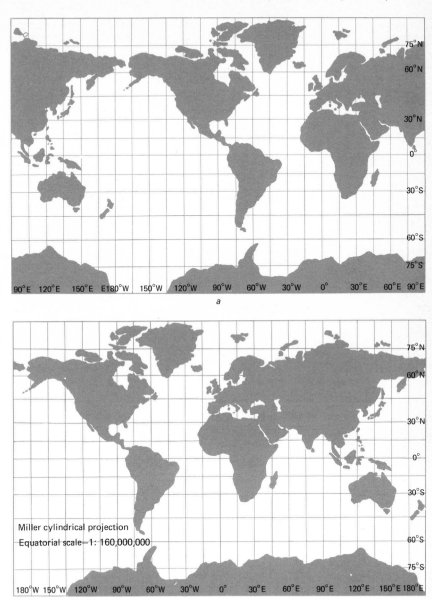

Figure 3-14 World views. Miller's cylindrical projection is used to show two different ways of looking at the world—the American (*a*) and the European (*b*). Note the importance attached to America's interocean location in *a*; also notice the location of Southeast Asia relative to the United States on each version. This projection is useful for areal distributions and shipping patterns.

where the labels "Europe" and "Asia" are placed. Very simple, very effective. The same technique is used in movies and television, but with much greater effect since the dark area can move and link up with small outposts. Ultimately the entire globe will be covered by the cancerous spread of this disease. This is also known as the "bleeding-map" technique. The Russians use the same technique, but to show the spread of imperialist colonial aggression.

In fact, if we change projections in midstream, from cylindrical to azimuthal, our perception of earth space can easily be changed from what America calls "containment" to what Russia calls "encirclement." Figure 3-4 is a polar projection, and is both informative and propagandistic. This time we put the "innocent" light-dot screen on Russia and her allies, and the "evil" heavy diagonal grid on "imperialist America and her running dogs." To emphasize the point, we then locate appropriate United States military bases and the missile-radar line, and the encirclement of the Soviet Union is readily apparent. We could have gone further and mapped an intensive series of latitudinal circles, or airplanes, missiles, and ships pointing toward Moscow. However, by retaining a certain amount of sophistication, the message can be readily conveyed and accepted unquestioningly by the Russian citizen that his freedom of spatial movement in the world is being severely restricted by the American military ring of steel. There are several other techniques involved here, like choice of symbols and placing of names, which help to create the gestalt of encirclement. By reversing the shading, the map would be perceived by the American as containment of Communist expansion. (Compare the shading with Figure 3-2 and Figure 3-10.)

MAPS AND POLITICS

The general public has great faith in information which is presented in cartographic form rather than in the written word, probably because it is easier to see at a glance what the "whole situation" is and thereby avoid having to read columns of print. Once the governmental "information agency," or whatever name is used, moves into the field of mapping, we enter the realm of propaganda maps. The inherent properties of maps to distort, exaggerate, or ignore facts are willfully exploited to drum up support for a particular policy or action. These characteristics are also used to propound geopolitical theories or concepts, and probably one of the best known is that of Mackinder.

Sir Halford Mackinder developed a theory of world power which remains to this day in modified form as the policy of containment noted above. In 1904, and again in 1919, Mackinder propounded a global viewpoint, based on the interconnectivity of the oceans, and the huge landmass of Eurasia (the "World Island"), the north central part of which he termed the "Heartland" or "Pivot Area." He theorized that since this large area was inaccessible to the navies of the world, thanks to the Arctic Ocean ("Icy Sea") and frozen rivers of Siberia, whosoever should rule this territory would have command over the world. The inner elipse of Figure 3-7 shows Mackinder's perception of the world. The centrality of the Heartland is emphasized firstly by repetition of North and South America at both the east and west edges of the map; secondly, the employment of a Mercator projection to exaggerate Siberia; and thirdly, the partial cutting off of Greenland and its de-emphasis by the lack of any name or shading. This view of the world by an individual basically familiar with the naval expression of military power contrasts markedly with the air-power concept (Figure 3-4), although encirclement of the central Pivot Area is still a concern of American foreign policy.

The cartographers working for the German Information Ministry during the 1930s produced a remarkable series of maps designed to influence both public opinion and their situational perception.[8] Figure 3-11 is adapted from one of these which was dated as the "high point" of the First World War. The gestalt effect of concentric circles centered approximately on Berlin is obvious. The reader perceptually closes the rings, and the "unnatural" constriction of Germany and its allies by the other powers of Europe is achieved. In the original, red was used for Germany, Austro-Hungary, Bulgaria, and Turkey, a color which indicated zeal or strength; yellow was used for those countries allied against Germany, with the probable implication of cowardice; and the neutrals were gray. On other maps America was colored green, possibly to imply stupidity or inexperience in world politics.[9]

If we move to the present, we might again look at one situation from a point of view other than that which Americans are accustomed to: the Russian invasion of Czechoslovakia in 1968 to protect the Czechs from revisionist liberals. Figure 3-15 has two maps. Map 3-15a shows the "normal" daily situation in Central Europe, with the Warsaw Pact countries in a dotted screen, the NATO countries in a diagonal grid, and the neutrals in a diagonal line matched to the grid. France is included with NATO because she still has substantial defense ties with other West European countries. Russian perception of the potential danger to her security caused by the liberalization and Western orientation of Czechoslovakia is shown on Map 3-15b. Simply by changing the shading from screen to grid, Czechoslovakia appears like a spearhead pointing toward the Ukraine. Further, since Czechoslovakia is the only East European country having borders with both the East and the West, loss of this territory would have divided Soviet control of the whole area in two halves and totally shattered its defense plans. The answer was obvious once the problem was expressed in map form; the potential danger could not be allowed to develop.

Using shading patterns of differing type and density to indicate danger spots which have to be eliminated is also a favorite technique that has frequently been

[8] Giselher Wirsing, (ed.), *Der Krieg 1939/41 in Karten*, Verlag Knorr und Hirth, Munich, 1941.
[9] Louis O. Quam, "The Use of Maps in Propaganda," *Journal of Geography*, vol. 42, pp. 21-32, 1943.

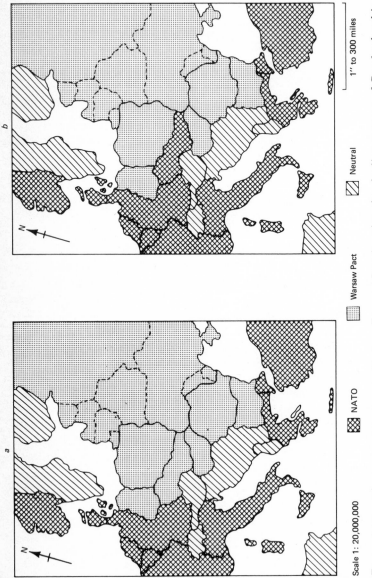

Scale 1: 20,000,000

◳ NATO   ▦ Warsaw Pact   ◩ Neutral

1″ to 300 miles

Figure 3-15 Czechoslovakia: key to Eastern Europe. By changing the shading pattern of Czechoslovakia from that of Warsaw Pact to NATO, its crucial strategic situation in Europe becomes readily apparent. From the Red Army's standpoint, the liberalization and potential Western orientation of Czechoslovakia made the Pact's defense stature untenable.

used in maps of Southeast Asia. Figure 3-9, page 48, is a composite of the kinds of maps which appeared in all the news media at the time of the joint American/South Vietnamese invasion of Cambodia in 1970. The diagonal line shading of the areas occupied by North Vietnamese and Viet Cong troops is an active threat amidst the white or lighter dot shadowing of Cambodia, Laos, Thailand, and South Vietnam, but the strong arrowed lines of the Allied thrusts indicate an unleashing of pent-up energy which will act like laser beams in cleaning out cancerous cells. Notice also how oversize labeling and the arrows draw your attention to the "Fishhook" and "Parrot's Beak" sanctuaries.

A WORD OF CAUTION

There is a difference between *reading* maps and *consulting* them. The ability to read a map is an art in itself; it must be learned and practiced. When the recipient is untrained, the conveyance of misinformation by a map can be far more invidious than even subtle words and phrases. The map satisfies his cognitive senses far more easily and effectively than does the written or spoken word. Nevertheless, the map is probably the most valuable single tool available to the geographer for the analysis of spatial relationships, and so both its positive and negative aspects must be adequately understood.

If the liberally educated person is required to learn how to handle the rudiments of English composition in order to adequately communicate facts and ideas, then it is obvious that such persons should also be able to appreciate the basics of map composition.[10] Just as students are warned to watch for discrepancies in the fads and styles of literature, so they should also develop the critical faculties of map appreciation.

Many of the maps which appear in the media are not drawn by cartographers, but rather by staff artists, draftsmen, and clerks. The essence of good cartography is accuracy, clarity, and relative simplicity, with the objective of portraying reality rather than the biases of those who draw the maps. Depending on the scale of a map, the amount of generalization will vary tremendously. The reader should be wary of maps that fill in masses of names in an attempt to show detail; it used to be that map buyers felt cheated if there were any blank spaces on a map, but a lack of data for an area may be very significant in and of itself. Remember also that on a small-scale map there is rarely any correlation between symbol and reality—a road through a mountainous region may show as a gentle curve and in fact be full of hairpins. Look for the North point: there is a tradition of orienting the top edge of a map to the north, but at larger scales this is not always the case; nor is the North point always parallel with the edge of the map. Beware of maps with pretty colors, touches of artistry, fancy lettering, contrived symbols like little men, and the lack of a grid indication or type of

[10] Arthur H. Robinson, *Geography in Undergraduate Education*, Association of American Geographers, Commission on College Geography, Washington, 1965.

projection. When in doubt about patterns, color, or black-and-white, reverse the shading sequence and see what happens—the message of the map may also be reversed. Do not be misled by simple or by overly complicated maps; they can be good or bad.

The intention in this chapter has been to provide a few hints for developing a critical eye when looking at a map. The ability to differentiate between good and bad maps may take a little practice, but it is well worth the effort. The only way to really appreciate a map is to know its qualities, both positive and negative, at all scales. Maps are a shorthand way of representing part of the reality of the earth's surface, but the symbolic representation is of perceived reality. Maps do not always tell the truth, but the more one knows of the techniques and tricks involved in their production, the better able one is to ascertain the credibility level of the map, and the less likely one is to accept inferior products.

BIBLIOGRAPHY

Boggs, S. W.: "Cartohypnosis," *The Scientific Monthly*, June 1947.

Brown, Lloyd A.: *The Story of Maps*, Bonanza Books, New York, 1949.

Jenks, George F.: "Generalization in Statistical Mapping," *Annals of the Association of American Geographers*, vol. 53, pp. 15-26, 1963.

Mackinder, Halford J.: "The Geographical Pivot of History," *Geographical Journal*, vol. 23, pp. 421-437, 1904.

———: *Democratic Ideals and Reality*, Holt, New York, 1919.

Monkhouse, Francis J., and Henry R. Wilkinson: *Maps and Diagrams*, 2d ed., Methuen, London, 1963.

Quam, Louis O.: "The Use of Maps in Propaganda," *Journal of Geography*, vol. 42, pp. 21-32, 1943.

Raisz, Erwin: *Principles of Cartography*, McGraw-Hill, New York, 1962.

Robinson, Arthur H.: *Geography in Undergraduate Education*, Association of American Geographers, Commission on College Geography, Washington, 1965.

Robinson, Arthur H., and Randall D. Sale: *Elements of Cartography*, 3d ed., Wiley, New York, 1969.

Starkey, Otis P.: "Maps Are Liars," *New York Times Magazine*, Oct. 11, 1942.

Wirsing, Giselher (ed.): *Der Krieg 1939/41 in Karten*, Verlag Knorr und Hirth, Munich, 1941.

PART THREE

SPATIAL ORGANIZATION

We have seen in the preceding section that man's attitudes play an extremely important role in explaining the ways in which he structures his world: attitudes about the characteristics of a place, as well as personality traits, affect spatial behavior. In the following section a more general and at times more abstract view of spatial behavior is presented. An example will make this statement more clear. We can agree that at any single instant in time we can photograph the distribution of population in a city or region. For that moment, we can identify clusters of population which we may assume represent nodes or centers of activity, and also areas with few or no people, areas presumably peripheral to most persons at that instant. Furthermore, by taking such pictures in rapid succession and over long periods of time, we can identify areas which are consistently or at least regularly "nodal" and those areas which are consistently "peripheral" with respect to population distribution. Recall that we have not looked into motivations for movement, perceptions of persons toward places or linkages, or the attitudes which groups have toward their environment. We have noted only the actual flow of persons within our study area, and on the basis of such observations, we will infer characteristics to that area.

Many geographers have attempted to describe *patterns* like the distributions we just discussed and to explain the *processes* behind these patterns. One method of conceptualizing the spatial organization of a society is to consider the nodal areas, peripheral locations, and connecting links as a system or a group of interacting elements forming a whole. All systems include centers of activity or nodes, areas well connected to these nodes, and areas poorly connected to the nodes. The latter areas we have previously referred to as peripheral, or frontier, areas. It must be recalled that the way the system is bounded and similarly the scale of analysis will determine the extent to which a particular place is viewed as nodal. Thus, if the system is bounded by the corporate limits of the village, then the main street will be viewed as the most nodal area; if the county is viewed as the system, then the village main street will be much less nodal; and if the nation is considered to be the system, the village main street may be quite peripheral in the system. Likewise, the particular function under study affects the nodality of areas even within similarly bounded systems. Thus, a rural mountain area may be peripheral in a study of commuter traffic flows, but nodal in a study of recreation land use.

The organization of nodal places is said to be "hierarchical," or to form a hierarchy. By hierarchy, the geographer refers to the ordering of nodal places such that those places which are most nodal are fewest in number and those places which are less nodal are greater in number. Furthermore, the organization of places in a hierarchy suggests differing degrees of functional importance and control with respect to a surrounding area. For example, the typical hierarchy discussed by the urban geographer is that of American cities. New York City and to a lesser extent Los Angeles and Chicago are doubtless nodal with respect to the national system of cities, and even perhaps nodal within an international system of cities. These three cities exercise a great deal of commercial, financial, and even informational control over vast areas and contain a wide range of economic activity. At a lower level in the national hierarchy are regional nodes such as Boston, Atlanta, Seattle, Minneapolis-St. Paul, Kansas City, Dallas, and a number of other large metropolitan areas dominating regional economies. At a still lower level in this hierarchy are the even more numerous cities which provide fewer services at a still more local level such as Duluth, Lubbock, Jacksonville, Birmingham, Wichita Falls, and Auburn, Maine. American cities thus portray the rule of a hierarchical structure: the more nodal, the fewer in number; the wider the range of economic activities, the greater the population and area under its control.

But the most significant advantage of organizing the elements of our surroundings into a system of nodes and linkages is that we can portray flows through the system. Geographers are concerned not only with an unchanging or static structure, but also with the way in which the system operates, with the actual linkages that are the basis for our evaluation of the "nodality" of a place. The spread of an element, an idea, or a group of people through the system can be traced to gain insight into the presumed effects of distance on human interaction, or on seemingly irrational spatial behavior (perhaps the effect of differential perception of opportunities), and the effects of particular types of barriers, physical or cultural, to such movements. Such studies of *diffusion* give us further clues regarding the nature and effect of the hierarchical ordering of places.

The elemental concepts from which the more complex notions of spatial organization are derived have already been discussed. In the introductory chapter, we noted that distance, direction, and connectivity are the elements on which our concept of location and particularly such ideas as "center" or "node" versus "periphery" or "frontier" are based. The very use of the terms "frontier" or 'borderland" imply that there is a localization or concentration of activity in some places and a relative absence of activity in other places. Furthermore, ideas concerning circulation, or movement, are invoked when one studies the flows of goods or ideas or persons through the systematic organization of places. The essays in this section have been selected to illustrate with some rather familiar phenomena the importance of these concepts in the study of location and spatial process.

Students from many disciplines have noted the existence of hierarchical structures. Whether the hierarchy be the plant classifications of the botanists, the church structure of the Roman Catholics, or the less formal power structure in such social organizations as political parties and universities, it is apparent that a hierarchical structure is a pervasive form in human organization. We have already noted the use of the term hierarchy to characterize the size and economic base of American cities. Similarly, we can use such everyday items as newspapers not only to indicate boundaries of zones of influence, but also to predict the detail of local news that will be available to people at particular places. The first of these usages of the newspaper may be most familiar to us, for all we must do to delimit the zone of news influence of a particular large city is to note the places where the daily or Sunday newspaper from that city is sold. For example, we can delimit the zone of influence for Kansas City with respect to St. Louis by observing where along the route between these two cities one city's newspaper becomes the dominant large-city Sunday newspaper. The second use of newspapers, as an indicator of the degree of familiarity its readers have with other places, is a less obvious usage, but is elaborated in the first essay, "Hierarchy and Diffusion: The U.S. Sunday Newspaper." In this article the author presents a rather ingenious device for measuring distance in a "communications space," or, in other words, the degree to which information about two places is likely to be exchanged.

The next two essays develop the ideas of hierarchy with discussions of the flows of elements through the system. In both essays, spatial *diffusion* is discussed, but the examples of diffusion come from different centuries, and deal with quite disparate subjects. The second essay, "The Diffusion of Cholera in the United States in the Nineteenth Century," illustrates spatial diffusion through the urban hierarchy, as well as diffusion due to proximity in linear distance, often referred to as "contagious diffusion" or the "neighborhood effect." A source area is identified for two epidemics, and the effects of both proximity and urban hierarchy are illustrated and analyzed. The third essay moves to the 1950s, the era of rock and roll, to discuss the nodal areas, or "culture hearths," for this cultural trait which diffused "like a disease" through the system of radio stations and record companies. It is particularly interesting to note that while the urban hierarchy discussed in the study of the Sunday newspaper is in many respects similar to the hierarchy through which the cholera epidemic was spread, the nodes and peripheral areas which made up the hierarchy for rock and roll music are quite different. Hierarchy, it should be recalled, is a mental construct, used by researchers to simplify a vast network of interrelationships, and is thus not absolute over time or space, but is very much a function of the element which is being diffused.

An even sharper contrast in the location of nodes and peripheries is presented in the fourth essay, "Up from the Mines and Out from the Prairies." Concepts of hierarchy and diffusion elaborated upon in the first three essays should be used by the reader in this essay. Although the subject matter of the essay is in itself interesting, its importance lies in its analysis of the contrast between "production areas" and "consumption areas" in the United States football player market. Those places which would be considered extremely out-of-the-way in the previous hierarchy are often very important, even nodal, in the production of football players.

Finally, the overall effects of spatial organization are discussed in the important essay "Vietnam, Cuba, and the Ghetto." In this essay, the author describes the consistency that one can see in the spatial organization of revolutionary activity. It is proposed that the principles outlined here are general in their applicability, and can thus perhaps be considered a tool kit for the understanding of other current insurrections such as that in Northern Ireland. Noteworthy also is the application which this essay makes of locational principles in the organization of insurrection in the American metropolis.

The concepts of hierarchy, diffusion, connectivity, and nodality are useful for an understanding of the orderly patterns of spatial arrangements which characterize our environment. The first essay lays the foundation for the development of these concepts.

CHAPTER FOUR

HIERARCHY AND DIFFUSION

The U.S. Sunday Newspaper

VAUGHN LUECK

The source and content of the news we hear and read shape our ideas about our world and affect the ways in which we understand and structure our surroundings. In this context, the relative places in which we live in the urban hierarchy take on a vital significance, for the amount and quality of information about our surroundings varies according to the position of a city within the diffusion hierarchy. Let us examine the role newspapers play in structuring and maintaining this hierarchy of information.

THE CONCEPT OF HIERARCHY: NEWSPAPER CIRCULATION

Hierarchy is clearly present in newspaper circulation. Larger places send substantial numbers of newspapers to smaller places, but smaller places send relatively few papers up the hierarchy to larger ones. For example, approximately 5,000 copies of the daily edition of the *New York Times* circulate in the Chicago area, while only about 300 copies of the *Chicago Tribune* circulate in the New York area. About 2,000 copies of the *Tribune* circulate in the central Illinois city of Peoria, but only about 50 copies a day of the *Peoria Journal* reach Chicago. Moving even farther down the hierarchy, 3,200 copies of the *Peoria Journal* circulate in the county containing the town of Canton, Illinois (population 15,000), but less than 100 copies of the Canton paper travel the 35 miles to Peoria.

Such figures exemplify typical characteristics of flow hierarchies. Let us consider for a moment some of the terminology used to discuss these patterns and relationships. We can examine a hypothetical college administration as an example of a flow hierarchy. In such a hierarchy, commands typically move downward and information about operations of the firm moves upward. A directive from the president would ordinarily be issued to the vice presidents. They would in turn pass the president's orders on to their subordinates, possibly rewording them, clarifying them, or stressing the implications most pertinent to the operation of the division or department concerned. Conversely, information about the personnel division would ordinarily circulate first to the vice president for financial affairs. Such information would reach the president's ears only if the vice president deemed it sufficiently important. Two employees at an equal level, for example the chairman of the geology department and the director of athletics, would not ordinarily exchange information about college operations or give orders to one another except indirectly by way of one of the vice presidents or the president. This sort of relationship is the essential property of a flow hierarchy: *the dominance of vertical flow* over cross-linkages or horizontal flow.

Flow hierarchies may differ in some respects. In some hierarchies events pass through the network in an essentially unaltered fashion. For example, in a hierarchy of streams, the water entering minor tributaries is still water when it enters the ocean. Hierarchies of this type are *passive*. Most flow hierarchies involving human beings are *active*. That is, the elements flowing through the hierarchy are altered in quantity or quality of flow. In our hypothetical college, information given by third-level employees to the vice presidents is selected, edited, and generalized by the vice presidents before it is conveyed to the president.

Flow hierarchies can also be differentiated by their directionality. In some cases, the flow runs in only one direction, as in the example of the stream hierarchy. In most instances, however, hierarchies are two-directional, and flows move both upward and downward in the hierarchy, as in the example of the college. This example also illustrates that a flow hierarchy may be passive in one direction and active in another. Commands flow downward in a relatively unaltered fashion, but information moving upward through the hierarchy is acted upon at each upward level, edited, and generalized. When the president makes a policy decision concerning smoking in classrooms and transmits his orders to the vice presidents who in turn pass them on to their subordinates, the decision is implemented at all levels without substantial alteration. The situation for upward movement is quite different. If the professor of Latin sends the vice president for internal affairs a detailed itemized account of the stuffy atmosphere in his classroom, the filth resulting from ashes and crushed cigarettes, and the film of smoke residue covering the windows and walls, the president would learn only that the students smoking in classrooms were a problem because teachers were complaining about dirty rooms and as a result maintenance costs were rising. A flow hierarchy of this type is *downward passive* and *upward active*; flows are substantially altered only when moving upward in the hierarchy. In our case of the circulation of Chicago, Peoria, and Canton newspapers, there is also clearly a downward-passive and upward-active flow.

The intercity patterns of Sunday newspaper circulation can be portrayed as a tree map or tree (Figure 4-1). Such a tree can be created by drawing a line from each city publishing a Sunday newspaper to the city from which it receives the largest number of out-of-town newspapers. The level of a city, in the newspaper hierarchy, can be defined by the number of links separating it from New York. Chicago, according to this definition, is a second-order city, and Fargo, North Dakota, is a third-order city. The Sunday newspaper tree as a whole may be described as a three-level hierarchy with New York at the top.

New York's first-order position is primarily the result of the nationwide circulation of the Sunday *Times*. In Michigan, for example, about 9,000 copies of the Sunday *Times* reach Detroit, or about 7 for every 1,000 households. In Grand Rapids, Michigan's second largest city and at the third-level in the hierarchy, only about 2 households in 1,000 read the Sunday *Times*. A significant exception to this rule can be found in college towns, which have a much higher *Times* circulation than their size would warrant. Ann Arbor, Michigan, for example, has a *Times* circulation of 59 copies per 1,000 households, over eight times the Detroit rate. Despite high *Times* penetration rates, no college town reaches second-order status because they are all penetrated to an even greater extent by papers published in second-order cities.

For the most part second-order cities are those commonly recognized as regional metropolises—such places as Atlanta, Dallas, Minneapolis-St. Paul, or San Francisco. These are the cities which have Federal Reserve Banks, major league sports teams, and home offices of major corporations; they are also most frequently chosen as the sites of branch offices for activities headquartered elsewhere. In short, they are focal points coordinating economic and social activity within their extensive regional spheres of influence.

Second-rank cities of the Northeast linked to New York have a somewhat different character. They are much smaller in size and are much more heavily penetrated by the Sunday *Times*. While directly linked to New York, these places are scarcely regional centers. If located elsewhere in the country, they would be classified as third-order because cities of their size usually receive heaviest circulation from second-order centers. Since they are located nearer to New York than to any regional center, New York assumes the role of a regional metropolis for these cities. It may also be observed that New York's national role gives it a decided advantage in competing with adjacent regional metropolises. The Carolinas, for example, are directly linked with New York despite the proximity of Atlanta.

Third-level publishing centers are usually small cities whose Sunday circulation is continued in an area surrounding the city of publication. However, some third-order cities, Kansas City, for example, are of substantial size and have subordinates of their own. The most elaborate case of this type is centered on

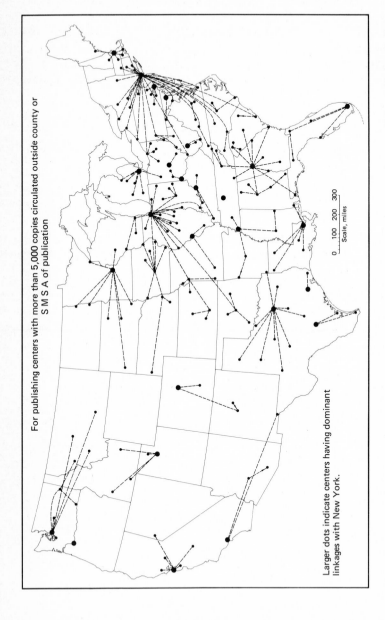

For publishing centers with more than 5,000 copies circulated outside county or S M S A of publication

Larger dots indicate centers having dominant linkages with New York.

0   100   200   300
Scale, miles

Figure 4-1 Tree map of the intercity patterns of Sunday newspaper circulation. This map shows the flow of Sunday newspapers from SMSA's to smaller cities.

Chicago, which has several third-order subordinates with subordinates of their own: seven for Des Moines, five for Kansas City, and three each for Milwaukee, Indianapolis, and Oklahoma City. Two of the fourth-order centers in this complex system even have fifth-level centers below them, which represent the lowest level to be found in this national hierarchy.

ISOLATION AND NEARNESS

The number of hierarchical steps or links separating two points within the hierarchy can be used as a measure of the isolation, because information is generalized and edited at each point where the links join. By this measure, two immediate subordinates of the same center would each have a distance of *one* from the center, but a distance of *two* from each other.

The probability of news of a given item diffusing to another place within the hierarchy is a *geometric* function of the distance between the two places. In other words, if half of the information arriving at a given city from its subordinates is edited before it is transmitted up the hierarchy, only one-fourth of the information would pass through a city two steps up the ladder, only one-eighth through one three steps up and so on. Taking one of the most mutually isolated pairs of cities in the newspaper hierarchy, Salina, Kansas, and Dothan, Alabama, which can only be joined by the very indirect eighth-step connection of Salina-Wichita-Kansas City-Chicago-New York-Atlanta-Birmingham-Montgomery-Dothan (see Figure 4-1), and assuming that nine-tenths of information occurring in a subordinate is edited by its superior when upward diffusion is occurring, and that one-half is edited when diffusion is downward, one comes to the striking conclusion that only one news item in sixteen thousand occurring in one city would diffuse to the other. It is not difficult to see that, if other media of diffusion have a similar type of hierarchical organization, the amount of spatial behavior linking two such cities is going to be very small.

The measure of distance from New York is particularly interesting, because it is essentially a measure of isolation within the hierarchy of national diffusion. If the diffusion of a given piece of information is to be nationwide, New York, as the national center, must either originate it or relay it. According to this measure, the most isolated places in the national network are the fifth-order centers: Scottsbluff and Lincoln, Nebraska; Salina and Hutchinson, Kansas; and Dothan, Alabama. In theory, information originating in these centers would be least likely to make national headlines, and national news will reach these places last and in the most modified form. It is interesting to note the correspondence of the isolation of these centers within the national newspaper hierarchy with the national stereotype (perhaps undeserved) of their general vicinity as cultural backwaters.

The isolation of these centers does not derive from their size, but from the indirectness of their linkage with New York. Many cities of comparable size have more direct linkages. To mention an extreme case, Erie, Pennsylvania, a second-order city, has about the same population as Lincoln, Nebraska, a fifth-order city. Similarly, centers along much of the eastern seaboard (Hartford, Syracuse, or Greensboro) are as "near" to the national information center as are the outlying larger regional metropolises. By the same token, Grand Rapids, Michigan, is more isolated than Salt Lake City, which is of comparable population size, but a regional center.

Although many provocative observations can be made from the tree of newspaper circulation, it is difficult to evaluate the significance of this particular example. Hierarchies of newspaper circulation may represent a wide variety of hierarchical diffusion patterns, as has been suggested here, or they may have little connection with other forms of diffusion. We really do not yet know much about the types of trees (or nontrees) into which the various media of diffusion, such as telephone calls or mail flow, are organized. However, the implications of recent research on the effects of poor access to information sources on unemployment and poverty make an increased awareness of the hierarchical structure of our sources of information not only an interesting, but a vital area for further careful study.

CHAPTER FIVE

THE DIFFUSION OF CHOLERA IN THE UNITED STATES IN THE NINETEENTH CENTURY*

G.F. PYLE

COMMENT

In the next essay, the subject matter and the time setting are different from the preceding selection, but the ideas and vocabulary are not. The combination of the neighborhood effect and the hierarchy of cities in the process of diffusion are particularly important concepts to note.

*"The Diffusion of Cholera in the United States in the Nineteenth Century," by Gerald F. Pyle, is adapted from *Geographical Analysis*, vol. 1, pp. 59-75, 1969, and is Copyright © 1969 by the Ohio State University Press. All rights reserved.

Two diffusion processes have been discussed. The first focuses on the frictional effects of distance and emphasizes diffusion sequences operating over space. The second has been studied less and is concerned with processes moving downward from larger to smaller centers in an urban system; this kind of sequence can be termed "hierarchical diffusion."

The example presented here shows that during the early years of the nineteenth century, when access was difficult and the urban system was undeveloped, cholera spread largely through the "neighborhood effect." By 1866, however, an urban hierarchy had emerged, and railroads already provided a modicum of rapid national integration. The cholera epidemic of that year diffused hierarchically.

CHOLERA

The occurrence of cholera is rooted in Asian antiquity. Three major cholera pandemics lashed out at the United States in the nineteenth century. The movement of the disease through the urban system was rapid. The recognized epidemic years of national proportions were 1832, 1849, and 1866. This study related differences in the diffusion of cholera in the United States to the country's evolving urban and transportation system.

Rosenberg offers a vivid presentation of the three successive waves of the disease in New York City. New York was an international port capable of receiving cholera from dozens of maritime sources, and some of the filthiest slums in the city were adjacent to the port facilities. It was only natural for New York City to be the first to feel the impact of an epidemic, and in most instances this is apparently what happened.

Although accounts for some cities are scanty, the shock of cholera was such that enough has been published to track the spread of each of the three epidemics from one urban center to another. Thus, an attempt can be made to isolate similarities in epidemic movements over time.

Cholera is a serious intestinal disease. Medical writers have often, conventionally, segmented cholera into several stages. As explained by De, the stages are characterized by (1) premonitory diarrhea, (2) copious evacuation, (3) collapse, (4) reaction, and (5) uremia. It is possible in acute circumstances for cholera to start with one of the latter stages, especially after an epidemic is fully developed. Conversely, a mild case may be manifested only by diarrhea.

Man is the prime reservoir for cholera. The several cholera vibrios which spread from one person to another are carried initially by human feces which contaminate water. Geographic conditions favoring the spread of the disease include warm temperatures and prolonged dry spells. The vibrios have a chance to flourish in warm alkaline mediums, and as epidemics spread, sources such as food and flies can carry the disease in addition to contaminated water.

May suggests several possible forms of immunity, but it is clear much is still unknown. The possible immunities are (1) natural, (2) excessive hydrochloric acid in the stomach, (3) inoculation, and (4) recent past history of the disease.

During the first part of the nineteenth century, Europeans in Asia received an exposure to a cholera pandemic from 1816 to 1823. This first in a series of pandemics receded only to penetrate all Europe and, eventually, North America, starting in 1826.

THE EPIDEMIC OF 1832 AND ITS PATH THROUGH THE URBAN SYSTEM

In 1832, the United States was barely more than a frontier country. Most major cities of the time were periodically drowned in mud. Pigs roamed the streets of New York. Sanitation as it is now known was virtually unheard of. However, the nucleus of the present urban system already existed.

The early 1830s were within the great water transportation era of the United States. Traffic was steady on the Ohio-Mississippi system, and the Hudson River and Erie Canal in New York carried heavy flows. The Great Lakes and Atlantic seaboard also were heavily utilized waterways. Poor sanitation coupled with a riverine orientation to produce conditions ripe for a cholera epidemic.

The path of cholera from one city to another in 1832 can be traced. The reconstruction of the epidemic is initially shown in Table 5-1. The "officially recognized entry dates" on the table are the first possible accounts of an epidemic which could be found for the cities listed. The very violent nature of a major epidemic suggests that early accounts are reasonably reliable in terms of when cholera first struck a city.

Population figures have been added to the table to demonstrate particular urban relationships among the cities. One relationship is obvious from examination of the population clusters: cholera struck larger cities and subsequently showed up adjacent to the larger cities. The result is a general hierarchy of "cholera fields" throughout the country.

There are, however, more noteworthy spatial relationships reflected in Table 5-1. When the cities shown on the table are plotted on a map of the United States, as has been done with Figure 5-1, it is possible to show patterns of movement from one city to the next. The dates in Table 5-1 indicate several separate movements.

CANADIAN ORIGIN

Montreal and Quebec shared the port facilities at Grosse Ile on the St. Lawrence River in 1832, and it was from here that the epidemic probably entered North America. The epidemic spread rapidly down the St. Lawrence River and continued until it reached Lake Champlain in the United States. By the time the epidemic entered Albany, it had traveled both from the north and from New

Table 5-1 Officially Recognized Entry Dates for Cholera: 1832 Epidemic

CITY	DATE	CITY SIZE
Plattsburgh, N.Y.	June 11	4,913
Burlington, Vt.	June 13	3,526
White Hall, N.Y.	June 14	2,888
Niagara, N.Y.	June 22	1,401
Erie, Pa.	June 26	1,329
New York City	June 26	202,589
Pittsburgh, Pa.	July 2	12,542
Albany, N.Y.	July 3	24,238
Philadelphia, Pa.	July 5	161,410
Richmond, Va.	July 6	16,060
Detroit, Mich.	July 6	2,222
Newark, N.J.	July 7	10,953
Cleveland, Ohio	July 10	1,076
Schenectady, N.Y.	July 12	11,405
Rochester N.Y.	July 12	9,269
Chicago, Ill.	July 12	4,470
New Haven, Conn.	July 14	10,180
New Brunswick, N.J.	July 14	7,830
Buffalo, N.Y.	July 15	8,653
Lockport, N.Y.	July 19	2,121
Hartford, Conn.	July 19	7,074
Frankfort, N.Y.	July 22	2,620
Newport, R.I.	July 24	8,010
Norfolk, Va.	July 24	14,998
Jersey City, N.J.	July 26	12,568
Annapolis, Md.	July 30	2,623
Providence, R.I.	July 31	16,836
Baltimore, Md.	August 4	80,625
Boston, Mass.	August 5	61,393
New Castle, Del.	August 6	2,463
Washington, D.C.	August 8	18,827
Andover, Mass.	August 18	4,540
Haverhill, Mass.	August 25	3,912
Rock Island, Ill.	August 26	
Cincinnati, Ohio	September 30	24,831
Covington, Ky.	October 4	743
Charleston, S.C.	Late October	30,286
Lexington, Ky.	November 6	6,104
Frankfort, Ky.	November 6	1,680
Baton Rouge, La.	November 8	9,809
New Orleans, La.	November 18	46,310
Bangor, Me.	December 26	2,863

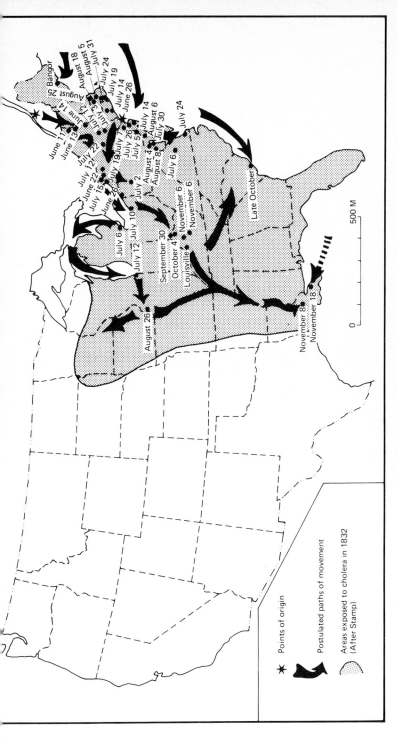

Figure 5-1 The movement of cholera in 1832. This map shows the paths followed by the 1832 cholera epidemic in the United States.

75

York City to the south. Meanwhile, the pestilence of Canadian origin moved across Lake Ontario and Lake Erie to Buffalo, Erie, and Pittsburgh. The time of the year during which Detroit, Chicago, and Rock Island reported outbreaks suggests Canadian origins (see Table 5-1). However, in many instances the original point of departure may have been New York City.

NEW YORK ORIGIN: INLAND WATERWAYS

There is some confusion within the literature as to whether cholera did or did not first appear in New York City in April 1832. It may simply have traveled down the Hudson River from Canadian sources in the early summer of that year. Official records indicate that cities in the Lake Champlain-Northern Hudson River area had outbreaks two weeks before New York City. However, the disease was firmly established in New York by late June, and it apparently moved up the Hudson Valley from that city. It then followed the Erie Canal to western New York State in the wake of the Canadian wave. The movement continued with traffic down the Ohio Canal to the Ohio and Mississippi Rivers, eventually to strike Baton Rouge and New Orleans in November. Meanwhile, the Atlantic seaboard was experiencing similar problems.

NEW YORK ORIGIN: EASTERN SEABOARD

The third path of cholera movement was outward from New York along the Atlantic Coast. The epidemic apparently spread from New York through New Jersey to Philadelphia and on to Baltimore, Virginia, and eventually, Charleston. It also spread north to Boston and New England. There were, however, many other possible methods of entry. One extreme example of other modes of cholera spread, and the strength of the vibrios is given by an account from Bangor, Maine:

During December 1832, a chest of clothing that had belonged to a sailor, who had died of cholera at a Baltic port, arrived at his home in a small village near Bangor, Me. The chest was opened, the clothing was distributed to his friends, and all who received the garments were taken with cholera and died.

The severity of the epidemic is illustrated in contemporary accounts from Philadelphia, which was hard hit by the epidemic. A report by the College of Physicians in 1832 shows that there were sporadic outbreaks of cholera before the 1832 epidemic. For the ten-year period ending in 1831, 2,437 deaths were attributed to cholera. Three general classes of sanitary regulation improvement— relating to place, habitation, and person—were suggested by the physicians because of the epidemic.

As indicated by Rosenberg, New York was drastically in need of sanitary improvements, and for years responsible citizens had agitated for a new water supply. When the epidemic hit the city, the slum areas were affected first, and it was felt the epidemic would stop in these areas. However, it occasionally crept into the homes of some finer folk through their servants' quarters.

The epidemic eventually hit people of most levels of the New York social hierarchy, just as it hit the various levels of society in many cities. The arrows in Figure 5-1 give an indication of its movement. Of equal importance is the shaded area. Taken from a rendition by Stamp, the shaded portion of the map shows areas of the United States eventually exposed to the epidemic. In the long run, status meant little.

The cholera data for 1832 can be examined in other ways in an attempt to better understand spatial movements. The time sequence from Table 5-1 was utilized to postulate paths of movement and points of origin. If the populations of these cities, classed into three groups in accordance with point of origin, are plotted against time of exposure, no definite relationship appears to exist. The points are widely scattered.

However, if distance from point of origin is plotted against time of epidemic recognition (Figure 5-1), the three paths of movement show up once again. Clearly, in 1832 distance was more important than city size.

There are many possible reasons for the relationship above. Two seem to stand out. The transportation system in 1832 was immature, that is, it was not comprehensive by modern standards, and the urban system, as noted by Borchert, was still evolving.

The importance of the time lag is further explained by the fact that the epidemic wintered over in the Kentucky Bluegrass area, and cholera ravaged that region through most of 1833.

THE EPIDEMIC OF 1849

The next epidemic diffused through the better-structured United States urban system of 1849. In the late 1840s water transportation was still very important in the United States. Railroads were spreading, but many parts of the country now considered as the Midwest were not yet connected to the East by rail.

From 1842 to 1862 cholera once more raked the world as a pandemic. The disease, originating in South Asia, was spread by pilgrimages, commercial travel vessels, warships, and related transportation movements. There is clear evidence that the disease entered the United States at two points within a nine-day period of time. New York was attacked on December 2, 1848, and New Orleans felt the first effects on December 11.

Table 5-2 has been constructed to show the spatial relationships reflected in the 1849 cholera epidemic in this country. Two things are clear: (1) smaller cities immediately adjacent to large cities contracted the disease after the primary centers; and (2) the disease filtered down the urban hierarchy. Closer examination reveals *two* paths of filtration: one through the interior waterways system, and a second one along the Atlantic seaboard.

Table 5-2 Officially Recognized Entry Dates for Cholera: 1849 Epidemic

CITY	DATE	CITY SIZE
New York City	Dec. 1, 1848	515,547
New Orleans, La.	Dec. 11, 1848	116,375
Louisville, Ky.	Dec. 22, 1848	43,194
Cincinnati, Ohio	Dec. 25, 1848	115,436
St. Louis, Mo.	Dec. 27, 1848	77,860
Nashville, Tenn.	Jan. 20, 1849	10,165
Mobile, Ala.	January 1849	20,515
Quincy, Ill.	March 1849	6,902
Cairo, Ill.	Apr. 14, 1849	242
Chicago, Ill.	Apr. 29, 1849	29,963
Philadelphia, Pa.	May 22, 1849	340,045
Baltimore, Md.	May 22, 1849	169,054
Buffalo, N.Y.	May 30, 1849	42,261
Richmond, Va.	May 30, 1849	27,570
Norfolk, Va.	May 30, 1849	14,326
Boston, Mass.	June 4, 1849	136,881
Newark, N.J.	June 4, 1849	38,894
Sandusky, Ohio	July 8, 1849	1,040
Frankfort, Ky.	July 14, 1849	3,308
Detroit, Mich.	Aug. 14, 1849	21,019
Casper, Wyo.	Spring 1850	
Sacramento, Calif.	October 1850	6,820
San Francisco, Calif.	Late 1850	34,776

INTERIOR WATERWAYS

Figure 5-2 indicates the extent of this path of movement. Although the wave of New Orleans origin entered nine days after the eastern epidemic, it traveled farther and lasted longer. Cholera moved rapidly up the Mississippi and Ohio Rivers. By January 1849, it had reached Cincinnati. It traveled from there through the interior of Ohio. It moved eventually up the Illinois River to Chicago and from there it spread to the East, probably by Great Lakes steamboats. It did not arrive in Detroit until August. In addition, it followed the pioneers west. The disease finally spread into Sacramento in October 1850, and from there it quickly moved to San Francisco.

Little was known about the disease. A report prepared by the City Physician of Boston stated that cholera was not contagious. Most of the people who died of cholera were said to be from the class with a high proportion of "foreigners" who paid little attention to public facts. To no one's surprise, most of the persons who died of cholera were classed as "intemperate."

THE EASTERN SEABOARD MOVEMENTS

After a lag of almost six months, the epidemic spread rapidly along the Atlantic seaboard. The dates for entry into specific Eastern cities form a definite cluster within Table 5-2, and the time lag shows up most clearly in Figure 5-2. Why the long lag? The temperature could have been low enough to control spread, or perhaps the lag was merely the result of bad reporting. One thing was clear: once the epidemic started to spread, there was no stopping it.

Within New York, the epidemic was apparently more widespread. In May 1849, the New York Board of Health appointed a Sanatory [*sic*] Committee to investigate the epidemic. The ensuing report shows that the first major concentration of the disease was noted in the "Five Points" slum area. From there it diffused outward. There were 15,219 deaths traced either directly to some form of cholera or indirectly to symptomatically related maladies. The chief cause of cholera was thought to exist in the atmosphere.

Even by the end of this second major pandemic, the miasmatic approach prevailed. And if cholera was not caused by bad air (malaria), then it was thought to be due to one's lack of piety. However, shortly after the 1849 epidemic, John Snow in London worked out a plausible scheme for understanding cholera. Snow's approach is a well-known study in urban medical geography.

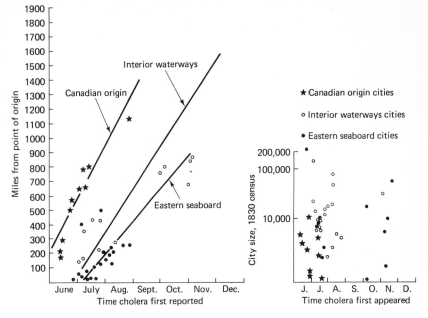

Figure 5-2   The movement of cholera through the 1832 urban system. This illustration compares the role distance played in the diffusion of cholera with the effect of hierarchic diffusion.

Snow recognized the spatial variability of cholera cases as they related to the location of water pumps. He noticed the area around the Broad Street pump was especially bad, and thus he had the pump handle removed. The number of cases immediately went down. Although Snow entertained no serious notions of vibrios, he started a successful sanitation campaign, having discovered one method of arresting the spread of cholera.

Once again, time of entry and population have been compared. The urban-system interrelationships were much clearer in 1849 than they were in 1832. Figure 5-2 shows the two paths of movement and how they reflect the growing urban hierarchy. This suggests that city size by 1849 was as important as distance from point of origin in the spread of cholera along both paths of movement.

THE EPIDEMIC OF 1866

By 1866, the railroads connecting the eastern part of the United States were essentially completed. The Mississippi River had been bridged. It was possible to move from one part of the country to another by land at a relatively rapid rate. An integrated national urban system had now formed.

On May 2, 1866, cholera again entered New York City. For the national epidemic which followed, New York could easily have been the point of origin and dispersal. The dates recorded in Table 5-3 demonstrate a definite tendency outward from New York toward smaller cities. The familiar hierarchical pattern is also reflected by the "cholera fields" presented in Table 5-3. In addition, Figure 5-3 shows an even more striking movement with time down the urban hierarchy. Postulated paths of movement and the affected area are also given in Figure 5-3.

One path of movement outward from New York to Detroit, Cincinnati, and Chicago is suggested. It also probably traveled down the Ohio and Mississippi Rivers to Vicksburg. It moved from Chicago to St. Louis and the West. Many Texas cities felt severe epidemics for the first time. Not only were many of them raw frontier towns with inadequate sanitation, but they also supported large army populations.

The epidemic also arrived from New Orleans and spread along the Gulf Coast area to Galveston and Brownsville. Texas, then, could have received the epidemic from two directions. The disease also moved up the Mississippi to Vicksburg, placing that town in a position similar to that of Albany and Buffalo in 1832. The disease had previously moved along the Atlantic piedmont to Atlanta and on into the shattered South.

In 1865, miasmatic theories continued to be accepted. However, experience with previous epidemics served to control somewhat the spread of cholera within New York in 1866. In a report published in that city, certain "cholera fields" (this is a reference to parts of the city) were recognized. Strong measures were taken to improve sanitation, and as a result the epidemic was not so severe as

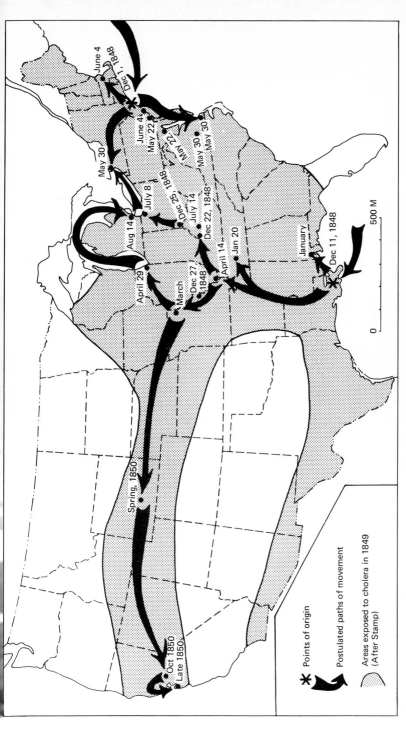

Figure 5-3 The movement of cholera in 1849. This map shows the paths of the 1849 cholera epidemic as it spread through the United States.

81

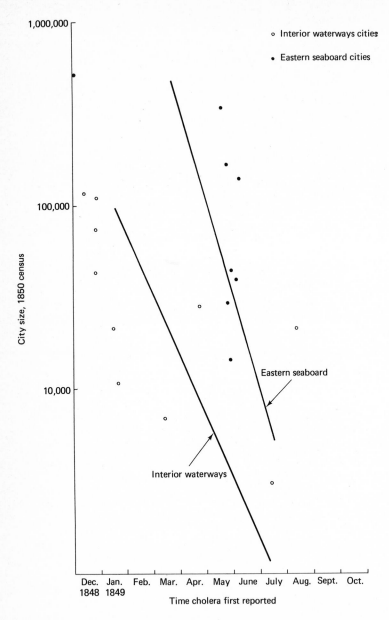

Figure 5-4   The movement of cholera through the 1849 urban system. This figure illustrates the correlation between city size (position in urban hierarchy) and the spread of cholera.

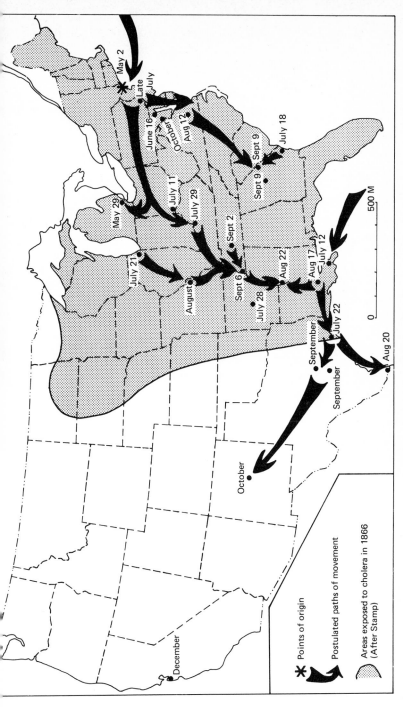

Figure 5-5 The movement of cholera in 1866. This map shows the paths of the 1866 epidemic as it spread through the United States.

83

Table 5-3 Officially Recognized Entry Dates for Cholera: 1866 Epidemic

CITY	DATE	CITY SIZE
New York City	May 2	942,292
Detroit, Mich.	May 29	79,577
Baltimore, Md.	June 16	267,354
Cincinnati, Ohio	July 11	216,239
New Orleans, La.	July 12	191,418
Savannah, Ga.	July 18	28,235
Chicago, Ill.	July 21	298,977
Galveston, Tex.	July 22	13,818
Little Rock, Ark.	July 28	12,380
Louisville, Ky.	July 29	100,753
Philadelphia, Pa.	Late July	674,022
Richmond, Va.	Aug. 12	51,038
Baton Rouge, La.	Aug. 17	6,498
Brownsville, Tex.	Aug. 20	4,905
Vicksburg, Miss.	Aug. 22	12,443
St. Louis, Mo.	August	310,864
Nashville, Tenn.	Sept. 2	25,865
Memphis, Tenn.	Sept. 6	40,226
Augusta, Ga.	Sept. 9	15,389
Atlanta, Ga.	Sept. 9	21,789
San Antonio, Tex.	September	12,256
Austin, Tex.	September	4,428
Washington, D.C.	October	109,199
Albuquerque, N.M.	October	1,307
San Francisco, Calif.	December	149,473

those of previous years. This was in spite of the fact that New York had a population of almost 1 million.

The United States was visited again by cholera in 1873, but it was not so widespread. Sporadic outbreaks and isolated cases appeared until shortly after the turn of the century when the disease disappeared from this country.

CONCLUSIONS

Several relationships about cholera diffusion and urbanization stand out. As the disease spread in a different way during each epidemic, contact with the environment was also changing. In 1832, contact with the natural environment was close, transportation was crude, and the urban hierarchy had not yet evolved. In 1849, the disease moved down the evolving hierarchy in two ways, thus reflecting more control over the environment and some integration of the

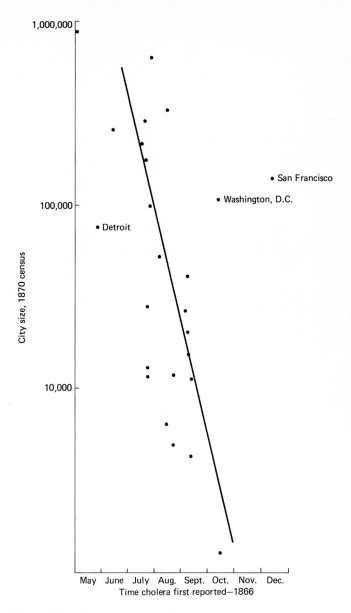

Figure 5-6   The movement of cholera through the 1866 urban system. This figure illustrates the correlation between city size (position in urban hierarchy) and the spread of cholera.

urban system since 1832. The 1866 epidemic shows a completed hierarchy. City size was a prime factor in the spread of cholera over space and through time. Differences in the spread of the epidemic were thus related to a changing transportation and urban environment.

CHAPTER SIX

DIFFUSION AND POPULAR CULTURE

Comments on
the Spatial Aspects
of Rock Music

RICHARD V. FRANCAVIGLIA

COMMENT

The previous essay offers some insights into the notion of
hierarchy by tracing the diffusion of a disease through the
hierarchy of American cities. In the following essay, the
nodes and connections within the same system of cities
change since the trait being diffused is different. In the
example of rock music it is somewhat more difficult to
identify the specific linkages between areas of origin and
destination because the rate at which rock music spread
throughout the United States was very rapid. Note the location of the areas of origin, or in this case "culture hearths,"
and try to account for the differences in the focuses for the
spread of cholera in the nineteenth century and the spread
of rock and roll music in the 1950s.

THE MYTH

Incredible as it may seem, rock and roll music has already passed into the history of popular culture. Springing from humble roots in the early 1950s, by the end of the decade it had captured and dominated a substantial part of the record industry. By the early 1960s, rock and roll was "king." A group sang about its sweeping the entire nation and penetrating deep into the hearts of everyone where it would remain and "never, no never" change. Rock and roll would stand!

Despite this proclamation, however, rock and roll music had a life-span of about ten years, from 1953 to 1963. By the middle-to-late sixties, people were already becoming nostalgic about the "oldies but goodies" and "vintage rock." The sound which was to be so permanent had been replaced by harder rock music. It did not last forever, but its influences will be felt in popular music into the future.

Contrary to the general notion, rock and roll may have swept this land, but it reached only certain hearts, albeit millions. The rate of acceptance of rock and roll by this nation's youth varied in both time and space. Like most elements of a culture, rock and roll originated in a specific place and spread to other parts of the region occupied by the culture. The original area is called a "culture hearth"; the spreading process is called "diffusion."

THE SOUND: SOURCE

Those who do not like contemporary music will be surprised to learn that rock and roll music was quite a bit more complex and interesting than its simple and basic name. Students of rock and roll have noted that, in its accentuation of notes and in its basic structure, it was primarily a fusion of two major types of music, both of them originating in the American South. The first was the classic black "rhythm and blues" with its "low down" beat and wailing, soulful lyrics. Rhythm and blues had been around since at least the 1930s and 1940s. The second ingredient in rock and roll was rockabilly, an up-tempo form of country western music. Rockabilly was also a part of Southern culture. West Tennessee was an important center for it.

By the early 1950s both styles were well developed. It is claimed that white rockabilly singers were so impressed with the popularity that rhythm and blues began experiencing in the early 1950s they began to copy black singers, and effectively combined the two styles. Rock and roll was born.

The juxtaposition of white rockabilly and black rhythm and blues in the Delta Area of the South reflected pronounced racial segregation, yet the two kinds of music originated in a fairly confined area surrounding Memphis. The upper Delta Area is certainly one of the single most important hearth areas in American music history. When rock and roll was born, local singers were there to answer the call. Out of any dozen rock and roll performers in the early years, at least half a dozen were likely to be from this area. Those singers have been immortalized: Little Richard, Fats Domino, Chuck Berry, Elvis Presley, Jerry Lee Lewis, to name but a few. Black and white alike, they changed the shape, meaning, and content of American music.

SOME CARRIERS: D.J.'S AND DISCS

Rock and roll was apparently introduced into white culture after a growing number of youths in various cities began listening to black rhythm and blues records. This interest began to erode the prejudicial "standards" against black music, especially earthy black music. This first contact of white youth with black culture set the stage for a wide variety of songs, lyrics, dances, and expressions which had at one time been taboo in white culture. In 1952, Alan Freed, a disc jockey in Cleveland, Ohio, is said to have become fascinated by the large numbers of white youth listening to, and buying, "race" records as they were then called. Race records were in reality rhythm and blues records sung by black singers and recorded on independent labels. The songs and the records were catching on: an "R and B" concert in Cleveland that year drew 30,000 people—most of them white!

Alan Freed is to be credited with disseminating these musical sounds to a wider, basically white, audience. In 1954, he moved to New York City and started his own show. It featured large doses of previously frowned upon, or prohibited, black music. It also featured the new rock and roll records by both black and white performers. It was a huge success. In the course of about a year, the complexion of popular music in New York began to change. Other major metropolitan areas soon had their own rock and roll shows. In Los Angeles, for example, the Johnny Otis show gained a wide audience.

Rock and roll music actually had two major modes of diffusion. The first was over the airwaves. Local black radio stations, and later stations owned by whites, kept listeners aware of the latest musical sounds. The availability of a radio really made the difference. The popularity of television relegated the radio to the kids' room. Little did parents realize what many a teen-ager was listening to in the small hours of the night.

The other mode of diffusion was the 45 rpm record. It was a flat donut-shaped disc with a big hole in the middle. When played on the old Victrola (after the insertion of a converter disc), the new sounds issuing from the old machine made parents cringe. Songs like "I Want a Bowlegged Woman" contrasted strongly with "On Top of Old Smokey."

These wobbly little records with bright-colored exotic labels such as "Excello" and "Aladdin" seemed to come from nowhere. They cost 49 to 98 cents. They could easily be carried around and played anywhere and everywhere. They, along with radio stations, were responsible for the diffusion of a new musical sound.

SOME SOUND BARRIERS: THE REJECTION OF A TRAIT

But if rock and roll was accepted by millions of eager young people, it was also rejected by just as many, or more. In its early days, it was considered a disease of epidemic proportions—something like cholera, but even worse. According to many people, it represented a conspiracy or plot by black people to undermine the morals of white youth. It was given derogatory names like "jungle music" and "nigger music." This was true not only in rural areas and the American South in general, but also in the major Northern cities.

In many rural areas rock and roll either was forbidden or simply had little appeal. Country and western and rockabilly were uncontested as the only music worth listening to. It took several years for that barrier to break down. But it did. In the South itself, the resentment against rock and roll was widespread. Written parental consent was obligatory before young people could dance to rock and roll music in Atlanta, Georgia.

Even in the supposedly liberal Northern cities, rock and roll music encountered heavy opposition. Alan Freed was arrested in Boston for allegedly inciting a riot, and one Chicago disc jockey broke rock and roll records over the air. Larry Ford noted that "rock and roll was banned on radio stations from Houston to New Haven."[1] But no matter how hard the going, it seemed that rough times strengthened opposition against the establishment. Acceptance of rock and roll was connected with a fascination with an almost alien black culture; continued acceptance of rock and roll meant a protest against established social values.

AND SOMETHING ABOUT THE ACCEPTORS

Rock and roll may have been forbidden and outlawed in many places, but it simply wouldn't stay banned. It was played, defiantly at times. In spite of massive pressure, it gained wide acceptance. Parents said "no"; kids said "yes." The kids won. But this is not to say that they all were converted into rock and roll buffs in one fell swoop. It took time.

It has been pointed out that almost anything, a new philosophical idea or a new type of lawnmower, finds its way into any society at different rates. In the case of rock and roll, the sociologist David Riesman noted that a very special kind of person listened to the music in its early days. They were an intensely interested avant-garde, a group of young people with inquiring minds—the kinds of young people who twisted their radio dials away from standard "hit parade" stations and onto the earthy, heavy rhythm and blues sounds. These kids led the trend; they were innovators.

These young people had actually experimented with the values of another culture. Wailing, pleading songs—some of them frankly erotic—were fascinating.

[1] Larry Ford "Geographic Factors in the Origin, Evolution, and Diffusion of Rock and Roll Music," *Journal of Geography*, vol. 70, p. 461, 1971.

"Work with Me Anny" and "Anny Had a Baby" were particularly delightful. There was nothing like them on the hit parade. The stuff was dynamite. Kids began to tell each other about the songs. More and more began to tune in.

The music started becoming popular, and when it did, songs began to get something of an antiseptic treatment so that they might have a larger sales potential. Thus, while a female singer had previously pleaded "roll with me Henry," it later became "dance with me Henry." If the world wasn't safe from rock and roll, then rock and roll would become safe for the world. And yet, rock and roll's basically erotic beat could not be disguised. Even the name itself is said to have originated in those good old records with lyrics like "my baby rocks me with a steady roll." But rock and roll was what a larger and larger number of people wanted, and no amount of purification or dilution could dull their enthusiasm.

It took about two years, but by 1955 rock and roll's early acceptors had been joined by a rapidly growing majority. By 1956 almost everybody knew what it was. Millions liked it. The demand for rock and roll records was so high that many companies had trouble keeping the popular ones in supply. Imagine the heartbreak: it might be a week or ten days before "Long Tall Sally" would be back on the shelves.

By the end of the 1950s rock and roll's audience had grown to a substantial percentage of the record-buying public. Rock and roll records sold by the millions, not the thousands as they had done just a few years earlier. But the growth rate of newly converted rock and roll fans began to slow. The same enthusiasm was still there, but a saturation point had been reached. The majority were converted and rock and roll's phenomenal boom period was over. It had become accepted and a part of the establishment.

The growth curve of rock and roll, then, is really the classic S-shaped curve that characterizes most innovations, popular ideas, and fads. There are three major components: (1) early acceptance, (2) majority acceptance, and (3) saturation. Although rock and roll survived for a decade from 1953 to 1963, most of its followers were gained in the three-year period from 1955 to 1958; hence the S-shaped curve instead of a straight line.

A BATTLE OF THE SOUNDS: CONFLICT IN THE SOURCES OF DISTRIBUTION

Most early rock and roll fans were blissfully unaware of the tremendous struggle that gripped the record industry during the 1950s between the "majors" and the "independents." The majors were the large, well-established companies, such as Decca and MGM, which catered to majority tastes in music. Some of the majors had been around since the turn of the century. They were based in the large cities: New York, Los Angeles, and Chicago. Their music appealed to a large, white buying market. Their songs stressed eternal or platonic love and everyday trite situations. Societal values were never questioned. Records pushed by the majors were optimistic, sweet, and clean.

The independents, on the other hand, were mavericks. Usually small, aggressive, and consciously catering to an ethnic buying market, they sold records by black singers telling of loose women, physical love, and hardships. There were several important independent companies in the South, as well as a few in Northern cities like Los Angeles and Chicago. But by far the largest number were in New York City, where about a million blacks lived (Figure 6-1). When these kinds of records first became popular, the distributors expanded from a primarily black market area to wider distribution in suburban neighborhood record stores. Some of the more earthy records were literally sold under the counter in the suburban areas.

When it was realized that there was no stopping the sale of rock and roll records, the majors responded to the independent's success by attempting to capture the market. Out and out copies of songs began appearing, most of them by white singers who purged songs of their sexual connotations and made them palatable to large numbers of people. These were called "cover" records.

Some singers like Pat Boone and Frankie Avalon got their start with this kind of mitigated music. Many of the imitators became more successful than the original performers! With the power of well-organized distribution systems behind them, as well as respectability, these records by major companies cut hard into the market that had been established by the independents.

Rock and roll succeeded in becoming middle class. And it was the contention of some that once it did, it really died. It became contrived, forced, and phony. Whatever the case, however, the cover records made by the majors did succeed in getting the basic sound of rock and roll accepted by the older generation. But by then its authenticity had been lost.

NEW PLACES AND SOUNDS: REGENERATION NODES

The rock and roll of the purists—the real vintage rock—may have perished in the early 1960s. But popular music with a hard, driving beat and wild lyrics certainly did not. Rock music, as distinct from rock and roll, emerged victorious. And like rock and roll, it experienced locational shifts. We now know that with rock and roll the centers of activity periodically migrated. For a year or so Philadelphia was a major center; then Los Angeles became important, and so on. One can deduce major shifts by looking at several variables: the location of recording studios, the recruitment of local talent with special attributes, and the perpetuation of local dance styles and place names in records.

ONE IN PARTICULAR: A LOOK AT A NODAL CENTER

The Los Angeles area of California became a major center of rock music in the early 1960s. It essentially replaced Philadelphia, the leader of the late 1950s. Certain symbolic moves epitomized the shift: Dick Clark's "American Band-

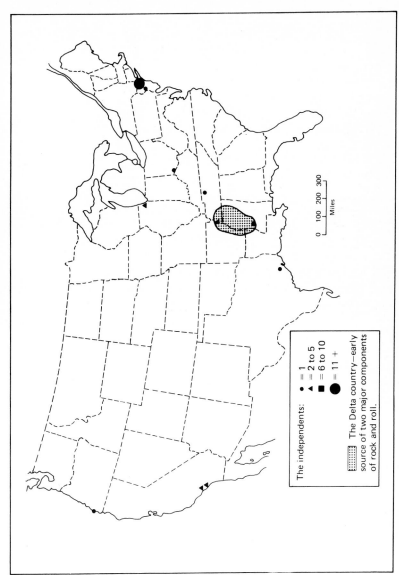

Figure 6-1 The location of independent record companies. This map shows the number and location of independent companies, together with the Delta Country, the source region of early rock and roll.

The independents:
- • = 1
- ▲ = 2 to 5
- ■ = 6 to 10
- ● = 11 +

The Delta country—early source of two major components of rock and roll.

0 100 200 300
Miles

stand" TV show moved from "Philly" to "L.A." Performers who were once associated with Philadelphia gained a California image: Frankie Avalon ceased being the cute Italian kid from Philadelphia and became the hero of the California beach-blanket set. A new image was in the making.

There was a strong local creativity which pulled Los Angeles into the center of the popular music market. By the early 1960s southern Californians were accustomed to hearing "local records" in addition to the national hits. It was well known that Jan and Arnie (later to be called Jan and Dean) made their first records in their garage in Torrance, a suburb of Los Angeles. This had local appeal and stressed the enterprising initiative of two southern California boys. Their songs, however, were not about southern California. They were about girls—big girls and little girls.

But in 1962, several local songs about a distinctively California life began appearing on the local charts. These bore names like "Surfin" and "The Lonely Surfer." The new songs used local place names (e.g., Huntington Beach, Pasadena, Rincon) which were curious and exotic to anyone living east of the Sierras. Groups like Dick Dale and the Dell-Tones, who recorded surf records exclusively, were big hits locally. They were little known outside of southern California.

But southern Californians soon began steeping the rest of the United States in their argot and even their attitudes. Some local songs soon became national hits. By 1962 New Yorkers were aware that "New York's a lonely town, when you're the only surfer boy around," and that "from Central Park to Pasadena's such a long way." Local surf expressions (e.g., "shooting the curl," "woody," "hanging ten") became familiar from coast to coast.

Even if one lived where there was no surf, the answer was simple: sidewalk surfing. This craze, which started in California, swept the United States in the early 1960s. There were, of course, records about it. "Sidewalk Surfing" by Jan and Dean became a number one record in 1964. A rash of surf and surf monster movies gave visual import to the zany California image: bikini-clad girls, surfboards, and guitars. "Surfer Girl" by the Beach Boys was a national hit song in 1963.

California has always had another glamour image associated with it: cars. The automobile was serenaded in numerous records that originated in southern California in the early 1960s. The Beach Boys "409" and "Little Deuce Coup" were classics, as was "GTO" by Ronnie and the Daytonas. Names of local race tracks like Pomona and Riverside became part of the aura of these songs. The southern California car records were climaxed by Jan and Dean's "Little Old Lady from Pasadena." Picture a little old lady with a garden of gardenias and a rickety old garage. In her garage is nothing less than a "brand new shiny red super-stock Dodge." This little old lady, probably wearing the inevitable tennis shoes, is revealed to us as "the terror of Colorado Boulevard." By the mid-1960s, if a young person didn't know about these bits of California culture, he was probably "out of it."

Surf, cars, girls—this was the California image. The Beach Boys' "California Girls" epitomized California chauvinism. Their song is a narration of a worldwide search for exciting young women. After their epic quest we are told there is none that could compare to the bikini-clad, suntanned girls of southern California. Going one step further, they wish all girls could be California girls.

For a period of about three years, from 1963 until 1966, California was the most sung-about state in the Union. It also had large numbers of local bands and rock groups on the top charts. "California Dreamin' " immortalized the situation, as did "Warm California Nights." With the acceptance and perpetuation of the California syndrome, however, came the inevitable usurping of the local independent companies' market by the majors. Songs about California began to lose their spontaneity and authenticity.

California provides an excellent example of the shifting importance of nodes of activity. Los Angeles itself, by the late 1960s, had lost its tremendous influence. The San Francisco area became far more important. Songs by northern Californians about northern California were "in." If Los Angeles concerned itself with girls and machinery, San Francisco was associated with heavier themes: communal living, protesting established authority, and experimentation with drugs. Songs like "Warm San Franciscan Nights," "Down in Monterey," and "Mendocino" and "Dock of the Bay" vividly demonstrated the appeal and influence that northern California had on the youth culture.

SUMMARY

Books have been written about popular music and its deeper cultural implications. I have used it only as an example of the kinds of processes that are involved in culture spread. The idea of a hearth, let's say that highly creative area in western Tennessee, Mississippi, and northern Louisiana, is geographically at the roots of the origins of rock and roll and later rock music. The British singers like the Beatles and the Animals admitted they emulated people like Chuck Berry at least early in their careers. They tried to capture the spontaneity of the early rock and roll sounds which originated in the Delta country.

Rock and roll and rock music have experienced tremendous changes in internal centers of activity. For a while it was "Motown" and more than a dozen creative local groups from the Detroit area which gave the music such a "soulful," rocking character. Before that it was Philadelphia. At one time or another New York, Los Angeles, and Chicago have been important subcenters. Along with San Francisco, they exemplify the meaning of a changing node.

Rock and roll, like any other culture trait, took time to diffuse. Traits reach certain segments of the population at different times. Although national hits are usually just that, there are still lags in the acceptance of certain records in certain places. Record companies and radio stations can only "push" so hard. Some records have made it better in some places than others, as a look at any top-40 charts from any dozen American cities will show. What was "number one" three weeks ago in Portland, Oregon, may surprisingly have just reached the top of the charts in Cleveland today. The most heavily played song on a juke box in Burlington, Iowa, may be a record that people in San Bernandino, California, don't play very much. Despite the seemingly monolithic nature of record companies—and the proliferation of rock record stations owned by one corporation which tries to musically link the United States (such as KFWB, KEWB, KBWB, and KDWB)—the distribution of the sounds we listen to are still stubbornly varied. A curiosity about that kind of variability lies at the roots of cultural geography. Studying items of popular culture—such as rock and roll music— provides an excellent way to get at some of the ways that the realities, images, and myths that affect our daily lives get to us—and either "turn us on" or "turn us off."

CHAPTER SEVEN

UP FROM THE MINES AND OUT FROM THE PRAIRIES

Some Geographical Implications of
Football in the United States*

JOHN F. ROONEY, JR.

COMMENT

In the two previous essays, we have seen how places are
linked together by a combination of proximity in space and
by the circulation of persons and ideas. In the next selection, the author discusses the geography of football in the
United States, combining the effects of proximity and connectivity in his analysis of this perhaps more familiar spatial
system.

*Abridged from the *Geographical Review*, vol. 59, pp. 471-492, 1969, reproduced by
permission.

The geographical aspects of sports are many and varied, but have received little academic attention. Like politics, money, hamburgers, and comic strips, interest and participation in athletics are integral parts of our culture.

There is spatial variation in the emphasis on the major sporting activities in the United States. This variation has been speculated about but never objectively assessed. Sports enthusiasts have long argued over the existence of areas that might be termed "hotbeds" of sporting activity. We associate the Bluegrass Country of Kentucky with the production of thoroughbred horses and the South with stockcar racing. We have been told that Indiana, Pennsylvania, and California are leading states in the production of basketball, football, and baseball players. But we don't know what accounts for this unequal ouput of good athletes.

Football is an American institution. It is the players and the fans; it is traditions; it is anecdotes and legends; it is a television bonanza and an intrinsic part of the American scene; it has a massive economic impact on many areas. Football is played, watched, and discussed heatedly (and even sometimes intelligently) by a substantial part of our population. In 1968 the attendance at college and professional football games surpassed 30 million persons. In that year more than 10 million persons attended high school football games in Texas alone, the place where "football mania" is perhaps at its peak. Television brings an average of five games a week into the homes of millions from early September to mid-February: an avid viewer can watch from two to four professional games on a single Sunday afternoon. The season has been extended to the point where games are now being played in every month except March, April, and May.

THE PRODUCTION OF PLAYERS

Although there is nationwide interest in football, some areas stand out for the quality of the talent they produce. Missouri, with a population of 4.5 million, has only one major college team, while Utah, with a population of less than a million, has four. Since the location of big-time football schools bears little relation to population size, high-caliber college football is now found in virtually all sections of the United States. The former dominance of the Ivy League, and later of the Big Ten and Pacific Coast Conferences, no longer exists. Universities in states with relatively small populations such as Wyoming, Arizona, and New Mexico now field teams that can compete with any in the country. These and many other universities support football programs too large to be maintained with local athletes. As a result, talent flows from surplus areas to deficit areas.

In the present study, measurement of the producing capacities of various sections of the United States has been based on the examination of team rosters, which list the players by high school attended. A six-year recruiting sample of approximately 14,500 players from 136 teams was used to delineate athletic productivity on both a total and a per-capita basis by state, county, city, SMSA, and county-based regions.[1]

WHERE THEY COME FROM

The map of varsity football production suggests a strong relationship between player origin and urban areas (Figure 7-1). Major cities such as New York, Chicago, Los Angeles, Houston, and Pittsburgh stand out, while many rural areas produce few players. The origin of professional football players is geographically similar to the situation of college players (Figure 7-2). However, the Southeast, particularly Mississippi, Louisiana and Texas, has a relatively high professional output compared with their college-player production.

A study of the per-capita output of players tends to produce a more meaningful pattern. Based on a 1960 national population of 180 million, the average production of college football players during the six-year period was approximately one for every 12,500 people. Thus, if a state or county were turning out players at the rate of one for every 25,000 persons, it would be operating at only 0.50 of the national rate. A ratio of one football player for every 6,250 persons would amount to 2.00 times the norm. If the national norm is represented by an index value of 1.00, the states that contain major universities range from 1.74 in Ohio to 0.47 in New York. Counties with at least one player range from 26.48 for Morgan, Utah, to 0.10 for Bronx, New York.

The map of per-capital production of college players conveys a somewhat different image than that portrayed in the map of gross production (Figure 7-3). Dominance by big cities has all but disappeared, except for Atlanta, Cincinnati, Cleveland, Dallas, Toledo, and Pittsburgh. Many of the leading cities based on output (Buffalo, Chicago, Los Angeles, Miami, and San Diego) are simply producing football talent in proportion to their populations. On the other hand, the five boroughs of New York City, which together accounted for only 80 players, are operating at the incredibly low rate of 13 percent of the national norm. Other major cities that are producing at rates less than 60 percent of the norm are Baltimore, Boston, Detroit, Kansas City, Milwaukee, Philadelphia, San Francisco, and St. Louis.

Many suburban areas stand in marked contrast to the central cities. For

---

[1] The six-year sample was based on two mutually exclusive roster samples taken between 1961 and 1967 for each team. Teams were selected on the basis of the National Collegiate Athletic Association major college ratings. Several college-division teams (whose recruiting budgets are smaller than those of schools rated "major" by the NCAA) were included in the sample in cases where their schedules and performances against major college teams seemed to justify it. It is assumed that differences in player ability tend to cancel each other out when such a large sample is used. Differences in the areal distribution of professional and college player origin suggest a slight underrepresentation in the South and an overrepresentation in the Northeast.

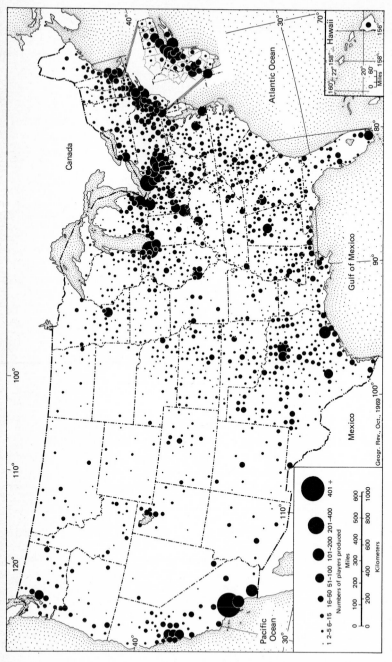

Figure 7-1 The origin of major college and university varsity football players by location of high school attended. This map shows the high schools that produced the largest numbers of college players—the "hotbeds" of high school football are those places covered by a concentration of black circles.

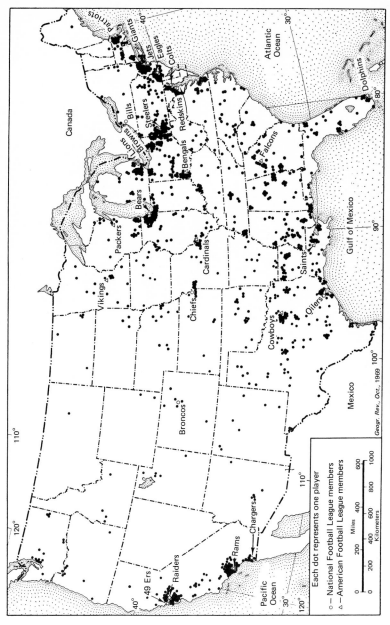

Figure 7-2 The origin of professional football players by location of high school attended. This map shows the high schools that produced the largest number of professional football players.

Geogr. Rev., Oct., 1969

101

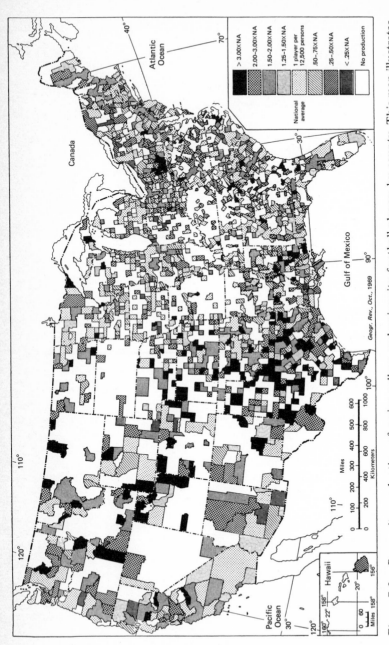

Figure 7-3 Per-capita production of major college and university football players by county. This map illustrates the effect which the distribution of population has on the number of football players produced. On this map the counties shaded black are the "hotbeds." Notice that some of the places producing large numbers of players (Figure 7-1) do not have a high per-capita production rate.

Geogr. Rev., Oct., 1969

example, the counties around New York City have a rate fifteen times greater than the city. The areas to the east of San Francisco (San Jose and Richmond), the Orange County complex southeast of Los Angeles, and Boston's western suburbs (Waltham, Newton, and Lexington) all generate football players at a significantly higher rate than the central cities. Extremely high per-capita output is confined to a few areas, but above-average performance is fairly widespread (Figure 7-4). Low and spotty output is characteristic of the Midwest, New York, Appalachia, and the Mid-South.

While it is possible to study the pattern of states of origin of football players, an examination by city and county units is more revealing. The leading cities in total player output during the six-year period were Los Angeles, Chicago, Pittsburgh, and Cleveland (Table 7-1). Although Los Angeles and Chicago produce an enormous amount of football talent, both are within 15 percent of the national average on a per-capita bases. Toledo, Pittsburgh, and Cleveland, however, support high school football programs that are turning out college players at a rate much higher than the national average. Other cities that rank high on a per-capita basis are Cincinnati, Dallas, Atlanta, and San Jose.

Counties that turn out players in large quantities (five or more a year) and at per-capita rates in excess of the national average are rare (Table 7-2). Five of the

Table 7-1 The Leading Cities or Urban Counties in the Total Production of College Football Players

CITY OR URBAN COUNTY	NUMBER OF PLAYERS	PER-CAPITA RATE
Los Angeles	492	1.02
Chicago	354	.86
Pittsburgh	333	2.56
Cleveland	247	1.83
Houston	130	1.30
Cincinnati	129	1.86
Detroit	127	.60
Middlesex County, Mass.		
(Waltham, Lexington, Newton)	122	1.23
Dallas	112	1.47
Bergen County, N.J.		
(Bergenfield, Teaneck, Hackensack)	109	1.75
Toledo	109	2.81
Orange County, Calif.		
(Anaheim, Santa Ana)	104	1.85
Nassau County, N.Y.	104	1.00
San Diego, Calif.	102	1.25
Miami, Fla.	94	1.26

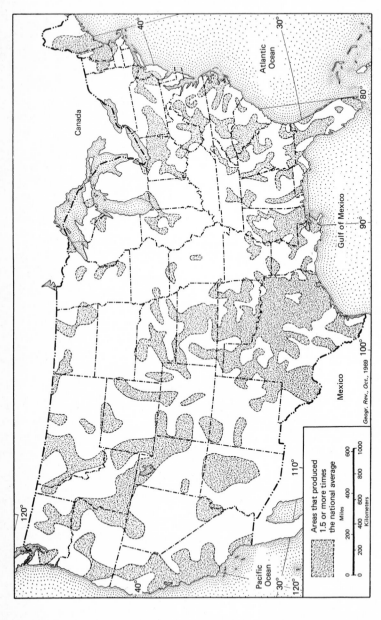

Figure 7-4 Generalized pattern of above average per-capita production of major college and university varsity football players. This map isolates the "hotbeds" of high school football shown in Figure 7-3. Notice the distortion embodied into this pattern by the large counties in the Western United States.

Areas that produced
1.5 or more times
the national average

Geogr. Rev., Oct., 1969

Table 7-2 Counties That Rank High in Total and Per-Capita Output of College Football Players

RANK	COUNTY	MAJOR CITIES	NUMBER OF PLAYERS	PER-CAPITA RATE
1	Jefferson, Ohio	Steubenville	37	4.66
2	Beaver, Pa.	Aliquippa	66	3.99
3	Potter, Tex.	Amarillo	33	3.57
4	Harrison, Miss.	Biloxi, Gulfport	32	3.35
5	Galveston, Tex.	Galveston, Texas City	37	3.30
6	Westmorland, Pa.	Monessen, Jeannette, Latrobe, Irwin	91	3.23
7	Washington, Pa.	Washington	54	3.11
8	Fayette, Pa.	Uniontown	41	3.03
9	Lucas, Ohio	Toledo	109	2.81
10	Trumbull, Ohio	Warren	43	2.58
11	Allegheny, Pa.	Pittsburgh	333	2.56
12	Hillsborough, N.H.	Manchester, Nashua	35	2.46
COUNTIES WITH HIGH PER-CAPITA RATES ONLY				
	Morgan, Utah	Morgan	6	26.48
	Rockwall, Tex.	Rockwall	7	14.91
	Young, Tex.	Graham, Newcastle, Olney	14	10.15
	Jones, Miss.	Laurel, Ellisville	8	7.40
	Simpson, Miss.	Mendenhall, Magee	11	6.90
	Burleson, Tex.	Caldwell, Somerville	6	6.88
	Hutchinson, Tex.	Borger, Phillips	17	6.15
	Transylvania, N.C.	Brevard	8	6.10
	Moore, Tex.	Dumas, Sunroy	7	6.00
	Andrews, Tex.	Andrews	6	5.58
	Victoria, Tex.	Victoria	20	5.38

top twelve are in western Pennsylvania, three are in Ohio, two in Texas, and the others in Mississippi and New Hampshire. Steubenville, Ohio, and Aliquippa, Pennsylvania, the two leaders, are some 25 miles apart. In fact, seven of the twelve counties are located in the steel region of western Pennsylvania and eastern Ohio. A belt that stretches from Johnstown, Pennsylvania, through the Pittsburgh region, across the panhandle of West Virginia, and via Youngstown to Cleveland accounts for 1,250 ball players, representing a production 2.5 times the national average. Thus from an area with a population of slightly more than 6 million came nearly 9 percent of the nation's major-college recruits, and they went anywhere to play.

There are several other districts that might be deemed football hotbeds on the merits of their total and per-capita production. The southern Mississippi zone accounted for 101 players, a per-capita index of 3.20. The Simpson County index was an amazing 6.90 (Table 7-2).

Four highly productive regions can be delineated in Texas. The northeastern part of the state had a per-capita index of 2.90, with an output of 163 players. Rockwall is the second leading county in the United States, with a per-capita rating of 14.91. A second area, centering on Midland and Odessa, includes the sparsely populated counties south of the Pecos River and stretches northward through Big Spring and Lamesa to Denver City. In this football-happy section, college players have been produced at a rate of 3.5 times the national norm. The central Texas region includes also a part of western Oklahoma and contains thirty-two counties. This sprawling region sent forth 153 players and registered a per-capita rate of 3.25. In the panhandle, an eight-county area centered on Amarillo and Borger accounted for 71 players, a production at a rate over four times the national average.

Another highly productive region embraces northern Utah, southeastern Idaho, and southwestern Wyoming. Its total production amounted to only 83 players, but the per-capita rate was 3.20. The productivity in this region seems to be closely associated with the Mormon emphasis on physical fitness and competitive sports.

The last region of national significance on the basis of per-capita productivity is an area east of San Francisco Bay. This area had a per-capita index of 2.35, well above the California average of 1.15. The total output was 157 players, nearly half of whom came from Contra Costa County.

WHERE THEY GO

The migration of high school players to colleges throughout the United States can be explained by two factors. First, and most obvious, is the geographical variation in the production of talent; second, the unequal spatial distribution of highly financed university football programs (Table 7-3). Most of the Western states, as well as smaller New England states, the South Atlantic belt, and the Great Plains, emphasize sports.

New York, New Jersey, and the Midwest show less emphasis: the relatively populous states of Minnesota, Wisconsin, and Missouri each have only one top-quality football team. Such spatial variation in football interest, together with the desire of many athletes to live in other parts of the country, has created streams from areas of surplus high school production to areas where quality football programs are carried on despite limited high school output. The role of alumni and coaches is an important determinant in recruiting. The increased mobility of both these groups has complicated still further the pattern of flows of athletes around the country.

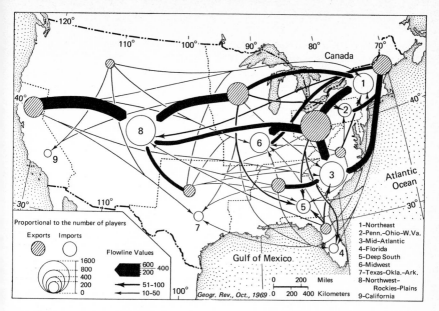

Figure 7-5 Interregional migration of major college and university football players. This map illustrates the manner in which parts of the nation interact through the movement of football players. There are obvious exporting and importing regions.

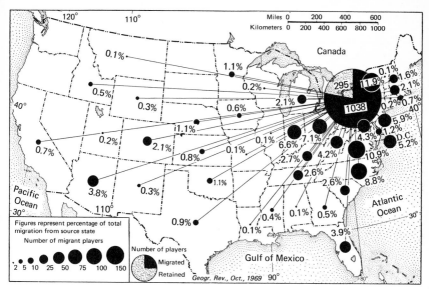

Figure 7-6 Migration of major college and university football players from Pennsylvania. One of the primary exporting states, Pennsylvania supplies players to all but six of the states shown on the map.

By subdividing the United States into nine production and consumption regions, we can obtain a broad view of interregional migration (Figure 7-5). The most important player flows originate in Pennsylvania-Ohio, California, the Midwest, and the Northeast. The Pennsylvania-Ohio region is the chief supplier of the South-Atlantic universities and a major exporter to the Northeast, the Midwest, and the West. Pennsylvania (Figure 7-6), which exports more than 75 percent of its high school players, is a leading source of athletes for the Atlantic Coast and Southern Conferences, the Ivy League, Indiana, Florida, and even Arizona. In fact, there were Pennsylvanians playing in all but five of the states with major recruiting budgets.

Table 7-3 Per-Capita Emphasis on Major College Football by States

RANK	STATE	NO. OF TEAMS	INDEX OF EMPHASIS*
1	Utah	4	5.94
2	New Hampshire	2	4.36
3	Wyoming	1	4.01
4	Idaho	2	3.98
5	Vermont	1	3.39
6	Rhode Island	2	3.08
7	Arizona	3	3.05
8	Delaware	1	2.97
9	New Mexico	2	2.78
10	Colorado	3	2.26
11	South Carolina	4	2.22
12	North Dakota	1	2.09
13	Montana	1	1.96
14	Mississippi	3	1.82
14	Kansas	3	1.82
16	North Carolina	6	1.74
17	District of Columbia	1	1.73
18	Oklahoma	3	1.71
19	Virginia	5	1.67
20	Oregon	2	1.50
21	West Virginia	2	1.42
22	Texas	10	1.38
23	Maine	1	1.37
24	Massachusetts	5	1.29
25	Ohio	9	1.23

*The index of emphasis for each state is derived by dividing the number of teams a state has by the number it should theoretically be supporting relative to its population. 1.00=norm.

California high school players go mainly to Pacific Coast universities and to the Western Athletic Conference. Utah alone absorbs 25 percent, and together with Washington and Oregon consumes well over half the California total. The impact of California decreases rapidly with distance; migration virtually stops at the Great Plains. However, distance appears to be no obstacle to the persistent recruiting efforts of Notre Dame and Naval Academy alumni, as demonstrated by the Indiana and Maryland figures.

Midwestern talent has been recruited primarily by schools in the Big Eight and Western Athletic Conferences, with Illinois providing most of the surplus. The Midwest is also a major source for the Northeast. The Ivy League schools,

Table 7-3 (continued)

RANK	STATE	NO. OF TEAMS	INDEX OF EMPHASIS*
26	Tennessee	3	1.11
27	Connecticut	2	1.04
28	Iowa	2	0.96
29	Nebraska	1	0.94
30	Washington	2	0.93
31	Kentucky	2	0.87
32	Indiana	3	0.85
33	Maryland	2	0.85
34	California	10	0.84
35	Louisiana	2	0.81
35	Alabama	2	0.81
37	Florida	3	0.80
38	Arkansas	1	0.74
39	Pennsylvania	6	0.70
40	Georgia	2	0.67
41	Michigan	3	0.51
42	New York	6	0.47
43	New Jersey	2	0.44
44	Illinois	3	0.39
44	Minnesota	1	0.39
46	Wisconsin	1	0.34
47	Missouri	1	0.31
48	Alaska	0	
48	Hawaii	0	
48	Nevada	0	
48	South Dakota	0	

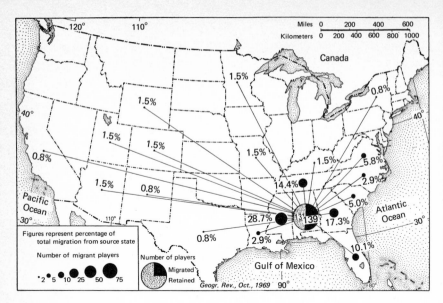

Figure 7-7 Migration of major college and university football players from Alabama. Alabama boys travel to few states. Those who do leave avoid the Northeast, Midwest, Great Plains, and West Coast.

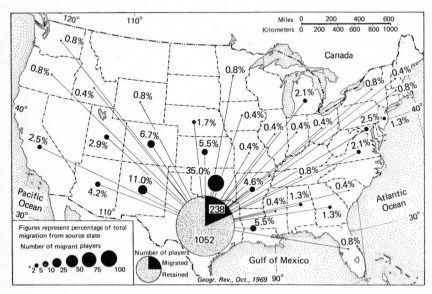

Figure 7-8 Migration of major college and university football players from Texas. Although Texans play ball in many states, they are primarily found in the West. Interestingly, while boys from Pennsylvania play football in Texas, boys from Texas are not invited to Pennsylvania.

especially Dartmouth and Yale, have been aggressive in seeking out athletes from this region. Much of the Northeastern outflow goes to the Atlantic Coast and Southern Conference states. The football teams in these conferences are highly dependent on New York and New Jersey talent.

Only minor flows of players stem from the Deep South, Texas, and Florida, and considering the number of schools and people in the Deep South, there has been little contact with other areas. Alabama is an example of the limited out-migration (Figure 7-7). It is obvious that most of the exports go no farther than the culturally similar South-Atlantic zone. On the other hand "Yankees" seldom penetrate farther than Tennessee. Until recently a substantial proportion of the Southern exports were blacks who went to schools in the Midwest. Big Ten records document the accomplishments of many blacks who would otherwise have been denied the opportunity of playing first-class college football. Today, however, the emergence of high-caliber football at predominantly black schools such as Grambling, Texas Southern, Jackson State, and Florida A & M has stemmed the tide of out-migration. In Texas most of the huge high school player output is employed at home (Figure 7-8), and those who leave seldom stray far. In contrast to Pennsylvania, Texas retains more than 80 percent of its athletes. But as the reputation of the state's high school football spreads, we can probably expect to see more Texas players making the move east.

More than 50 percent of the interregional movement of players is prompted by the deficit spending of universities in the vast Plains-Rockies-Northwest region, and in the smaller South-Atlantic zone. A total of 1,340 migrants entered the Western area, and nearly a thousand went to the South-Atlantic. Aside from the two large deficit areas, most of the interregional flow balances out, with the Midwestern and Northeastern exports roughly equaling their imports. Nevertheless, the magnitude of player flows is indicative of the heated competition for, and the cost of, acquiring football talent in the present market. Thus, distinctive parts of our nation are linked by the movement of these specialized persons. Like other examples of spatial distribution and interaction this phenomenon is open to geographic analysis and explication.

CHAPTER EIGHT

VIETNAM, CUBA, AND THE GHETTO

ROBERT W. McCOLL

COMMENT   The spatial configurations which describe the movement of disease, culture traits, and athletes are of course important, for we can trace the extent to which places are linked in particular contexts and can project potential linkages in other situations. The utility of specifying such linkages is dramatically illustrated for such issues as civil disorder or revolution. The last essay in this section illustrates that connectivity and situation as well as site characteristics loom large in the organization of militant movements in the 1950s and 1960s in Cuba, the urban ghetto, and Vietnam.

Geopolitics is not dead.

It is very much alive and practiced in every revolutionary and guerrilla movement from the battlefields of Vietnam and Latin America to the riots in our own cities in the United States.

Geopolitics, the role of geography in influencing and explaining political actions, gives an insight into elements that underlie modern militant movements—such as those in Vietnam, Cuba, and the ghettos in American cities.

One of the most distinguishing features of modern revolutionary and guerrilla warfare is the insurgent's ability to control a part of the country. In these areas he has been able to successfully exclude government troops and officials. Three important questions may be posed:

First, how are such "liberated areas" created?

Second, is there any consistent pattern or explanation for the location of these bases? and

Third, how are these bases used by the insurgent?

To answer these questions, one must look at both political and geographic conditions.

The insurgent believes he has lost the ability to use legal or open means of protest against the government or its policies, and thus some form of overt action has become necessary to correct the situation. This is the political motivation behind his action. The actual location of his act will coincide with the geographic concentration of the ethnic, religious, linguistic, or economic group most committed to the same program of change.

When such a group is concentrated in a specific geographical area such as the mountains of Vietnam, the sugar plantations of Cuba, or the ghettos of a city, a physical territorial base is created from which the insurgent may direct organization and action for the revolution.

The insurgent is able to prevent or limit government penetration and action within that portion of the country, state, or city. He is thus able to "demonstrate" that the existing government does not hold the loyalty of "all" the people and that it cannot even maintain control of its own territory.

The logic then continues that the existing government should not be recognized as the legal government, but should be overthrown and replaced.

In revolutionary movements in Asia, Africa, and Latin America, and according to written works of such men as Mao Tse-tung, Vo Nguyen Giap, and Che Guevara, the location of insurgent guerrilla bases have the following properties:

1. Liberated areas are concentrated in locations that have had previous political or revolutionary activity.
2. Political stability should be lacking at either the local or national level.
3. Each liberated area must be selected to provide access to key political targets and symbols of power and authority such as cities, the capital, public transportation, and public services.

113

4. If local political authority is strong, then the liberated area must be situated in areas where such authority is weak or confused, e.g., at provincial, international, or municipal boundaries.
5. Terrain should be chosen that will provide for the personal safety of the group.
6. Such military areas should be self-contained and self-sufficient.

Once created, the liberated areas provide not only inviolable sanctuaries for the rebel and his armed followers, but the basis for the creation of a state within the state—a model of how things will be once the insurgents take control.

Citing only highlights from recent revolutions in Cuba and Vietnam, one can demonstrate how the geopolitical elements listed above are used in practice.

In both Cuba and Vietnam, the insurgents created distinct physical guerrilla bases located in the countryside. From these bases they were able to force the ruling government to withdraw to the cities.

In each country the initial rebellion occurred not only in provinces and cities where discontent among the local population was at a maximum, but also in the hometown or home province of the eventual hero of the revolution. In Vietnam this event was an uprising in Nghe An, the home province of Ho Chi Minh. In Cuba the initial attack was on the Moncada barracks in Santiago de Cuba, the provincial capital of Oriente and the hometown of Castro. Although these first uprisings failed, these leaders and their fellow participants continued the revolutions. Castro returned to Oriente in 1956 to begin a new (and, as it happened, final) revolution. Ho Chi Minh wandered from Vietnam to France, the United States, the Soviet Union, China, and finally back to Vietnam where he eventually emerged victorious in overthrowing a hated colonial government.

Each base was concentrated in an area with previous rebel or political activity. In Cuba, this area was in the Sierra Maestra mountains of the Oriente province. In Vietnam, the close correspondence between former Viet Minh areas and the present guerrilla bases demonstrates the importance of previous political experience in the location of a liberated area.

In the case of both Cuba and Vietnam, political stability was often lacking in the remote areas of the mountains and jungles, as well as among minority ethnic groups like the black sugar workers in Oriente and the various ethnic and religious groups found throughout Vietnam.

Each guerrilla base not only provided direct access to a major city, but was often in a position to interrupt or destroy vital communications and transportation systems.

In Cuba rebel bases were primarily located in the mountains, almost regardless of provincial boundaries. In most other countries, especially Vietnam, such bases were concentrated along both national and provincial boundaries. This means that if the police were in hot pursuit, the insurgent need only cross the "jurisdictional" line to become someone else's problem.

Guerrilla bases are autonomous; they contain their own schools, hospitals, printing presses, and factories for manufacturing daily necessities such as cigars in Cuba and clothing and sandals in Vietnam. When the population of the base becomes too large either for security or for continued self-sufficiency, a group is sent out to establish a new base or rebel colony.

Through the creation of such bases and the process of "colonization," the insurgent movement is able to expand its control over larger geographic areas. Each base acts as a center with access to villages and people on all of its margins.

Eventually a centralized coordinating system, or "insurgent state," is created to link the growing number of bases. The insurgent state creates its own provinces, counties, and municipalities, and selects officials to administer these areas. The state has a cause that is often represented by a symbol recognized throughout the country. In Cuba, the symbol was the beard. During the height of the revolution, a beard was sufficient cause for arrest and often summary execution. In Vietnam, this symbol is a flag dominated by a yellow star whose five points represent the five elements fighting in the revolution: workers, farmers, soldiers, students, and intellectuals.

Once established, the insurgent state may begin open and large-scale attacks upon government forces. This is a period of formal rather than guerrilla warfare. The attacks represent an effort to settle the final issue of who rules the country both de facto and de jure.

While the average American city may seem a long way from the jungles of Vietnam or Cuba, the following parallels can be drawn between national revolutions and recent urban civil disorders.

The insurgent is in both cases a local man. In the American city, he is a resident of the inner city, or ghetto. He organizes and leads the actions of people who feel their needs are not being met by the legal government. If the city is now divided into its "terrain" features, we find that the central business district and the ghetto are the mountains and forests. Here it is possible to hide and to move with great facility. There are hundreds of windows, rooftops, and dark paths that can be used for attack or escape. Outlying residential suburbs are too far away to be readily accessible, and their limited network of highways makes it relatively easy for police to control traffic and to conduct search operations. Consequently, such districts represent exposed and unsafe terrain.

Since the inner city and the central business district are the home of the potential insurgent, this is where he will strike first. As the insurgent movement gains attention and a following, and the movement is able to demonstrate the ineffectiveness of the police and local government, other persons with similar grievances will join forces.

In the cities the time for action is not tied to the agricultural calendar, but nonetheless shows a seasonal rhythm. An urban insurrection will normally occur during a time when the unemployment rate is high. In the city, this period coincides with summer months when the community suddenly is faced with a surge of potential labor that has been released by the closing of schools for summer vacation. These are the potential troops or masses that will man the barricades and carry out acts of violence. Contrary to popular opinion, these disturbances are not the result of the long, hot summer. Climatic conditions merely add to a sense of frustration; they do not cause it.

While it is often assumed that once the process of social disintegration and insurrection has begun it is irreversible, there is a great deal of evidence to the contrary. We have seen failures, often magnificent failures, of guerrilla wars in Malaya, the Philippines, Greece, and Bolivia. In the instances of Bolivia and Greece, these defeats were the result of military actions alone. In the other cases the defeat was accomplished through the combination of peaceful social and economic reforms and the military actions of hard-core rebels, who would be satisfied with nothing short of anarchy or a new government—their government.

Locational analysis adds another dimension and perspective to an understanding of insurgencies. It is now even possible to predict the general areas in which these activities will be initiated. The ultimate value of such prediction, however, lies in the ability to initiate and carry out preemptive political, social, and economic changes that will remove the basis for insurrection and the need for the mass destruction which usually results from efforts to put down such an insurrection.

PART FOUR

GEOGRAPHIC BACKGROUND TO CONTEMPORARY PROBLEMS

All the problems facing contemporary Americans have their geographical aspects, for they all occur in space and involve interaction between man and the environment. They are therefore open to our questions. As an academic discipline, geography has not been any more successful than the other disciplines in solving social problems. There are two reasons for this. First, the confines of a discipline do not allow the perspective necessary to confront complex problems, and second, academic disciplines are not organized to solve social problems. Instead they develop methods, concepts, and models that are used by people we can call practitioners or problem solvers. The two groups of practitioners most closely associated with geography are urban/regional planners and conservationists. Geography contributes much to their work.

In recent years geographers have become more concerned with using their methods and concepts directly. The four essays in this section are examples of this attitude. The first two deal with relatively new concerns to geographers—urban riots and poverty. The latter two topics—population and man's effects on climate—are somewhat more traditional.

We all regret the conditions that called forth the essay by John Adams on civil disorders. Urban geographers have been primarily concerned with the problems of locating cities and determining their internal spatial structure. In the mid-1960s catastrophic events directed our attention toward new questions. The riots indicated that the urban system was undergoing severe strain, and pessimists prophesied its imminent downfall. All the academic disciplines have turned their attention to these problems and much has been written about them, although few remedies have been developed.

In "Geography of Riots and Civil Disorder in the 1960s," John Adams described a situation where human expectations for space were not fulfilled by their environment. Although several explanations for these riots have been offered, they do not answer the "where-why" questions of geographers to the satisfaction of Dr. Adams. To him, an explanation must involve a fine appreciation for patterns of spatial behavior and the circulation system within the urban area. In addition to the concepts of spatial analysis used, we also see some of the most dramatic applications of the concepts of environmental perception on the effects of crowding. As population continues to grow, decision makers and social scientists are becoming more concerned with problems of crowding and the spatial behavior of large numbers of people. At present we suspect human tolerances for crowding are culturally determined. We also suspect crowding beyond the culturally perceived levels of tolerance will produce some form of pathological behavior. Presently our sources of information are experimental animal populations. The Adams essay is one of the earliest attempts to apply the concepts of spatial analysis and environmental perception to a dire problem of American society. It is followed in this section by three more general essays about contemporary problems, which also use geographic concepts, but at different scales.

Most people's interest in poverty centers on finding ways to avoid it. Although the vast majority of us share a distaste for this condition, our society has been unable to ensure itself against it. Even though volumes filling entire libraries have been written describing the miseries of poverty, its causes, and methods to combat it, we are unable to control it. While the essay on low-income families in rural America contains no panacea, it brings to bear the questions and concepts of geography on the problem of poverty in the hope that this reformulation of information will further our search for solutions.

Unfortunately, poverty is not easily defined. Consequently, the authors have begun with a discussion of the various opinions on what poverty really means and then have adopted a working definition which is used throughout the essay. Having done this, they can ask the "where" question. At the time of writing, the 1970 income figures were not available for the nation. Therefore you may compare the data for 1960 with the most recent available and question the data for 1970 in the same fashion the authors examined that for 1960.

Because poverty is a topic too large for one discipline, the authors have summarized some of the opinions of a wide variety of scholars about the causes of poverty in various regions of the United States. After doing this, they develop a geographic perspective. The first explanation examined is environmental resources: poverty exists in those areas where there are too many people for the resource base needed to support them. This explanation was found wanting, for we see that areas with a meager set of natural resources are well-off and fertile areas such as the Mississippi Delta are impoverished. Second, concepts of spatial analysis and human spatial behavior are applied. We see low-income areas located on the margins of North America's circulation system. In terms of relative location they are very isolated because of limited interaction with areas of opportunity for financial advancement. The essay also indicates that *simple* solutions such as moving the rural poor to cities or urban functions to rural areas are not likely to succeed. If any improvement in the income of the people discussed in this essay is to be realized, both their relative location in our spatial system and their life-style must be changed.

Like poverty, the topic of population is too large for one discipline. Nonetheless, the spatial point of view is useful for organizing some of the information about people. Studies of population have been conducted at several scales, from global to neighborhood levels. We have seen that geographers' understanding of the significance of scale make them cognizant of the problems inherent in delineating the proper levels of generalization. For example, the generalization and simplification necessary to conduct an inquiry into the nature of the world's population have led many scholars to conclude that there is one population problem. Many geographers, however, believe that geography of the world's population is so complex that several "population problems" exist. They also believe that the solutions to one of these problems will not solve them all. Instead, each problem must be examined in and of itself, and its distinguishing features must be well understood before it can be likened to a situation elsewhere. This is not to say that remedies useful in one place cannot have wider applications, but we must not assume that they will. Therefore, in "Where Is Everybody?" the United States is used to illustrate the geographical approach because its population is of manageable scale and it is of special significance to its members. We will have difficulty comprehending the attributes and problems of another people if we do not first understand ourselves.

This essay concerns only the basic question of location. Obviously, questions concerning such qualities of the population as age, race, growth rates, and age-and-sex ratios should be asked. These questions, however, must be preceded by the "where" question because they are elaborations of the basic data. The location question has been answered in terms of absolute distance and direction. These distributions should be plotted in some sort of socioeconomic space. Perhaps the maps in this essay should be warped to conform with the distances in the hierarchy presented by Lueck. As you read the essay, think about the various dimensions that would be useful for locating people.

The present location of the American population is explained by the geographer as a result of a continuing process of spatial interaction. The sparsely populated lands of the American Indian were occupied by a rapidly expanding European population that was connected to North America by the shipping lanes. As the American population grew, other patterns of spatial interaction developed. Urbanization has localized the population in the recent decades. As urbanization continued and as transportation improved, amenity features in the landscape drew people to heretofore unoccupied or sparsely settled areas. Thus, the geographic viewpoints, especially scale and spatial interaction, allow us to predict with confidence the location of future Americans.

"Paradise Lost," the final essay in this section, is different from those that have preceded it because the authors have focused the questions and concepts of geography on man's interaction with the physical environment. Although many disciplines are interested in the quality of our environment, the geographic approach is distinct from others in four general ways. First, the geographers' awareness of the complexity of the interaction between man and the environment induces a reluctance to accept simplistic cause-and-effect propositions. Nonetheless, to examine this interaction we must synthesize a tremendous amount of information about both the physical and cultural elements of the landscape. The authors have attempted to aid you in this synthesis by presenting a model of interaction in the form of a simple diagram. This is the basis for the application of geographic concepts to air pollution.

The second distinguishing contributions of geography to studies of air pollution are the concepts of site and situation. The authors demonstrate how these can be used to aid our understanding of air pollution incidents. Naturally, relative location is a fundamental part of the discussion of this situation.

Scale is the third contribution of geographers. This concept is so important that the bulk of the discussion of air pollution is structured around it. Three levels—micro, meso, and macro—have been used in this context to organize a rather comprehensive summary of what is known about inadvertent weather modification and its effects on human beings. It is interesting to note that while the geographic questions are useful at three scales, the answers to them vary.

The concluding section of the essay brings us to the fourth contribution of the geographic approach. In it we see that the interaction between man and the environment must be considered in relation to human needs, perceptions, and goals as well as in relation to physical and biological terms. We note that pollution exists only when we see it, and our society's ethical structure determines the manner in which we treat the environment. The message is simple: our attitudes toward the environment must be examined in detail before we can begin a course of action in environmental advocacy.

CHAPTER NINE

THE GEOGRAPHY OF RIOTS AND CIVIL DISORDERS IN THE 1960s*

JOHN S. ADAMS

COMMENT   The following essay deals with people's protests about their situation in the urban system. We see how the frustrations of the urban blacks were fueled by the changes in the population structure of the black communities and the shrinking of the housing supply for those people. Adams describes the critical role blocked opportunities had in developing conditions conducive for disorders. Thus, the location pattern of civil disorders is established and explained, and finally, Adams considers the impact that environmental perception, especially the needs for personal space and environmental stimulation, had on the location of disturbances.

*Abridged by permission of the author and journal, from *Economic Geography*, vol. 48, no. 1, pp. 24-42, 1972.

"The sufferings that are endured patiently, as being inevitable, become intolerable the moment it appears there might be an escape. Reform then only serves to reveal more closely what still remains oppressive and now all the more unbearable. The suffering, it is true, has been reduced, but one's sensitivity has become more acute."

Alexis de Tocqueville

This paper explores the psychological and physical environments that surrounded the urban riots of the 1960s and presents an argument explaining why black neighborhoods at certain locations exploded while others remained tense but calm. The study concludes that during the decade urban black Americans experienced a widening gap between sharply rising expectations and limited capabilities. This "relative deprivation" gap varied from place to place within cities and apparently was greatest in neighborhoods which exploded first.

THE REVOLT OF THE GHETTOS, 1964-1968: THE PSYCHOLOGICAL SIDE[1]

The revolt of black America did not happen overnight; it began with an unfulfilled promise. Claude Brown, in *Manchild in the Promised Land*, began his portrayal of Harlem with this denial of the promise:

I want to talk about the first Northern urban generation of Negroes. I want to talk about the experiences of a misplaced generation of a misplaced people in an extremely complex, confused society. . . .

These migrants were told that unlimited opportunities for prosperity existed in New York and that there was no "color problem" there. They were told that Negroes lived in houses with bathrooms, electricity, running water, and indoor toilets. To them, this was the "promised land" that Mammy had been singing about in the cotton fields for many years. . . . There was a tremendous difference in the way people lived up north. There were too many people full of hate and bitterness crowded into a dirty, stinky, uncared-for closet-sized section of a great city. . . .

The children of these disillusioned colored pioneers inherited the total lot of their parents—the disappointments, the anger. To add to their misery, they had little hope of deliverance. For where does one run when he's already in the promised land?[2]

---

[1] The first part of this section draws heavily from Joseph Boskin, "The Revolt of the Urban Ghettos," *The Annals of the American Academy of Political and Social Science*, vol. 382, pp. 1-14, March 1969.

[2] Claude Brown, *Manchild in the Promised Land*, New American Library, New York, 1965, pp. vii-viii.

One runs to one's soul brother. Sentiment and experience fused in Harlem and in ghettos across the country. Metropolitan areas grew, ghettos expanded, whites escaped to the suburbs, more blacks arrived, and ghetto life deteriorated.

According to the "law of proper proportions," any living organism thrives at only one scale. Eventually it will collapse of its own weight if size is doubled, tripled, or quadrupled and proportions are held constant. The same laws of growth and proper proportions may apply to cities and ghettos. Let us say a city's black neighborhood comprised a compact zone covering a tenth of the city in 1920, and by 1960 the urbanized area and its black neighborhood had both tripled in size (Figure 9-1). Even though the black neighborhood is segregated from white neighborhoods in both cases, the activity area of an average black resident (schematically suggested by the ellipses in Figure 9-1) intersects a proportionately wider spectrum of the available urban experience in 1920 than in 1960. As the metropolis and the ghetto expand, activity areas of poor residents remain constant or shrink somewhat as public transportation deteriorates. In 1920, blacks and whites lived rather close to one another. By 1960, partly because of the geometry of human behavior and unregulated expansion of cities and ghettos, the centers of gravity of each city's black and white populations were drifting farther and farther apart.

What started out as a vigorous and varied urban experience ended as a monotonous ghetto existence for black newcomers to the Northern city. From Harlem to Watts, ghetto life became the common denominator, with its own life-style, language, and restricted range of experience. The ghetto became a dead end for many of its residents. It became an object of loathing, a mirror of a squalid existence. Feelings of helplessness and isolation recurred in city after

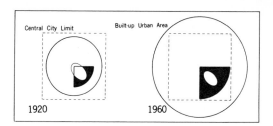

Figure 9-1   As a built-up urban area (circle) and its black neighborhood (solid color) expand, the activity space of an inner-city poor black resident (ellipse) intersects an ever smaller fraction of not only the available urban experience, but also the available experience inside the black neighborhood. In recent decades activity spaces of the poor may even have shrunk as public transportation service has deteriorated.

city. When asked what she would do if she had enough income one woman declared: "The first thing I would do myself is move out of the nieghborhood. I feel the entire neighborhood is more or less a trap."[3]

Compounding these antagonisms were the intensifying antiurban attitudes of whites, who were drawn to the city by economic necessity, but seized the first opportunity to escape to the suburbs. Meanwhile, not only were the poorest citizens poor, but they were black and located in those sections of the city vacated by earlier immigrant groups who had succeeded in translating upward social and economic mobility into geographic mobility. As Kenneth Clark wrote,

The poor are always alienated from normal society, and when the poor are Negro as they increasingly are in American cities, a double trauma exists—rejection on the basis of class and race is a danger to the stability of the society as a whole.[4]

The inauguration of John F. Kennedy in 1961 introduced the fervent rhetoric and promises of the New Frontier and a significant fraction of mesmerized Americans became convinced not only that change was possible, but that rapid improvement of their lot lay just around the corner. President Kennedy's death in 1963 interrupted that dream, but even more extravagant promises accompanied the unveiling of a plan for a war on poverty and a Great Society with full civil rights for all.

Gradually at first, then picking up steam, a sense of betrayal of expectations brought grievances into focus. To lower- and lower-middle-class blacks, the visibility of an affluent, comfortable middle class, exaggerated by mass media, induced dual feelings of emulation and smoldering resentment. After the riots, the Kerner Commission found in city after city the same complaints.[5]

The most intensely felt problems were:

1. Police practices, perceived as attacks against *personal dignity*
2. Unemployment and underemployment, perceived as attacks against *personal and family economic security*
3. Inadequate housing, perceived as an attack on the health, safety, and comfort of the family's *personal environment*

Such deep-seated, long-term malaise can lead to only one result in a decade of rapid change and rising expectations. Aaron Wildavsky summarized the situation in his recipe for violence:

---

[3] U.S. Commission on Civil Rights, *A Time to Listen . . . A Time to Act*, 1967, p. 6.

[4] Kenneth Clark, *Dark Ghetto*, Harper & Row, New York, 1964, p. 21.

[5] *Report of the National Advisory Commission on Civil Disorders*, Bantam, New York, 1968, p. 143.

Promise a lot; deliver a little. Lead people to believe they will be much better off, but let there be no dramatic improvement. Try a variety of small programs, each interesting but marginal in impact and severely underfinanced. Avoid any attempted solution remotely comparable in size to the dimensions of the problem you are trying to solve. . . . Get some poor people involved in local decision-making, only to discover that there is not enough at stake to be worth bothering about. Feel guilty about what has happened to black people; tell them you are surprised that they have not revolted before; express shock and dismay when they follow your advice. Go in for a little force, just enough to anger, not to discourage. Feel guilty again; say you are surprised that worse has not happened. Alternate with a little supression. Mix well, apply a match, and run. . . . [6]

DYSFUNCTIONAL POPULATION AND HOUSING CHANGES, 1950-1960: THE STAGE FOR UNREST

In most large cities the spatial organization of the housing supply resembles a series of distinct concentric zones around the downtown. High-density, lower-priced, and older housing is available in the inner rings; newer, lower-density, higher-priced units, mainly single-family detached dwellings, are concentrated in the outer rings.

The demand for housing is expressed sectorally. As each household passes through the stages of the family life cycle, its housing needs change and the household relocates, either *outward* to a larger, more expensive unit, or *inward* to a smaller, cheaper dwelling. Most households try to satisfy changed household requirements with a move as short as possible, and so a city's overall pattern of migration displays pronounced sectoral biases.

At the suburban edge of each sector, the addition of new housing provides upwardly mobile inner-city families with an opportunity to move outward. As they move outward, they vacate older housing which then becomes available to families localized nearer to the downtown core. Within each areal sector, the invasion-succession process is the principal means by which better housing "filters down" from the prosperous to the poor. In normal times housing filters smoothly; but from 1950 up into the 1960s the poor and the middle-class black neighborhoods experienced a housing squeeze of alarming proportions.

Let us examine the source of the housing squeeze. Residential structures have high durability and long lives. According to the 1960 census of housing, there were 58 million housing units in the United States. Thus, 1.5 million new housing starts in one year is only about 2.5 percent of the housing stock, a relatively small change in the total number which in the meantime is also affected by housing removals, especially in core areas of cities. If we consider the entire metropolitan housing market rather than its areal subdivisions, removals

[6]Daniel P. Moynihan, *Maximum Feasible Misunderstanding*, The Free Press, New York, 1969, p. ii.

generate a demand for replacement which is less important than either household formations or other influences on housing demand. In certain areal submarkets, however, demolition in one neighborhood is the principal stimulus for incremental demand in adjacent neighborhoods.

During the 1960s, demolitions due to public and private urban land development and urban highway construction proceeded at a brisk rate, but the building of new houses and the rates of vacancy varied widely, putting a serious crunch on the most active housing sectors. Despite *increasing* demands for more housing throughout the 1960s, annual new private housing starts reached a peak of 1.6 million in 1963 and then dropped to 1.2 million by 1966. By 1968, when only 1.5 million private units were started, the construction industry still had not reached its 1962 levels of production. Just when more housing was desperately needed, less was provided; and to make matters worse, in some neighborhoods housing was even being removed.

Vacancy rates are another indicator of the degree of pressure that demands exert on available supplies. The annual average rental vacancy rate for the United States rose from 5.1 percent in 1957 to 6.4 percent in 1959, and to 8.1 percent in the second quarter of 1961. Then, dropping as the market tightened and housing became scarce, the rate fell to 4.9 percent at the end of 1968. Vacancy rates for owner-occupied units were more stable, but they too reached a peak in 1963 and fell to 1.0 percent in 1968. From 1960 to 1968 mobile home shipments quadrupled in response to strong demand, but this particular alternative to low-income housing, virtually banned from cities' core housing areas, remained largely a rural or suburban option. Thus, blacks account for fewer than 2 percent of mobile home households.

Racial and ethnic ghettos usually develop in a city's most expansionist residential sectors.[7] At the turn of the twentieth century diverse ethnic groups clustered around the downtowns of American cities. Some groups, usually Jewish or white Anglo-Saxon Protestant, prospered more rapidly than others and moved outward as a group with disproportionate speed. Because they moved outward in such large numbers, they vacated entire neighborhoods which then stood ready for occupancy by the next wave of newcomers. Thus, today's black populations often occupy housing formerly used by the city's largest and most prosperous upwardly mobile groups.

Sometimes the outward movement is slowed down as it was during much of the 1960s. The expansion of the Indo-Chinese war after 1960 prompted major increases in the federal military budget. Increased federal spending coupled with deficit financing of the expanded war produced severe inflation which, despite tax increases, persisted and intensified until the end of the decade. Monetary controls were applied to the economy and tighter credit hit the home mortgage market. As government-insured interest rates on mortgages rose from 5 and 6

[7] Karl Taeuber and Alma Taeuber, *Negroes in Cities*, Aldine, Chicago, 1965.

percent to 9 and 10 percent, the construction of new suburban homes was drastically curtailed. The suburbs that had been growing fastest suffered the greatest curtailment, and thus the sectors wherein the black ghettos were located were hit the hardest. Filtering was sharply curtailed. From middle-class black neighborhoods, departures in the form of migration outward or to other cities, or of death, did not keep up either with arrivals or with the pressing need for additional space due to emigration from core areas, from other cities, or from the South, to births; or to infants and young children becoming young children and adolescents. Thus, *in certain parts* of black neighborhoods during the 1960s crowding radically increased without a safety valve. Severe congestion developed neither in the oldest core area nor in the advancing edges of the upper middle class, but instead in the middle zones as working-class and lower-middle-class blacks saw their situation deteriorate at precisely the time when they expected their lot to improve. These middle zones were precisely the places where violence erupted. To understand why violence flared in the middle zones rather than in other locations, let us examine the alternative theories of riot origin.

THEORIES OF RIOT ORIGIN

Some explanations of riot occurrence differentiate rioters from nonrioters. Other theories stress environmental circumstances, arguing that certain sets of conditions, if prevalent in a place, trigger violence. The most successful theories are psychological and emphasize the difference between what people think they have and what they feel they deserve.

The Riffraff Theory

The first theory is called the "riffraff theory." It argues that "rioters are irresponsible deviants: criminals, unassimilated migrants, emotionally disturbed persons or members of an underclass . . . peripheral to organized society with no broad social or political concerns, and views the frustration that leads to rioting as simply part of a long history of personal failure."[8] By sampling populations in the Detroit and Newark census tracts where violence and damage occurred, Kerner Commission interviewers found no differences between rioters and nonrioters that would support the riffraff theory. Instead, occupational aspirations of the rioters in Newark were higher than among nonrioters. Moreover, the vast majority of the rioters were Northerners, either born in the riot city or emigrants from another Northern city.

Relative Deprivation

The "relative deprivation theory" was rejected by the Kerner Commission for the same reason as the riffraff theory: it failed to distinguish rioters from non-

[8] N. S. Kaplan and J. M. Paige, "A Study of Ghetto Rioters," *Scientific American*, vol. 219, no. 2, p. 15, August 1968.

rioters in the census tracts which exploded. Relative deprivation is more complex than a simple "want-get" ratio suggests. The greater the deprivation a person perceives relative to what he feels are "justified expectations," the greater his discontent. Relative deprivation is not what the outside observer thinks people ought to be dissatisfied with. It is people's perception of a discrepancy between their level of expectations and the capabilities they realize. People become most intensely discontented, first, when they fail to get what they think they justly deserve, not just what they *want* in an ideal sense and second, when they feel they are making inadequate progress beyond their expectations, not whether they have actually attained them.

"Progressive deprivation," the third form of relative deprivation, often seems to be tied to revolutionary movements. Prolonged experience of increasing well-being generates intense expectations for continued increases. If changing circumstances mean that these expectations will not be satisfied, the likely consequence is intense discontent.

Applied to black populations and black neighborhoods, the relative deprivation theory can emphasize (1) the economic gap between blacks and white, which is a popular and somewhat invalid impression; (2) the gap between urban blacks and rural blacks, which is a discounted view and in any case fails to explain urban discontent; and (3) the perceived gap between upper-middle-class blacks and the blacks that rioted. The Kerner Commission found substantial and unexpected support for this third type of gap; the rioters used prosperous, successful blacks as their principal reference group.

Black Americans in the 1960s should have benefited from the most prolonged economic expansion in the nation's history, and they apparently did. Median income of nonwhite families as a percentage of white family income rose from 53 percent in 1961 to 62 percent in 1967. The percentage of nonwhite persons below the poverty line fell from 55 in 1961 to 35 in 1967. But just looking at income changes—the realizations or capabilities— misses half the point. Expectations changed too. As Boulding paraphrases Veblen: "We cannot assume that tastes are given in any dynamic theory . . . we cannot afford to neglect the processes by which cultures are created and by which preferences are learned."[9]

Blocked Opportunity

The third theory of riot origin stresses "blocked opportunities." It claims that black Americans have been systematically excluded from white society and the economic institutions controlled by whites. "This theory views white discrimination as a constant barrier to occupational mobility; thus, the Negroes who are most likely to react violently are those who want to better themselves. . . . "[10]

---

[9] Kenneth Boulding, "Economics as a Moral Science," *American Economic Review*, vol. 59, p. 2, March 1969.

[10] Kaplan and Paige, op. cit., p. 15.

The most useful theory of riot origin seems to be a combination of the second and third theories. The relative deprivation theory accounts for the level of intense discontent among the working-class and lower-middle-class blacks who are neither the poorest nor the most prosperous. The blocked opportunity theory accounts for the low level of capabilities or realization of personal, economic, and environmental rewards inside the American system.

Besides overt discrimination in many places, feelings of relative deprivation and blocked opportunity were sometimes aggravated in innocent ways as well. The exclusion of blacks from many construction jobs is frequently cited as a particularly glaring form of blocked opportunity. Because such jobs are highly visible, reputed to be lucrative, and seem relatively easy to learn, "justified expectations" on the part of blacks are that a representative fraction of all construction workers should be black. Yet many of these occupations have little if any room for newcomers, black or white (Table 9-1). Journeymen tradesmen, often anxious for their own jobs in the face of automation and declining employment, jealously guard their union membership as a birthright to pass on to whomever they choose. Yet from the black point of view, opportunities appear to be blocked just when aspirations are rising.

Table 9-1 Estimated Annual Average Employment in Selected Construction Trades, by Craft, 1951 and 1966. (Thousands)

	1951	1966
Brick masons, stone masons, and tile setters	163	164
Carpenters	808	658
Cement and concrete finishers	32	67
Electricians	111	194
Excavating, grading, and road machinery operators	95	237
Laborers	756	728
Painters, construction and maintenance, and paper hangers	348	320
Plasterers	65	35
Plumbers and pipe fitters	194	214
Roofers and slaters	47	50
Structural metal workers	32	49
Tinsmiths, coppersmiths, and sheet metal workers	35	48

SOURCE: *A Decent Home: The Report of the President's Committee on Urban Housing,* 1968, pp. 248-249.

THE LOCATION OF RIOTS AND CIVIL DISORDERS

Black Americans can be classified in socioeconomic terms or in locational terms. In socioeconomic terms the answer to the question "Who riots?" is an ambitious, hard working, but intensely dissatisfied group of working-class and lower-middle-class blacks who feel deprived and excluded from what they feel are justified expectations. In geographical terms the question becomes: "Why did some black neighborhoods explode while others remained quiet?"

The people who live in cities also live in neighborhoods, and although cities differ substantially from one another, the range of neighborhood diversity in any one city is much greater. Two neighborhood attributes which dramatize neighborhood diversity are (1) census tract population change between 1950 and 1960 and (2) the change in each tract's housing supply during the decade up to 1960 (Figure 9-2).

The *population change ratio* for a census tract is computed by dividing the tract's 1960 population by its 1950 population. An isopleth map of the ratio for each of seven Midwestern cities reveals that in every case the downtown is surrounded by a zone of sharp population decline which gives way to stability and then growth from the city edge into the suburbs. The deepest losses are concentrated in the all-white sectors (Figure 9-2). The black neighborhood develops in the most active housing sector (Figure 9-2). Housing filters down to lower-income black newcomers as the previous residents prosper and move as a group toward the suburbs. The faster the original residents prosper, the sooner they are able and anxious to abandon old housing for something better. New suburban housing is built wherever demand warrants; it is erected at the location where builders expect effective purchasing power to be strongest. The large volume of old housing units that are vacated in a sector attracts newcomers. If more are attracted than can be comfortably housed, the tract population change ratios are stabilized instead of dropping fast as they do in the more stagnant all-white sectors (Figure 9-3).

In Cleveland, the black population is concentrated east of downtown, and net population losses were highest on the west side. In Cincinnati the largest black neighborhoods lie to the northeast of downtown, but the largest population decline occurred in tracts north and southeast of downtown. In St. Louis the black sector is northwest of downtown, but the tracts with the most abrupt population declines in the 1950s were in the western and southern sectors.

A tract's *housing change ratio* equals the number of housing units in the tract in 1960 divided by the number in 1950. When mapped, Midwestern cities reveal four distinct housing zones (Figure 9-2). The number of housing units increased in zone I, which is a public and private renewal area; zone II underwent net housing losses in the 1950s; zone III was an area of stability where the few demolitions were canceled out by modest growth. Zone IV represents vigorous suburban expansion (Figure 9-4). Housing problems are concentrated in zones I

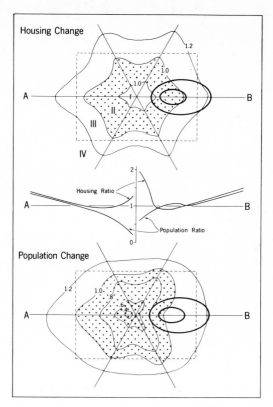

Figure 9-2 A map of housing change ratios (1960 housing units in a tract divided by 1950 units in the place) has four housing zones: zone I housing increased; zone II (stippled) housing declined; zone III was stable or had a modest housing increase; zone IV had vigorous suburban growth. The map of population change ratios (1960 tract population divided by 1950 tract population) reveals the sharpest losses (stippled) next to the downtown center and sharp increases in suburban areas. Dysfunctional change occurs when population ratios exceed housing ratios as they often did in the middle zones (small ellipse) of the black neighborhood (large ellipse).

and II of the active sectors containing black populations. Because black neighborhoods lie in the most active housing sectors, they are exceptionally visible to a substantial fraction of community economic and political leaders. Moreover, in Midwestern cities, the *center* of the downtown has migrated *from* its first loca-

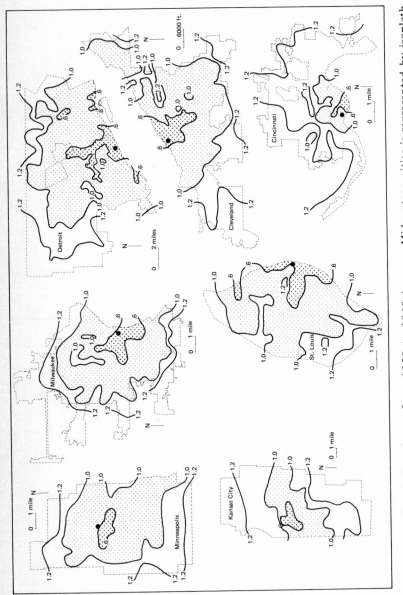

Figure 9-3 Population change from 1950 to 1960 in seven Midwestern cities is represented by isopleth values computed by dividing 1960 tract population by 1950 tract population. Stippled areas are zones of net population loss during the decade; compare Figure 9-2.

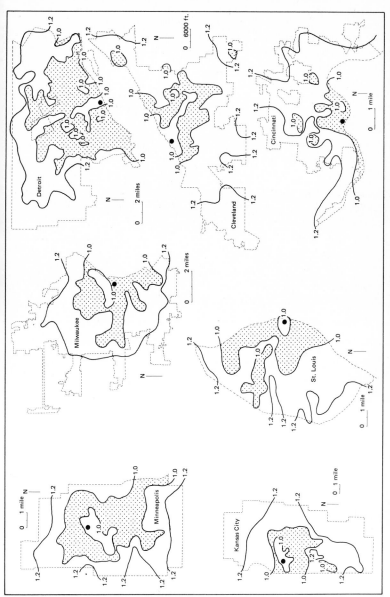

Figure 9-4   Housing change from 1950 to 1960 in seven Midwestern cities is represented by isopleth values computed by dividing the number of housing units in a tract in 1960 by the number in 1950. Stippled areas indicate net housing removal; compare Figure 9-2.

tion *toward* the center of gravity of the city's purchasing power. This direction of movement approximates the location of the most active housing sector. If there are two exceptionally active sectors, the direction of displacement of the downtown center represents a resolution of forces. A consequence of all this is that today's black neighborhoods lie between the vigorous retailing and service edge of the downtown and the mass upper-middle-class clientele that downtown tries to tap as employees and customers. Thus, downtown councils in Midwestern cities have been more anxious to support public and private renewal in black neighborhoods than in poor white sectors elsewhere. Expressways also displace housing, and the chances are high that it is black housing for at least two reasons: black neighborhoods as we have just seen usually lie between downtown and the largest concentrations of prosperous commuters and shoppers; and secondly, black neighborhoods and especially those close to downtown have had practically no political punch in city politics and are unable to get roads relocated when they threaten to cut neighborhoods in two.

In Cleveland, Cincinnati, and Detroit serious riots and civil disorders occurred midway between ancient emptying ghetto cores and youthful, prosperous advancing ghetto margins (Figure 9-5). Trapped in the middle zones were people with intense expectations who found the relative deprivation gap widening when it should have been diminishing. Housing was a major problem. In these middle zones the population ratio actually exceeded the housing ratio, and crowding as measured by persons per dwelling unit thereby increased. The squeeze was especially grim in Cleveland's Hough neighborhood. The middle zone in Cincinnati was only about 40 percent black, but nevertheless the crowding got worse. In the neighborhood at the center of the 1967 Detroit riot area, population rose from 22,000 in 1956 to 38,000 in 1967, while the available housing supply was stable to declining.[11] At the ghetto margins and in the white suburbs outside the city, young nuclear families live in single-family dwellings. In these circumstances when the population ratio exceeds the housing ratio, it is due to childbirth.

In Kansas City and Milwaukee the black neighborhood's expanding edge and its crowded midsection overlap (Figure 9-5). Yet when violence flared in the middle zone, it was at locations analogous to those in Cleveland, Detroit, and Cincinnati.

St. Louis and Minneapolis avoided serious disturbances between 1965 and 1968, but were included in the analysis to see how housing and population ratios in middle zones differed from patterns in riot cities. Census data for St. Louis reveal no increased crowding problems in the middle zones but only the evidence of typical family growth on the ghetto margins. Housing appears to have been

[11] United States Senate, Permanent Subcommittee on Investigation of the Committee on Government Operations, *Riots, Civil and Criminal Disorders, Hearings*, 1967-1969, vol. 5, p. 1276.

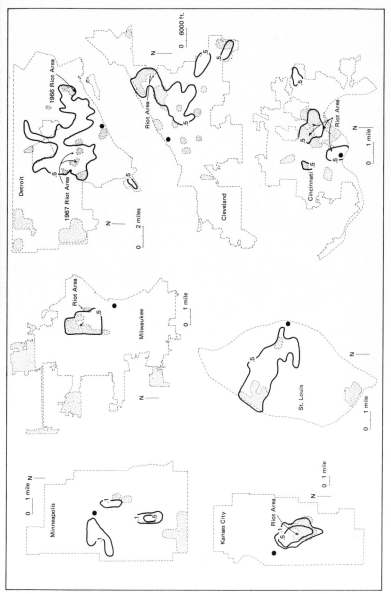

Figure 9-5   Riot locations found inside black neighborhoods. In areas enclosed by solid lines, the fraction of the population that is black exceeds the fraction shown. This fraction declines slowly toward the suburbs. In stippled areas the population ratio exceeds the housing ratio.

filtering smoothly up through 1960. In the case of Minneapolis, black population was so small in 1960 that in no census tract did black population reach 75 percent of the total. Black neighborhoods west and south of downtown reflect vigorous urban expansion mainly in these directions, but in no "black" tract did the population ratio exceed the housing ratio.

To summarize, only in certain black neighborhoods of certain cities did people experience the relative deprivation that accompanied abrupt and dysfunctional population changes in the 1960s. For the sample of cities examined, there is a striking correlation between the location of such dysfunctional changes and the outbreak of violence.

REFLECTIONS ON ENVIRONMENTAL STIMULATION AND THE NEED FOR PERSONAL SPACE

As with many social pathologies, our evidence about the riots of the 1960s resembles the tip of an iceberg—it gives only a hint of the structure that lurks below. We have barely scratched the surface in our understanding of the spatial organization of black neighborhoods, of the processes and behavior that produced them, or of the ways in which they influence learning as young people grow toward adulthood. It seems likely, however, that ghetto neighborhoods are a trap reinforced not only from outside but from within as well. According to Dubos, in every kind of neighborhood,

Man makes himself in the very act of responding to his environment through an uninterrupted series of feedback processes. . . . Early influences are of particular importance because man's body and brain are incompletely developed at the time of birth. It is well known that various forms of deprivation impair learning ability. By acting on a child during formative years, the environment shapes him physically and mentally and influences how he will function as an adult.[12]

Thus, if children are denied the opportunity to experience early in life the kind of stimuli needed for mental development, if they fail to acquire needed mental resources, their range of free choices as adults shrinks, perhaps to zero. As Dubos continues,

It is not right to say that lack of culture is responsible for the behavior of slum children or for their failure to be successful in our society. The more painful truth is that these children acquire early in life a slum culture from which escape is almost impossible. Their early surroundings and ways of life at a critical period in their development limit the range of manifestations of their innate endowment and thus destroy much of their potential freedom.[13]

[12] René Dubos, "The Crisis of Man in His Environment," *Ekistics*, vol. 27, p. 153, March 1969.

[13] Dubos, op. cit., p. 153.

Cities are created by man's need and ability to move, to interact, and to exchange. Yet after a city reaches a certain size, it becomes a cumbersome collection of functionally and spatially segregated districts. Its sheer size reduces it to an administrative abstraction. Interaction is thwarted as the number of "contact choices" (different persons, goods, services) offered to the average citizen within an hour's round trip declines. In the ideal city each resident's activity space should produce an optimum level of stimulation and opportunity. Visual monotony has adverse psychological consequences, especially for children who need a degree of diversity in their surroundings.

In addition to the psychological consequences of boring surroundings and excessive residential segregation, the social and physiological consequences of increased crowding (number of persons per dwelling unit) and high density (number of persons per unit area) are only dimly understood. Crowding experiments with rats and studies of animal crowding revealed pathologies that may be relevant to the problem of crowding and density in cities.[14]

Hall, in his work on proxemics (man's perception and use of space), observes that humans share with lower life-forms certain basic needs for territory.[15] Each man has around him an invisible series of space bubbles that expand and contract, depending on his emotional state, culture, activities, and social status.[16] People from different ethnic origins need spaces of different kinds. There are those who like to touch others and those who do not. There are those who like to be auditorially involved with everyone else and those who depend on architectural barriers to screen them from the world.

Besides ethnic differences in spatial requirements, there are variations from person to person in each culture. When Hall studied urban renewal's effects on slum dwellers, he found evidence indicating "that poor uneducated people have a much lower tolerance for being displaced than people of the middle class. Even a move across the street can be traumatic because it alters the pattern of social relationships."[17] Nowhere does he find evidence that public housing or urban renewal plans recognize the existence of different needs for different ethnic groups.

GEOGRAPHICAL PERSPECTIVES ON URBAN HOUSING POLICIES

If it can be shown that uncoordinated programs of tight money, urban renewal, and highway construction can have a disastrous aggregate impact on certain

---

[14] John B. Calhoun, "Population Density and Social Pathology," *Scientific American*, vol. 206, no. 2, pp. 139-148, February 1962; and J. Christian, "The Pathology of Overpopulation," *Military Medicine*, no. 7, pp. 571-603, July 1963.

[15] Edward T. Hall, "Human Needs and Inhuman Cities," *Ekistics*, vol. 27, pp. 181-184, March 1969.

[16] C. A. Doxiadis, "A City for Human Development," *Ekistics*, vol. 25, pp. 374-394, June 1968.

[17] Hall, op. cit., p. 182.

parts of the city, what should be done? The President's Committee on Urban Housing argued that federally assisted and public housing should be built where people want to live and where production costs are low. But it recognized that "the removal of existing constraints on freedom of location, such as racial discrimination and zoning abuses, is essential to the achievement of decent housing for all."[18] On the subject of the quality and location of government-assisted housing, care must be taken that it does not become an additional "storage bin for the poor."[19] Instead of exclusive reliance on public housing programs around the downtown core, additional sound housing could be supplied to the inner-city poor and working classes by speeding up filtering. Abundant new housing at the suburban margins of each residential sector stimulates out-migration from the central city portions of the sector. Vacated housing is thereby released to the poor who can afford housing only when they are subsidized or when prices are stabilized or depressed by rapid expansion in the amount of new housing supplied.

Yet solving the problem of housing quality is more than a supply and demand situation. The increasing isolation of ghetto children must be dealt with. The spatial arrangement of households inside human settlements may be the most basic item in preparing children to live and participate in diverse groups, to travel, to profit from their experiences, and to be at home in strange environments. Today, as the metropolis and its black neighborhoods expand, ghetto youngsters become progressively more cut off from a diverse, instructive, and racially integrated urban experience. Integrated schools become segregated; then segregated schools near the ghetto core start deteriorating. The busing of young schoolchildren is but a stopgap attempt to equalize educational opportunities that have been rendered unequal by economic and racial segregation. If busing is to succeed in overcoming ghetto isolation, care must be taken to avoid journeys which *seem* long to the child, whether they are or not, thereby affecting his perception of his accessibility to his home and mother.

Because of its full range of problems and promises, the metropolis is a useful model for tomorrow's world. For example, the urbanized-industrialized Northeast has been settled since the eighteenth century and has spread since then into Florida and the Gulf and West Coast areas. A United States map of net migration in the twentieth century shows that the edges gain at the expense of the older, settled interior. The metropolis with its old-style core of high-density residential and business activities is adjusting in a parallel way. Concentrations at the downtown center are dropping, and residential, commercial, and industrial efforts on the edges are spreading aggressively into the formerly agricultural countryside.

At a still more detailed scale we can consider the racial-ethnic ghetto as a

---

[18] *A Decent Home: The Report of the President's Committee on Urban Housing*, Washington, 1968, pp. 69-70.
[19] Ibid., p. 71.

metropolis in miniature. High densities at the core of the ghetto have been dropping sharply as jobs and houses have fallen into decay and ruin. The bright, the young, the successful, and the enterprising have pushed outward from the old ghetto core and have invaded adjacent residential territories on the outer edges of the ghetto territory. Looked at in this way we see the ghetto as a small expanding world, located within the metropolis, which itself constitutes a larger and expanding spatial unit. As these spatial changes occur, either society must regulate them, or the society will be regulated by their consequences. Our recent national experiences with violence reflect a vacillation between an anachronistic culture of violence that surrounds us and the perplexing culture of constant change that makes impossible demands on the ill-equipped. Violent aggression was once a useful form of coping with behavior, but in today's urban and technological age it produces maladaptive and destructive results.

CHAPTER TEN

FAMILIES WITH LOW INCOMES IN RURAL AMERICA

DAVID A. LANEGRAN
JOHN G. SNOWFIELD

COMMENT

While the people referred to in the previous essay reacted violently to the adverse conditions surrounding them, many Americans suffer silently. In many instances their living conditions are more miserable than those encountered in the ghetto, but because of their marginal location we seldom think of them and they are soon forgotten. In this essay the location of low-income families is described and geographic concepts are used to attempt to explain the pattern. However, the geographic approach will not solve the problem of poverty. The application of population measures to resource ratios and accessibility does not lead to any panacea. Poverty is a complex problem that involves the entire range of culture and environment. It therefore demands attention from all the academic disciplines. To date, geographers have made minor contributions to the search for solutions.

When important politicians pass through the land of the Oglala Sioux, local Bureau of Indian Affairs officials sometimes persuade Charlie Red Cloud to put on his feathered regalia and come into the reservation's main community, Pine Ridge, to have his picture taken shaking hands with the visiting dignitaries. . . . They never go out to his home for the ceremonial handshake and photo . . . to get there the visitor must pass between the city dump on the left and, on the right, a shiny pond into which the community of Pine Ridge poured its raw sewage for several years. From Chief Red Cloud's residence, one has a perfect view of both the dump and the lagoon of excrement.

Robert Sherrill, "The Lagoon of Excrement,"
The Nation, Nov. 10, 1969, pp. 500-501.

The best that can be said of rural poverty is that you may never see it. The green of Appalachia hides the hunger in the hollows. As you drive through the vacation lands of northern Minnesota, there is no way of knowing that one of the abandoned cars along the road is home for an Indian family. The ill-clad black children of the rural South will never be bussed to your school. As geographers we have tried to be dispassionate in our analysis of the distribution of those with low income. Further, we recognize that the tools and skills of our profession can only help us to understand the problem and can contribute but little to its solution. However, as human beings and as Americans we abominate the existence of such suffering and injustice in the United States and are ashamed for our country.

As with most important concepts, it is impossible to define poverty satisfactorily. In many parts of the world the overriding question is survival. By this standard, poverty is essentially absent from the United States. The definition of poverty also varies in a historical perspective; the contemporary American poor have access to goods and services that were inaccessible to the wealthiest of our ancestors.

Even if we consider only our own country at the present time, we find that poverty has many facets, not all reducible to money equivalents. Being poor is a complex of social and psychological factors; one is poor when he thinks he is poor. A graduate student on a $3,000 fellowship may lead a rich and full life, especially in the view of a student with a $2,000 grant, while an executive whose income is suddenly reduced from $100,000 to $80,000 may feel penury approaching. Another person may have an income above the average, but when he compares his possessions and life-style with those "typical" Americans he sees on television and in magazine advertisements, he finds his life to be mean and empty.

There remain many problems in classification even if we ignore perception. Consider money management. The authors of this article have noted, to their chagrin, that others with smaller incomes seem able to support fast cars and faster women—neither of which are accomplishments to which we can lay claim. In this context one notes Micawber's law, which demonstrates that two individuals with identical incomes may end up in drastically different financial circumstances. "My other piece of advice, Copperfield, you know. Annual income twenty pounds, annual expenditure nineteen, nineteen, six, result happiness. Annual income twenty pounds, annual expenditure twenty pounds ought and six, result misery."[1] Other difficulties occur when the subject of classification is the victim of occasional or cyclical poverty: the elderly, the disabled, the seasonal workers, the technologically unemployed, and those living off capital rather than income.

Being poor in the United States can be seen as either an absolute or a relative condition. That is to say, one can set a "poverty line:" if a family earns less than a given amount of money per year, it is decreed poor. On the other hand, one can describe the poor as being the lower 10 percent in income in a given year. In practice the definition tends to be more complicated than any of these. Those who have attempted to achieve a fixed or absolute poverty line have used money income alone or money income in conjunction with other variables such as the cost of food, family size, and location. Others have used the percentage of the family income spent for food, the possession of some material good such as an automobile, a standard of housing, or the payment of income tax. The Social Security Administration definition is based on the amount necessary to purchase a certain quantity of food. It considers family size, the age of the head of the family, and rural or urban residence.

Critics of a fixed poverty line dislike its arbitrary nature. Further, they argue that establishing such a level allows the poor to survive at an unchangingly low level, while the nonpoor continue to improve their lot. Rather than talk about those with an income below a certain sum, the critics would assert that those with the lowest aggregate income in any given year are poor. The problem is to determine the boundary. If one attempts to choose one figure in preference to another, one must go back to the same kind of considerations involved in arriving at a fixed poverty line. From the foregoing it is obvious that the selection of a poverty line is arbitrary. Nevertheless, to add a spatial dimension to our discussion of poverty in the United States, we have mapped the distribution of families with income under $3,000 in 1959, the then official poverty threshold (see Figure 10-1). This is not a map of the poor, but of people with low incomes.[2]

[1] Charles Dickens, *David Copperfield*, from *Complete Works*, vol. VI, Hern Books, New York, p. 209.
[2] Many sociologists prefer to use the concept of lower class to that of poverty. Their emphasis is on vulnerability to the factors and situations that shape one's life rather than on money income.

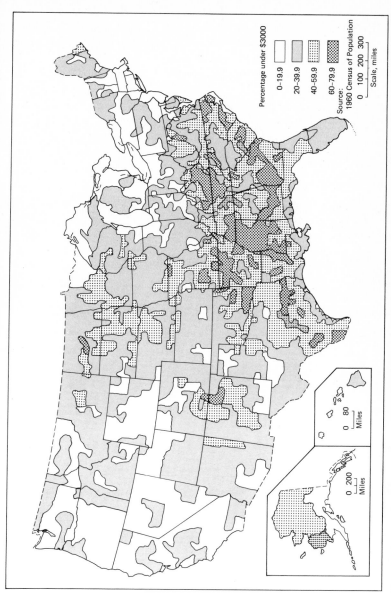

Figure 10-1   Percentage of families with income under $3,000 in 1959. This map is a generalization of the county data on income, and shows the extent of rural poverty in the United States.

Percentage under $3000

0-19.9

20-39.9

40-59.9

60-79.9

Source:
1960 Census of Population

0 100 200 300
Scale, miles

0   80
Miles

0   200
Miles

THE DISTRIBUTION OF LOW-INCOME PEOPLE IN RURAL AMERICA IN 1959

The distribution of the absolute numbers of low-income people in the United States is relatively simple.[3] Most of the low-income people in the country live in the East and the South, or in California. The South contained a disproportionate number of the low-income people. There were some 9.2 million families in the United States in 1959 with incomes of $3,000 or less; 4.5 million (46 percent) lived in the South. Only the sparsely populated Midwestern and Western states have light concentrations of low-income families.

Since, with the exception of the South, absolute numbers of the poor appear to be related to population density, it is perhaps more useful to look at the relative numbers of those with low income. Here a very different pattern emerges. Figure 10-1 shows the percentage of families with incomes of under $3,000 in 1959. A consideration of the problem at this scale provides an overview of the pattern. In addition, while people with low incomes are localized and isolated, their distribution is most understandable in the context of the national circulation system. Richard Peet has characterized a similar map as illustrating a center-periphery or heartland-hinterland distribution. Another geographer, attempting to explain these terms in a simple manner, summed it up as "Backwoods are backwards."[4] Thus the Northeastern and Midwestern manufacturing regions have proportionately fewer families with incomes under $3,000 than the surrounding rural areas.

LOW INCOME AND ACCESSIBILITY

These rural areas are poor partly because they are distant from the areas where the greatest opportunity to acquire wealth exists. They are marginal locations; the distance of their separation is more relative than absolute. One way of measuring the relative distance between marginal and nodal locations would be to use Vaughn Lueck's technique of counting the steps in a hierarchy of information flow. In such a system the number of steps separating two places is more important than the intervening earth space. Another technique would be to measure distance in terms of the units of energy necessary to overcome the separation, such as travel time or transport cost. Thus although Appalachia is fairly close to North America's main manufacturing belt in terms of straight-line earth distance, difficulties of terrain and a scarcity of good roads and other means of rapid transportation greatly increase the relative distance between the two areas. Other factors increasing distance are cultural barriers between groups such as differing languages or one group's attitude toward the other.

[3] Richard Morrill and Ernest Wohlenberg, "The Absolute Poverty of Areas and Races," *Antipode*, vol. 2, no. 2, pp. 61-67, December 1970.
[4] Jan O. M. Broek, *Geography: Its Scope and Spirit*, Merrill, Columbus, 1965, p. 31.

The relative distance between the low-income areas and opportunities for earning a better living is most important because opportunities in the objective environment do not become opportunities for an individual until he learns of them. If information about economic opportunities does not reach the poor, the effective distance between the people and the opportunity is nearly infinite.

ENVIRONMENTAL FACTORS AND POVERTY

It is a truism among geographers that the most important resources are human. Harry Caudill, author of *Night Comes to the Cumberlands*, has compared eastern Kentucky, a part of Appalachia, with Switzerland.[5] Both areas are approximately 15,000 square miles in size; both are mountainous and beautiful; and both contain brine beds. There the similarity ends. Kentucky has immense beds of coal, limestone, and silica-rich sandstone, and there are important reserves of petroleum and natural gas. The land is fertile. "There is probably not an acre of land in eastern Kentucky that, in its natural state, cannot grow something of utility and beauty."[6] In Switzerland, 24 percent of the land is barren, another quarter will grow timber of limited varieties, and very little of the remainder of the country is warm enough for really good crops. Yet Switzerland is one of the wealthiest regions in the world while supporting some 5½ million inhabitants. It is so desirable a place to live that it has some of the world's strictest immigration laws; yet inhabitants of eastern Kentucky are eager to leave. The rich alluvial lands of the Mississippi Delta and the wretched reservation land of the American Indians are each inhabited by people of low income. Thus, the consideration of environmental factors does little to explain the distribution of low-income families in the rural portions of America.

LOW-INCOME GROUPS AND REGIONS IN THE UNITED STATES

Within the rural periphery the map indicates several areas that can be termed low-income regions. Although poverty is common to these areas, they are occupied by diverse groups of people. There is considerable association between the counties with the largest number of families with incomes below $3,000 and the distribution of certain cultural groups, in particular, black rural Americans, Indian-Americans, and the group loosely characterized as Appalachians.

Certainly these groups do not contain all the rural poor in America, nor are all rural Americans poor. Rural nonfarm income, although below that of urban dwellers, was substantially higher than that of farm families. Large areas in the western United States have few families with incomes under $3,000.

The scale of farming and level of income are related. Small farms and farms without adequate capitalization for machinery or fertilizer are usually owned or

[5] Harry Caudill, "Appalachia: The Dismal Land," in *Poverty Views from the Left*, Jeremy Larner and Irving Howe (eds.), Morrow, New York, 1968, pp. 264-273.
[6] Ibid., p. 266.

operated by people with low income. The problem of low income, then, is not entirely regional or cultural. Other factors, even less specifically related to place than is farm size, appear to link rural inhabitants to poverty: age of the head of the household, education, race, and value systems.[7]

However, rural blacks, American Indians, and Appalachians, and the regions they inhabit, most clearly exhibit the problems that beset other rural Americans. Each of these groups has lived in its region for an extended period of time. The omission in this article of their unique cultural histories, which would aid in the understanding of their present circumstances, is the result of space limitations. In considering the plight of these groups, it must be remembered that low income is not only part of their present existence, but a tradition.

APPALACHIA AND THE OZARKS

I had a bad cough all the time, like you do when you work down in the mines. After a while you stop thinking about it. . . . I took some pills when it got bad, but most of the time I showed up first thing in the morning and stuck it out to the end. And I miss those days. Time went fast, and there was money around, enough to pay the bills and live real decent like and feel like a man, like somebody who was doing at least something with his life.

Then they mechanized and they started strip mining all over with those machines, and we were through, me and all my friends. And ever since it's been the same. We're lucky to be alive each day.[8]

Appalachia is an indefinitely bounded region stretching from southern New York to central Alabama and Georgia. It is characterized by rugged terrain, cutover land, poor communications, subsistence farming, coal mining, and inhabitants of Scots-Irish descent.

Several factors combine to make Appalachia unattractive to the development of industries that would employ the labor force no longer needed by the coal mines. It suffers from poor accessibility, the rather low educational level of its inhabitants, and a lack of indigenous capital. In addition, the area may not be suitable for large-scale modern agriculture. The results of federal programs to improve accessibility and to take advantage of the recreational possibilities of the region are not yet clear.

A recent study defined the Ozarks as four physiographic regions: the Ozark Uplands, the Arkansas River Valley, the Ouachita Mountains, and border coun-

[7] John F. Kain and Joseph J. Pershy, "The North's Stake in Southern Rural Poverty," in *Rural Poverty in the United States: A Report by the President's National Advisory Commission on Rural Poverty*, 1968, p. 303.

[8] Robert Coles, "Appalachia: Hunger in the Hollows," *New Republic*, vol. 159, no. 19, 1966, pp. 16-17.

ties.[9] The region is predominantly rural, with only 39 percent of the population living in urban areas. A high proportion of the land is cutover or inferior timber, and much of the land appears unsuited to profitable agriculture. Despite this, small subsistence farms are prevalent. Here the age of the inhabitants is perhaps the most serious problem. Older retired people make up a large percentage of the low-income population. This in turn relates to education: many of the old were in school when a grade school education was considered sufficient preparation for work.

Areas with similar problems are the Great Lakes cutover region and northern New England. These are areas of white rural poverty, with a primitive farming economy, supplemented by timbering, mining, seasonal recreation work, and public welfare. Life in the northern areas is even more difficult because of the severe winters.

LOW-INCOME BLACKS IN THE RURAL SOUTH

Driving south on U.S. 61 through western Mississippi the grim picture of what is taking place in rural America today comes into sharp focus. Abandoned share-croppers' shacks sit in empty, barren delta fields; many of their long-time occupants having moved either to the fringes of nearby metropolitan areas like Memphis or to the North. Occasionally one sees a house with a porch swing, a line of clothes flapping in the chill breeze, a wire fence with pieces of corrugated tin wedged between the strands to act as a wind breaker for the frail wooden structure beyond. In poverty and in the fear of leaving the land for the unknown a handful of the people have stayed.[10]

Low income is characteristic of both white and black inhabitants of the rural South. Although only 12 percent of all American families had incomes of $3,000 or less in 1959, 26% of the families in the rural South were in this category. The income of blacks in the South is on the average substantially lower than whites. Seventy-eight percent of all Southern rural black families had incomes below $3,000 per year, compared to 39 percent of the white families.

Two of the areas reported on in a recent government study were the Mississippi Delta and South Carolina, the latter being considered representative of the southern coastal plain.[11] About one-half of the families interviewed in these two regions were black. On the Delta, about 84 percent of the black families were poor; in South Carolina, 78 percent were in this category. It appears that race

[9] *Rural Poverty in Three Southern Regions*, U.S. Department of Agriculture Economic Report no. 176, 1970, p. 2.
[10] Albert V. Krebs, Jr., "On the Road in Mississippi," *Catholic World*, vol. 212, no. 1,272, March 1971, p. 297.
[11] Ibid.

overrides and intensifies the relative effect of other factors linked to poverty such as sex of head of household. In the Delta and in South Carolina many of the blacks are landless, working as farm laborers and sharecroppers. The increasing scale and mechanization of the farms remove employment opportunity. While educational levels are strongly correlated with poverty status among whites, they are much less so among blacks. The authors of *Rural Poverty in Three Southern Regions* found that when the various factors generally associated with poverty, such as age, occupation, and household size, are cross-classified by race, many of the relationships between these factors and poverty are reduced in the strength of their association. That is to say, race would appear to be the overriding influence affecting poverty in these areas.

THE TRIBAL LANDS OF THE AMERICAN INDIAN

Grandma Tobacco ... was drying the hooves and anklebones from a cow. There was no meat on the bones but she said she would boil the hooves and bones and a few strips of hide and make soup for them later this winter. There was no plumbing in her hut. She carries water from a creek a mile and a half down the hill. She is 77. [12]

One has a difficult time describing the distribution of the American Indian, except to say that most Indians live on reservations and most reservations are scattered throughout the western United States. In the early part of the twentieth century a number of American geographers, called "environmental determinists," argued that the physical environment of a region determined the culture of the region's inhabitants, i.e., poor lands produce poor people. The mutual poverty of the reservations and the Indians who inhabit them would have supported this view. Perhaps a better explanation is the greed of the whites who left to the Indians only the least fertile and productive regions of the country.

Most Indian-Americans have low incomes. Nearly three out of five rural Indian families, twice as many as other rural residents, had incomes less than $3,000 in 1959. Approximately 70 percent of Indians live in rural areas. Although they are distributed throughout the United States, the greatest concentration, some two-fifths of the total Indian population, is in the Southwest. Most Indians are very young. In 1960, some 45 percent of the rural Indian population was composed of children fourteen years old or younger. Indian families are larger than the average. Over one-fourth of rural Indian families have seven members or more. [13]

Life expectancy is lower among American Indians than among other rural residents; infant mortality is higher. Over one-half of Indian children must learn

---

[12] Sherrill, op. cit., p. 502.
[13] *Rural Indian Americans in Poverty*, Department of Agriculture Economic Research Service, Agriculture Economic Report no. 167, courtesy of Charlotte Bauer, A.C.L.

English as a second language. The concepts, skills, and attitudes they are taught in school are frequently foreign to their culture. It is not surprising then that over one-fourth of rural American Indians are deemed functionally illiterate.

The political status of Indians differs from that of other persons with low income. There are some 315 Indian tribal groups that function as quasi-sovereign nations under treaty and have a special relationship to the Bureau of Indian Affairs. An even more complicated political and cultural factor is the individual Indian's loyalty to his tribe. Traditionalists demand a return to the open council, a revival of Indian religions, and the replacement of white laws with Indian customs. Others, sometimes educated by church or foundation funding, have tended to adopt the values of the larger American society. National, regional, and state Indian organizations tend to set diverse goals for their people.

Little is known about rural American Indians living off the reservation. What evidence there is suggests that they suffer greater destitution than Indians on the reservation. Contemporary Indian policy has been characterized as tending "to prevent the Indian from participation at all in the modern economy, even from competing for the lowliest jobs in the city."[14] Although few would defend the reservation system, it may be the least of a number of evils. The Indians themselves consistently oppose the termination of the Bureau of Indian Affairs and the idea of giving them their "freedom." More than 60 percent of the 100,000 rural off-reservation Indians live in Oklahoma and North Carolina. Case studies of nonreservation Indian families in Oklahoma showed that their income was almost universally low, much of it coming from public assistance. The families were large, their housing was bad, and the plumbing was inadequate or nonexistent.

SPATIAL SYSTEMS AND LOW INCOME

Given the intensity of rural poverty in the United States, one wonders why the poor do not move to the city where there is more opportunity. In fact, many of them do. The loss of black population from the South probably exceeds that of the loss of Irish from Ireland following the famine. Today portions of Appalachia face almost complete depopulation.

On the surface, this might be seen as some kind of solution. The departure of "surplus population" increases the ratio of resources to population for the remaining inhabitants while providing opportunities to those who leave. The United States Department of Labor has funded a number of projects to further this kind of mobility, recruiting blacks and Indians from North Carolina and Mexican-Americans and Indians from Arizona and relocating them in urban areas. It is not yet certain what the long-term results of these efforts will be.[15]

[14] Richard L. Morrill, "Geographical Aspects of Poverty in the United States," *Proceedings of the Association of American Geographers*, vol. 1, pp. 117-121, 1969.

[15] Donald Schon, "Assimilation of Migrants into Urban Centers," in *Rural Poverty in the United States*, op. cit., pp. 267-287.

Promoters of migration as a solution to the problem of poverty neglect the question of the skills and abilities of the migrant. Frequently those who depart are the most productive and vigorous in their society. The rural-urban migration tends to be selective, leaving behind the old, the very young, the disabled, and the most poorly educated. Although they possess qualities that the source region cannot afford to lose, the migrants may not be equipped for city life. One study has concluded:

The North's biggest cities attract large numbers of rural Negroes from the Core South. Smaller northern areas draw disproportionately large numbers of Appalachian whites. Ironically, it is these groups that are relatively the worst prepared for coping with the complexities of the industrial metropolitan North. The educational achievement of each is inferior to the majority of the southern population from which they come. Negroes of the Core South are especially disadvantaged in this respect. In analyzing the distribution of poverty in the north-central region of the country, we found that a substantial fraction of the metropolitan North's poor were born and educated in the South. [16]

The alternative to migration is to bring the opportunities to the rural areas. Two geographers have argued that the approach most likely to alleviate the problem of poverty in rural areas is the location of a new set of cities scattered over the countryside. [17]

There is some question as to the efficacy of such plans if there is not a concurrent change in the social-cultural characteristics and personal spatial behavior of those with low incomes. The idea that poverty can be solved by moving the poor to the city or the city to the poor rests on the assumption that spatial and occupational shifts improve the lot of those who change. However, one study indicates that the characteristics which make one poor in farming have the same result in nonfarm employment. [18] This study found considerable movement back to rural areas by those who had tried the city and failed. Its conclusion was "many are called, but few are chosen."

When we first approached the problem of low income, we suspected that the rural poor would have rather limited systems of personal spatial circulation. We have concluded that personal spatial systems must be viewed qualitatively as well as quantitatively. The rural poor vary considerably in their mobility. Some, particularly the old and the very poorly educated, may have travel patterns not very different from those of the medieval peasant. Migrant laborers on the other hand travel extended distances. Too frequently their way stations and destina-

---

[16] Kain, op. cit., p. 303.
[17] Richard Peet, "Poor, Hungry America," *The Professional Geographer*, vol. XXIII, pp. 99-104, April 1971, and Morrill, loc. cit.
[18] Dale E. Hathaway and Brian E. Perkins, "Occupational Mobility and Migration from Agriculture," in *Rural Poverty in the United States*, op. cit., pp. 185-237.

tions are places of deprivation equal to their point of origin. Those with low incomes often lack the ability to manipulate their environment, the hierarchies of power or advancement, and the sources of information about opportunities. Many geographers focus on the failures of our society as well as the failure of the poor to operate within the system. Morrill and Wohlenberg argue that poverty stems from inequitable distribution of wealth and power in the United States.[19]

CONCLUSION

One of the basic problems that we face is discovering who are the poor. At the present time we deal with those with low incomes, but low income is not synonymous with poverty. When we look at the distribution of those persons with low incomes, we find that in general there is a core of the more affluent and a periphery of areas where families of low income predominate. The rural areas with the largest concentrations of low-income families tend to be inhabited by groups whose social-cultural and demographic characteristics isolate them from opportunities to make money. There is some question as to whether moving the poor to the cities or the bringing of the cities to the rural poor will materially increase their economic well-being. Considering the wide diversity among low income groups, one suspects that only a combination of programs over a long period of time will result in major improvements.

[19] Richard Morrill and Ernest Wohlenberg, *Geography of Poverty*, McGraw-Hill, New York, 1972.

CHAPTER ELEVEN

WHERE IS EVERYBODY?

A Geographer's View
of the Population
of the United States

DAVID A. LANEGRAN

COMMENT

Like the preceding essay, "Where is Everybody?" does not
deal with one specific problem but instead presents the
geographical background of the American population. In it
we see how the character of the environment and man's
utilization of it have helped produce the present distribution of people in the United States. We also see how
changes in patterns of accessibility have affected the location of people and that although these processes are illustrated in a historical or developmental context, they are
still affecting us.

Clearly the population of the United States is not evenly spread over the land (see Figure 11-1). Its density reflects the availability of resources, the type of economic activity, and the circulation system in each area. The population is concentrated in the eastern portion of the area occupied by the contiguous forty-eight states, especially within a rectangle bounded on the north by a line from Boston to Milwaukee, on the west by a line from Milwaukee to St. Louis, and on the south from St. Louis to a point just south of Washington, D.C. A second concentration occurs on the Pacific Coast. Alaska, the Great Plains, the Western mountains, and the arid basins of the Southwest have a small permanent population.

Within the densely populated regions, people are clustered in urban areas. Over 70 percent of the people in the United States live in metropolitan areas (a city of 50,000 or more and the contiguous closely settled areas surrounding it). The major concentrations are the great conurbations: megalopolis or the urbanized northeastern seaboard stretching from Boston to Washington; the developing megalopolis along the Great Lakes, from Milwaukee-Chicago to Detroit to Toledo, Cleveland, and Pittsburgh; and southern California, from San Diego to San Francisco. Other urban clusters are found on the coasts of Florida and the Gulf Coast of Texas and Louisiana. In addition to these are the outlying centers of Phoenix, Seattle, Denver, Dallas-Fort Worth, Kansas City, and Minneapolis-St. Paul. The greatest rural densities are found between the Great Lakes and the Ohio River in the Carolina piedmont and in the upper Mississippi Delta. The "empty" areas are the rugged western mountains, the nonagricultural land of the Southwest, and the high plains. In the East, the northern forest and cutover land are sparsely settled, as are the Ozark and Appalachian Highland areas and the Florida swamps. Spatial phenomena are best described in graphic form. Therefore the map should be carefully consulted before reading further.

A task of geography is to discover spatial patterns and to determine the factors that underpin a given distribution. In the case of population, as with most spatial phenomena, the factors are a combination of interactions between man and the land, especially the exploitation of resources and a complex set of spatial interactions. The presence or absence of people in any given area is a result of the site features of that place and its situation, the set of relationships that link it with other parts of the nation. By the same token the pattern of American population reflects the location of people and resources elsewhere in the world.

The population of any area changes through natural increase (the number of deaths subtracted from the number of births) and immigration (people either entering or leaving the area). The distribution of people in the United States is the result of the operation of these two processes.

Except for the last two to three centuries, America north of central Mexico has been lightly settled. The Indians occupied the land with a combined hunting and agricultural economic system. This way of life allowed a maximum popula-

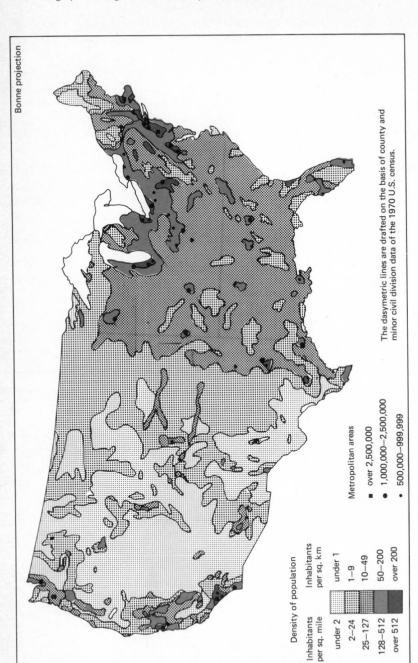

Figure 11-1   Density of population in the United States in 1970. This map is a generalization of the county data.

tion density of approximately one person per square mile. Conflicts, disease, and vagaries of climate held the population below the theoretical carrying capacity of the land. Modern scholars estimate that before the arrival of Columbus approximately 1 million Indians occupied the 7 million square miles north of the Rio Grande.

The Indians were localized in four general areas. Fishing peoples lived at relatively high densities along the Pacific Coast of present-day British Columbia and Washington. These people harvested the rich coastal waters and developed a very intricate social structure. In the dry American Southwest agriculturalists grew irrigated corn, squash, and beans in the valleys of permanent streams. In the Great Lakes and St. Lawrence region lived the famous Eastern Woodland Indians who hunted and tilled the earth. These Indians developed a complex social and governmental system. The fourth major concentration was in the Southeastern United States where the Cherokee and other agriculturists lived in large permanent villages.

The technology developed by the Indians enabled them to live off the land while at the same time remaining in a state of dynamic equilibrium with the environment. To be sure, they disrupted their environment by clearing fields in the forest and burning grasslands. Nevertheless, these changes did not alter the fundamental relationship between man and the land. Unless the technology of the Indian peoples changed enough to enable them to exploit more resources, the population of North America could not increase. We will never know what sorts of technology the Indians would have developed if they had not been disturbed by the Europeans, for the coming of the Europeans to America was to prove fatal to the Indian way of life.

In the sixteenth and seventeenth centuries Europe underwent great changes. Its merchants and navies linked it to most of the world, bringing to Europe the wealth and knowledge of the Asian, African, and American peoples. The great intellectual awakening and changes in the social structure created conditions favorable for the economic and political expansion of Europe's nation-states. Gradual improvement of living conditions produced an increase in the European population. This increase was the result of a decline in the death rate, a decline caused by improved sanitation and public health measures.

Throughout most of man's history, life has been precarious. High death rates have been the rule, especially for the young (life has always proved fatal for the old). In many preindustrial societies infant mortality rates reached 50 percent. This means that half of the babies born did not live to survive their first year. In preindustrial populations, like that of Europe before 1800, human labor was very valuable. In these populations birth rates were high because married couples sought to have large numbers of children to help support the family and to maintain the couple in their dotage. However, if 50 percent of the babies died before they grew to puberty, a woman would have to bear twice the number of babies she wanted. If she wanted ten children, she would have to give birth to twenty live babies. If we allow for occasional miscarriages, she may have had to be pregnant two dozen times to accomplish her goal. Is it any wonder that our great grandmothers lost their girlish figures and have such grim expressions in old photographs?

As Europe prospered, living conditions improved, and most importantly food became more readily available. Many food plants such as the potato, tomato, and corn were introduced to Europe from the Americas. These new food resources enabled the population of Europe to grow. In addition to improved supplies of food, housing conditions improved somwhat during these years, and the first efforts to clean up the urban water supplies were made. With the improvement in sanitation there was a decline in communicable diseases which of course reduced the death rate. Most of the reduction in the number of deaths occurred because of a decrease in infant mortality rates. Although the death rate began to decline in the eighteenth century, birth rates remained high, and the population began to grow. As death rates continued to decline, the population of Europe grew at an increasing rate. High rates of population growth followed the spread of industrialization and commercialization to the east and south from Northwest Europe.

The result of the growing population of Europe and of the existence of an attractive, relatively empty continent just across the ocean was the great Atlantic migration. The migration was a unique event in the history of man: the transplantation of a people and the occupation of a land mass three times the size of Europe.

The Indians were not particularly hospitable to the surplus Europeans. In any case, the invasion of the whites was disastrous to them. European diseases and superior military technology greatly reduced the numbers of Indians east of the Mississippi River. The survivors were forced to move to the Great Plains. Europeans also brought black people to the continent as slaves, who formed an important part of the colonial population.

Colonization essentially means linking the "mother country" to places that supply resources or markets. These places are held together through trade and movements of people. In North America the first Europeans took over and fortified the Indian circulation (transportation and communication) system of canoe routes and pack trails. They then connected this system to new focuses on the coast, the ports, which were really part of the European circulation system. By first capturing and then elaborating the Indian circulation system, the Europeans were able to exploit the resources of the continent very efficiently. They were so efficient that the resources were exhausted in many places. The subsequent modifications of the North American circulation system have not altered its basic European focus. As hazards to settlement were removed or reduced and the circulation system developed, the European population increased at a rapid and consistent rate.

The first census takers counted 3.9 million people in the United States (see

Table 11-1). Most of these people lived within 250 miles of the Atlantic Coast. Less than 5 percent of the population lived west of the Appalachian Mountains. Needless to say, they wanted to be as close to Europe as possible. The eastern seaboard has to this day remained the most densely populated area in the country. As the population grew, it expanded westward. By 1800 three tongues of settlement reached through the mountains: one in the Mohawk Valley of New York, a cluster around the present site of Pittsburgh, and a strip in Kentucky. Beyond these were the scattered posts and forts of the traders and military forces. In 1800 the North-Central states had 51,000 people. Throughout the rest of the nineteenth century this area would grow faster than the older settled areas in the East and South.

This population was essentially rural, and there were very few clusters of people. In 1790 the United States contained twenty-four urban places. Two of these had a population of over 25,000. By 1800 there were thirty-three urban places, with a combined total population of 322,271. Three of these cities had over 25,000 people. Philadelphia, the largest, had 70,000 inhabitants, while London at the same time had 800,000.

As the century progressed, the Republic expanded its territory. With the Gadsden Purchase in 1853 the area occupied by the contiguous forty-eight states was placed completely under the control of the United States government. Alaska and Hawaii were both acquired before the end of the century. Although the gross area of the United States increased from 888,811 square miles in 1800 to 3,022,387 square miles in 1860, the population grew even faster. There were approximately twenty-six million more Americans in 1860 than there were in 1800. This growth was the result of natural increase and immigration. Unfortunately we have no information about death rates in nineteenth-century America. We do know that the birth rate fell from 55/1,000 in 1800 (white only) to 41.4/1,000 (white only) and 44.3/1,000 (total population) in 1860. In order for the population to have grown, the death rate must have declined along with the birth rate.

Immigration was of fundamental importance to the growth of the population (see Table 11-2). Some five million people entered the United States officially during the first sixty years of the nineteenth century. The impact of these new arrivals on the population cannot be adequately measured by these figures, for they brought with them skills and ideas that made the nation work. Over half of those who entered the country during these years came in the last two decades. During the 1850s the immigration was twice that of the 1830s. The flow of people was interrupted by the Civil War but increased afterward. This migration was the result of three things: unpleasant conditions in Europe pushing people out, relatively attractive conditions in North America drawing people across the Atlantic, and a circulation system that made the movement of these people feasible. During the 1840s, famine followed the failure of the Irish potato crop. Irish farmers, forced off their land, were drawn to the United States by promises

Table 11-1 Population and Area: 1790-1940

(Area figures represent area on indicated date including in some cases considerable areas not then organized or settled, and not covered by the census. Area figures have been adjusted to bring them into agreement with remeasurements made in 1940.)

CENSUS DATE	RESIDENT POPULATION					AREA (SQUARE MILES)		
	NUMBER	PER SQUARE MILE OF LAND	INCREASE OVER PRECEDING CENSUS			GROSS	LAND	WATER
			NUMBER	PERCENT				
Conterminous U.S. (†)								
1790 (Aug. 2)	3,929,214	4.5	(*)	(*)		888,811	864,746	24,065
1800 (Aug. 4)	5,308,483	6.1	1,379,269	35.1		888,811	864,746	24,065
1810 (Aug. 6)	7,239,881	4.3	1,931,398	36.4		1,716,003	1,681,828	34,175
1820 (Aug. 7)	9,638,453	5.5	2,398,572	33.1		1,788,006	1,749,462	38,544
1830 (June 1)	12,866,020	7.4	3,227,567	33.5		1,788,006	1,749,462	38,544
1840 (June 1)	17,069,453	9.8	4,203,433	32.7		1,788,006	1,749,462	38,544

Year							
1850 (June 1)	23,191,876	7.9	6,122,423	35.9	2,992,747	2,940,042	52,705
1860 (June 1)	31,443,321	10.6	8,251,445	35.6	3,022,387	2,969,640	52,747
1870 (June 1)	39,818,449(†)	13.4(‡)	8,375,128	26.6	3,022,387	2,969,640	52,747
1880 (June 1)	50,155,783	16.9	10,337,334	26.0	3,022,387	2,969,640	52,747
1890 (June 1)	62,947,714	21.2	12,791,931	25.5	3,022,387	2,969,640	52,747
1900 (June 1)	75,994,575	25.6	13,046,861	20.7	3,022,387	2,969,834	52,553
1910 (Apr. 15)	91,972,266	31.0	15,977,691	21.0	3,022,387	2,969,565	52,822
1920 (Jan. 1)	105,710,620	35.6	13,738,354	14.9	3,022,387	2,969,451	52,936
1930 (Apr. 1)	122,775,046	41.2	17,064,426	16.1	3,022,387	2,977,128	45,259
1940 (Apr. 1)	131,669,275	44.2	8,894,229	7.2	3,022,387	2,977,128	45,259

(*) Not applicable.

(†) Excludes Alaska and Hawaii.

(‡) Revised to include adjustments for underenumeration in Southern states; unrevised number is 38,558,371.

Source: "Statistical Abstract of the United States, 1970", U.S. Department of Commerce, p. 5.

of employment associated with the economic booms of the forties. The connection between Ireland and America is both interesting and complex. During the seventeenth and eighteenth centuries, the population of Ireland expanded because of the adoption of a New World plant, the potato. Later, after an essentially one-crop economy had been established, the potato blight, a New World disease, destroyed the agricultural base of the Irish. The surplus population left for "Amerikai," an ironic turn of events. Other factors pushing Europeans were

Table 11-2 Recorded Immigration, by Continents: 1819-1940

(In thousands. Data are for years ending June 30, except as noted. 1819 to 1867, figures represent alien passengers arriving in steerage; 1868 to 1891 and 1895 to 1897, immigrant aliens arriving; 1892 to 1894 and 1898 to 1940, immigrant aliens admitted; 1819 to 1868, by nationality; 1869 to 1898, by country of origin or nationality; 1899 to 1940, by country of last permanent residence.)

PERIOD	TOTAL[a]	EUROPE	AMERICA	ASIA	AUSTRA-LIA AND NEW ZEALAND	PACIFIC ISLANDS	AFRICA
Total, 1819 to 1940	40,173	33,764	5,038	982	71	20	37
1819 to 1820[b]	8	8					
1821 to 1830[b]	143	99	12				
1831 to 1840[c]	599	496	33				
1841 to 1850[d]	1,713	1,598	62				
1851 to 1860[d]	2,598	2,453	75	41			
1861 to 1870[e]	2,315	2,065	167	65			
1871 to 1880	2,812	2,272	404	124	10	1	
1881 to 1890	5,247	4,737	427[f]	68	7	6	1
1891 to 1900	3,688	3,559	39[f]	71	3	1	
1901 to 1910	8,795	8,136	362	244	12	1	7
1911 to 1920	5,736	4,377	1,144	193	12	1	8
1921 to 1930	4,107	2,478	1,517	97	8		6
1931 to 1940	528	348	160	15	2		2

[a]Includes some immigrants of unspecified origins.
[b]October 1 to September 30.
[c]October 1, 1830, to Dec. 1, 1840.
[d]Calendar years.
[e]Jan. 1, 1861, to June 30, 1870.
[f]No reports of British, North American, or Mexican immigrants, 1886 to 1893.

Source: Conrad Taeuber and Irene B. Taeuber, *The Changing Population of the United States,* New York, Wiley, 1958, p. 53.

the political restrictions of East European empires and the attempts to encourage the lower classes to leave England.

Although there were 392 urban places in the United States in 1860, these immigrants came to an agricultural nation. In 1860, 6,216,518 people lived in urban places, while four times as many people (25,226,803) lived in rural territory. Agriculturists occupied ("occupied" areas are defined as having at least two people per square mile) most of the land east of the Mississippi. Only the rugged mountain country, the Northern forests, south Florida, and the marshy Gulf Coast were unoccupied. West of the Mississippi the population was confined to southeastern Minnesota, eastern Iowa, the lowland regions of Missouri and Arkansas, upland Louisiana, and east Texas. Further west there was a center of Spanish-speaking people in the upper Rio Grande Valley and a Mormon cluster in the Salt Lake area. On the West Coast the great valleys were settled, and a fringe of people lived along southern California's golden coast. This pattern reflects two factors: settlement occurred from east to west; and in the arid West human occupance depends upon the location of water resources.

In the remaining decades of the century this pattern of population intensified, and the frontier continued to move westward. By 1870 the edge of the settled area had expanded into central Minnesota and upper Michigan. All of Iowa was occupied as well as eastern Nebraska and eastern Kansas. Texans expanded southwestward but remained in the eastern third of their state. The Colorado piedmont was opened and West Coast centers continued to expand. At the turn of the century the eastern portion of the Great Plains was occupied; the Colorado and Utah piedmont centers expanded while the mining centers of the Western mountains were founded. The West Coast concentrations coalesced, and the oases of the arid Southwest were settled. Indian Territory was opened to white settlement, and the last large block of good land was passed into the hands of the whites. After 1900 only the most inhospitable places remained unoccupied. Such forbidding places as the western Dakotas, northern Maine, Nevada, and southern Florida, especially the area around Miami, were empty. The Bureau of the Census officially closed the frontier after the 1900 census; the first stage of the great western movement came to an end.

After a slight dip during the 1860s, immigration continued at a rapid pace. As both the numbers and the rates of immigration increased in the late nineteenth and early twentieth centuries, the source regions for immigrants changed. The first change was the end of the black immigration. Although the importation of slaves was made illegal in 1808, slaves were smuggled into the country as late as the 1840s. Thus the black immigration ended just when the greatest number of Europeans began to arrive. In 1790 blacks made up 19.3 percent of the population. In 1900 they accounted for 11.6 percent, and in 1970 they were 11.1 percent of the population.

As mentioned previously, the flow of European migrants was the result of economic development, population growth, and political pressures. Therefore the source of European migrants followed the industrialization and urbanization of the continent. As can be seen in Table 11-3, early migrants came from Western and Northern Europe. During the nineteenth century the economies of these countries expanded. As the forces pushing people from these countries lost their power, the volume of immigration declined. Although there is some variation from country to country, the peak of migration from Northern and Western Europe came in the 1880's when 3.8 million people entered the United States. When the Northern and Western European immigration was at its peak, immigrants from the rest of Europe began to enter the country. After 1890 the tide of immigration came from Southern and Eastern Europe. In the first decade of the twentieth century, immigrants from these areas outnumbered their Northern and Western cousins three to one. This changed pattern of origins alarmed the earlier immigrants and their descendants. In 1920 a quota system was established to restore immigration to the proportionate ethnic composition of the 1920 white population of the United States and to restrict the number of immigrants.

The massive flows of immigration were a transitory phase in the development of the nation. The flows which had the greatest impact on the land and govern-

Table 11-3 Reported Emigration from Europe, by Major Regions: 1819-1940

(In thousands)

| YEAR | REGIONS | | | | |
	ALL EUROPE	NORTH AND WEST	EAST AND CENTRAL	SOUTH	OTHER
Total, 1819 to 1940	33,764	19,457	8,549	5,715	43
1819 to 1820	8	8			
1821 to 1830	99	96		3	
1831 to 1840	496	490		5	
1841 to 1850	1,598	1,592	1	5	
1851 to 1860	2,453	2,431	2	20	
1861 to 1870	2,065	2,032	12	21	
1871 to 1880	2,272	2,070	126	75	1
1881 to 1890	4,737	3,779	627	331	1
1891 to 1900	3,559	1,643	1,211	704	
1901 to 1910	8,136	1,910	3,915	2,310	1
1911 to 1920	4,377	998	1,918	1,452	8
1921 to 1930	2,478	1,300	590	565	23
1931 to 1940	348	205	58	84	2

Source: Conrad Taeuber and Irene B. Taeuber, *The Changing Population of the United States,* New York, Wiley, 1958, p. 57.

ment of the nation were those which took place before the Civil War. However, in absolute numbers the important immigrations came after the Civil War. From 1790 to 1840 less than one million immigrants arrived. Almost 10 million came between 1840 and 1880, but the great wave of 23.5 million came between 1880 and 1920. By the end of World War I the era in which unskilled and uneducated labor could move at will had ended.

The immigrants from Southern and Eastern Europe, although agriculturists, came to live in the large cities of the industrialized Northeast. The land of opportunity was urban—an ethnic quarter of a crowded city. In 1920, for the first time in the history of the nation, people living in urban places outnumbered those living in rural areas 54,157,973 to 51,552,647.

Having examined the great international migration and the westward expansion of the American population, we can now turn our attention to urbanization, one of the primary factors in the localization of people. As we have seen, the location of resources influenced the overall distribution of the population. Within this general framework cities provide focuses for concentrations of people. American cities have always served as points for collecting, processing, and distributing goods, services, and ideas. The size and growth rate of a particular city is affected by the size and resource base of its hinterland, or tributary, area, and the available technology of transportation and industry. To a large measure the size of a city's hinterland is determined by transportation technology, and of course industrial technology determines what elements of the earth's crust are resources. Cities occur at nodes or intersections in a circulation system. Because these locations depend upon the circulation system and because cities provide the focal points for the location of people in the United States, we can analyze the urbanization and distribution of people in terms of four eras of transportation and industrial technology.[1]

The first era, called the "sail and wagon era," lasted from 1790 to 1830. In this period people relied on small sailing ships for coastal trade and smaller sailing sloops for riverine traffic. Goods could be floated down the large river systems from the interior with ease, but upstream travel was difficult and therefore expensive. Primitive trails and roads made overland travel slow and difficult. Because most of the population during these years lived along the seaboard, urban clusters were ports either on the Atlantic or the Ohio and lower Mississippi rivers. These cities had small hinterlands and were primarily concerned with mercantile activities, exporting agricultural products and importing and transhipping manufactured goods. No one city dominated the nation: New York, Philadelphia, and Boston were all about the same size at the beginning of the era. Towns were located on the waterways at power sites, mining sites, stream crossings, and crossroads.

[1] John R. Borchert, "American Metropolitan Evolution," *Geographical Review*, vol. 57, pp. 301-332, 1967.

During the "steamboat and iron horse era," from 1830 to 1880, river travel improved tremendously. Because of the steamboat, scheduled service both upstream and downstream was possible on practically all rivers. Oceanic steamships required larger and better-equipped harbors. Consequently the smaller ports were eclipsed by those of larger cities. A series of regional rail networks were developed, focused on large rivers or seaports. The largest cities were concentrated east of the Appalachians, although the Midwestern and West Coast cities were established during this period.

Cities located in transportation corridors either on the rail network or along rivers were most attractive to new arrivals from Europe and for people leaving the farms. Other local points of population growth occurred around sources of water power, coal mines, and crossroads amid rich farmland.

The third era, the "steel rail" or "long haul," lasted from 1880 to 1920. It was during this period that the cities of the plains and mountain region were established. In older settled areas the coal towns of western Pennsylvania and West Virginia boomed. Rails linked the nation together for the first time. The agricultural frontier closed, and industrialization proceeded very rapidly. Cities were no longer completely commercial centers, but took on industrial functions. These industrial and railroad cities of the Northeastern quarter of the country attracted the 23.5 million European migrants. Older river towns, cut off by the new transportation system, stagnated. The hauling of coal over long distances enabled ports to have power for manufacturing, and as a result these sites grew. Markets for manufactured goods became increasingly important; large cities became larger by inertia. Although rural to urban migration began in the previous era, it increased rapidly during these years. In 1880 approximately 50 percent of the total labor force was employed in agriculture, but by 1920 this figure had dropped to 27 percent. As people began to leave the rural areas and the small towns, the farm trade centers began to decline.

The "air-auto-amenity era" began in 1920, and its end is not in sight. Several technological changes have occurred in this epoch that have affected the location of people. Most significant has been the great decentralization of transportation brought about by the widespread use of the automobile. Today cars, station wagons, pickup trucks, and house trailers have put us all in the transportation industry. This has produced a major redistribution of accessibility. A location on the rail network is no longer crucial. Instead, distance from population centers has become the prime determinant of accessibility. A second major change was the mechanization of agriculture. As farming became increasingly mechanized, employment in agriculture continued to decline in this epoch. In 1970 approximately 5 percent of the total labor force worked on farms. Expenditure on national defense increased through the period from 1 percent of the gross national product in 1920 to 9 percent in 1970. While employment in manufacturing, transportation, and agriculture decreased, employment in the government, military, and service industries increased.

These changes have had many effects on the distribution of both cities and people in the country. The biggest change has been the retreat from the rural areas, especially marginal agricultural areas and mining sites where minerals have either been exhausted or are no longer needed. People leaving these places moved to the growing urban areas and have entered the service industries. In the past there has been a consistent need for former agriculturists in cities. When the immigration of European peasants ended in 1920, North American peasants, subsistence farmers from the Northern forests, the Southern hills or coastal plains, and the high Western plains began to move to the cities. This rural-to-urban migration has dominated the localization of the American population.

Within the nationwide movement from country to city there have been several interchanges that warrant attention. The movement from the Southern plains to California during the 1930s gained the nation's attention through the art of John Steinbeck and Woody Guthrie. This movement was triggered by a combination of a drought, continued mechanization of agriculture, and a general economic depression, and was complemented by the pull of promised employment in the specialized agricultural areas of southern California. Although the plainsmen were eventually absorbed into the state's economic system, they paid a price of much hardship and suffering, and the indignity of hearing two American regional insults, "Okie" and "Arkie."

During World War I the cheapest labor available in the United States was located in the Southeast—the black subsistence farmers. The South, because of its high rate of natural increase and limited economic opportunity, has always been an area of out-migration. At the beginning of the fourth era, wartime labor shortages led industrialists to induce people out of the South; most of these people were black. Although blacks had always lived outside the Southeast, until the fourth era the percentage had been small. In 1900, 90 percent of American blacks lived in the South; in 1920, 85 percent were still in the South. The first blacks to move were those closest to the industrial centers, those in the border states. Their destinations were Chicago, Detroit, Toledo, Cleveland, Pittsburgh, and the cities of the northeastern seaboard. The movement of blacks was slowed during the 1930s by white opposition and by the Depression. Spurred by the war economy, the migration began again in the early 1940s. By this time, however, the potential migrants of the border states had already moved, and the Deep South became the primary source region. Los Angeles and the West Coast manufacturing cities were a new destination. The migration of the forties was dramatic. For example 260,000 blacks left Mississippi during the decade, almost one-quarter of the 1940 black population. The black migration from the South follows three general paths: one from the Atlantic Coast to megalopolis; another from Mississippi, Alabama, Tennessee, Kentucky, and western Georgia to the Great Lakes conurbation; the third from Louisiana, Arkansas, Oklahoma, and Texas to southern California.

The population of the northern Great Plains has had an absolute decline (Figure 11-2). This decline is due entirely to out-migration. The Dakotas were settled under the Homestead Act of 1863, a law designed to create a class of

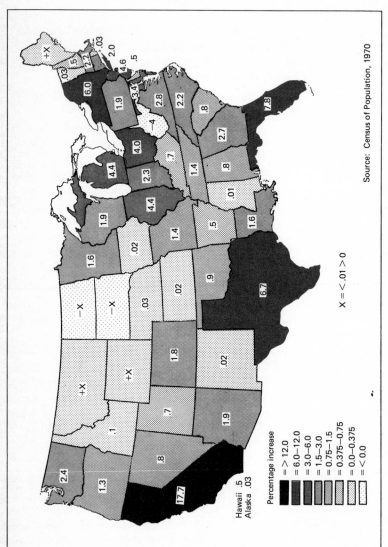

Figure 11-2 Percentage of national population increase by state 1960-1970. This map shows what portion of the national increase in the ten-year period was produced by the growth within the forty-eight contiguous states. California clearly had the greatest increase.

yeoman farmers. In the fourth era, farmers dispensed with horses as a source of power. Since they no longer had to care for animals and since crops can be grown only in the summer (the land and atmosphere both freeze in the winter), there was no reason for farmers to stay on the land throughout the year. Typically, farm families began to move to nearby towns, and the farmers commuted to their fields. Gradually they moved to more distant and larger cities. Some even bought land further south, moved their families out of the Dakotas, and returned north only for the planting and harvesting operations.

Migration theory tells us that migrants move to the closest opportunity; the number of migrants decreases with the distance from the point of origin. This phenomenon can be seen with the movement of North Dakotans. The greatest number of people move to the nearby metropolitan area, Minneapolis and St. Paul. However, large numbers of migrants spurn the industrial cities of the Great Lakes and move to southern California. Once in California they settle near their friends and live in a style they are accustomed to. For example, 20 percent of the 28,000 inhabitants of Lodi, California, are reputed to be from the Dakotas. One of the most famous individuals involved in this movement is Lawrence Welk. Welk was once a small-town bandsman who traveled from town to town seeking his fortune. He eventually found the nation's largest concentration of Dakotans and assorted Midwesterners in the Los Angeles area. These homesick middle Americans made his music famous and Welk wealthy.

Dakotans went to California in search of jobs, but they also went in search of amenities, specifically a better climate. Their movement is indicative of the third major migration pattern in the United States, the move toward amenities. The transportation developments of the fourth era opened up many new areas to urbanization. The most exciting example of this is southern Florida, an area that had remained unoccupied for most of the nation's history. As the population of the United States became more affluent and as life expectancy increased, retirement areas became more important places of population growth. Pensions can be collected anywhere in the country, so these retirement communities are found in the areas with the most attractive climates—southern California, coastal Florida, and Arizona. California, with its expanding economy, is a beacon for migrants from all over the United States. It is the leading example of population growth in an amenity area.

Urbanization has been accompanied by suburbanization. Although suburbanization does not alter the distribution of people at the national scale, it is important in individual states and in sections of the country.

These are the factors that have produced the present distribution of people in the United States. Natural increase has been the primary determinant of the numbers of people, and migration has determined their location. There have been four significant patterns in the migration: the European immigration, the westward movement, the rural-to-urban movement with its special variations, and the movement to amenity locations. From the present distribution and the factors that underlie it, we can attempt to forecast its future.

The task of predicting the American population of the future has fallen on the government demographers of the Census Bureau. Theirs is no easy task. Having given up trying to make exact predictions of the population for a given time in the future, they issue sets of projections based on differing fertility rates (the number of births per 1,000 women aged 15 to 44). The estimates of the population in the year 2000, 30 years from now, differ by 54 million people (see Table 11-4).

The basic assumption behind series B is that the birth rates will soon return to the high levels characteristic of the "baby boom" years of the 1940s and 1950s, and that these rates will remain high until the end of the century. This calls for a second-generation baby boom. Series C assumes a return to the moderately high birth rates of the 1960s. These series call for an annual increase of 1.4 percent per year. In 1969 the population increased 1.0 percent. Series D calls for a continual moderate decline in fertility rates until 2.45 children per woman is reached. This rate is well above the 2.10 required for replacement. Assuming an average immigration figure of 400,000 per year, the population in 2000 would be 281 million. Series E calls for a reduction of fertility rates until the replacement rate is reached. This seems to be the minimum estimate. Another series exists, series X, which is based on the same assumptions as those of Series E except it has included an end to immigration. This estimate calls for a population of 250 million in 2000, some 16 million fewer than series E. In issuing these four forecasts the Census Bureau has essentially said, "Here are the possible ranges for population growth; take the one that suits you best."

Table 11-4 Projections of Total Population: 1960-2000

(Population in thousands. Total population including Armed Forces abroad.)

YEAR (JULY 7)	SERIES B	SERIES C	SERIES D	SERIES E
Projections:				
1970*	205,456	205,357	205,167	205,070
1975	219,101	217,557	215,588	214,735
1980	236,797	232,412	227,510	225,510
1985	256,980	249,248	240,925	236,918
1990	277,286	266,319	254,720	247,726
1995	297,884	283,180	267,951	257,345
2000	320,780	300,789	280,740	266,281

*A preliminary estimate for July 1, 1970, is 205,391.

Source: "The Future Population of the United States," *Population Bulletin*, vol. 27, p. 14, 1971.

There is little reason to expect any major shifts in the location of people in the next decades. The large metropolitan areas will continue to attract people. Although some redistribution is likely to occur within the urban areas, the general trend toward increased urbanization will persist. This country has never had an explicit population policy, although many programs have had great effect on both the size and location of the population. However, if the national government would adopt some sort of relocation policy, its success would seem highly unlikely. Even the planned nation of Great Britain could not stop the growth of Greater London. In addition, the Soviet Union has had little success in limiting the growth of Moscow.

In the United States the areas that are now densely settled will remain centers of population. Southern California, Phoenix, the Gulf Coast, and Florida will continue to grow as more people become able to move to warmer climates (see Figure 11-2). The decline of the population in rural areas will undoubtedly level off in the next decade or so as some floor or minimum population necessary for agriculture is reached. It is very difficult to predict the exact figure, but it will be a very small fraction of the population. In any case, areas that now have more than two persons per square mile will not become uninhabited.

As personal mobility increases, seasonal homes in recreational areas will become more common. This fact will probably not be reflected in the map of population density, which is based on legal residence. Perhaps some of the depressed population engaged in marginal agriculture and mining activities will relocate in cities but will make up only a minor part of the total picture.

In general, the map of population density for the year 2000 will look much like that for 1970. The only major difference will be that the Great Lakes and seaboard megalopolis will be joined into one vast urbanized area.

CHAPTER TWELVE

PARADISE LOST

A Geographic Look
at the Environment

RICHARD SKAGGS
DAVID A. LANEGRAN

COMMENT

The following essay is different from those that have preceded it because the authors focus the questions and concepts of geography on man's interaction with the physical environment. The localization in space of this interaction fascinates geographers, and examination of it is their contribution to the study of environmental problems. In order to examine this interaction we must synthesize a tremendous amount of information about both the physical and cultural elements of the landscapes. The authors have attempted to aid you in this synthesis by presenting a model of interaction in the form of a diagram. This is the basis for the following section in which the authors apply geographical concepts to air pollution. We see how site and situation aid in our understanding of air pollution incidents, and of the primary role which distance plays in the problem. The authors use the concept of scale to organize a rather comprehensive summary of what is known about inadvertent weather modification and its effects on human beings. It is interesting to note that while the geographic questions are useful at the three scales, the answers to them vary. The concluding section of the essay brings us back to the notion of environmental perception and its effect on our behavior. Its message is simple: our attitudes toward the environment must be examined in detail before we can begin a course of action in environmental advocacy. Read this essay in a place with windows, look out the windows frequently, and breathe deeply.

Southern California! To most residents of the United States living north of Miami the Los Angeles area was once thought of as a modern Garden of Eden. While there are rainstorms in the winter which may cause flooding, it never snows, and summers are always warm and sunny. The warm ocean beaches are occupied by California blondes and surfers, and only occasionally by garbage. The surrounding mountains and their valleys provide scenic sites for houses and good places to develop the dams and reservoirs necessary to store the winter rains to be used during the dry summers. The urbanized area offers employment opportunities, and the world's most developed freeway system allows residents to move their cars freely around the metropolitan area. Is it any wonder that until recent years many Midwesterners wanted to live there?

There are a few problems, nevertheless. Los Angeles is located on one of the earth's most active earthquake zones. Periodic movements in the earth's crust tend to disturb dams, hillsides, and buildings. Despite the hopes of Floridians, however, there is no chance that California will split off the continent and drift out to sea.

During the dry summers, the uncultivated vegetation surrounding the homes on the hillsides and mountain slopes becomes highly combustible. The presence of large numbers of people in an inflammable countryside means fire.

The winter rains put an end to the summer and fall fires. When the rains fall on the hillsides denuded by fire, the soil washes downslope to help fill in reservoirs. Occasionally this erosion takes on a spectacular form, and great mudslides engulf valley houses while cliffside homes move gradually toward the sea.

Innumerable cars in southern California release tons of material into the atmosphere of the region. These pollutants are prevented from dispersing horizontally out of the area by the surrounding mountains and the daily oscillation of winds. Thus the only way this material can escape and disperse is through upward movement. Occasionally, the atmospheric temperature at a certain elevation begins to increase with increasing elevation instead of decreasing as would be expected. This is significant because gases will rise in the atmosphere only as long as they are warmer than the surrounding air. When warm gases encounter the inversion, they stop rising because they are no longer warmer than the air above them. The inversion layer acts like a giant sewer cover trapping the pollutants beneath it. When the inversion is lower than the mountain tops, the trap is closed. Pollution is caused by human activity. Although the same set of physical conditions existed before 1940, air pollution was not a problem.

In Los Angeles the various elements of the physical and cultural landscapes interact and work upon one another. It is this interaction as it is localized on the surface of the earth that fascinates geographers. Although many people are concerned with the quality of our environment, the geographer's questions set his interests apart. His attention is focused on this interaction in space. Although spatial arrangement and interactions are properties of the environment, they do not exist as physical phenomena in the way things like soil and water do.

In order to come to grips with environmental problems we must attempt to synthesize a tremendous amount of information. Such an attempt should include a soundly based understanding of environmental disturbances coupled with knowledge of social, economic, and political systems. One way to attempt this synthesis is by diagramming and simplifying the complex set of interactions into a system of elements and interactions (see Figure 12-1). The interactions are called feedback and may be either positive or negative. That is, the influence of element A on element B can either stimulate or repress B. By the same token, element B may stimulate or repress A.

With this scheme in mind let us consider air pollution. We can begin with an input of microscopic particles into the atmosphere, which result from such human activity as steel making, driving cars, or plowing fields. These particles will become a part of the atmosphere and will affect its basic functions, such as the flow of radiant energy to and from the earth's surface. As a result of their effect on the atmospheric process, an output such as decreased mean temperature *may* occur. This possible decrease in temperature will in turn trigger feedback loops, either positive or negative, of cultural and natural origin.

One feedback loop might result in an attempt to counter the temperature reduction by producing more energy and food. Such activity would in turn have the effect of fostering the problem by producing more particles, a positive feedback. On the other hand, technology might be changed to reduce the particle production and provide a negative feedback.

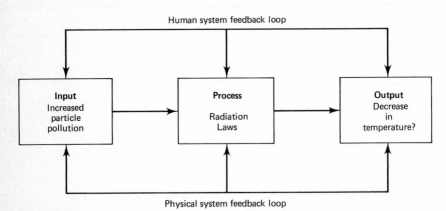

Figure 12-1 Flow diagram of changes in an environmental system with feedback loops. In this system a change in the things put into the atmosphere, such as increased pollution, affects the temperature through the process of the radiation balance. The pollution may cause more energy to be held in the atmosphere, thereby increasing the temperature. If such a temperature change occurs, people may choose to reduce the amount of pollution they put into the atmosphere.

In the physical system a positive feedback would result from decreased temperature causing a diminishing of vegetation ground cover. This would expose more of the earth's surface to wind erosion and thereby increase the amount of dust particles in the atmosphere. Conversely in those areas where a decrease in temperature would result in a reduction of water evaporated from the earth's surface, the vegetation cover would increase. This would diminish the amount of surface exposed to wind erosion and decrease the amount of dust particles in the atmosphere. Of course both positive and negative feedback loops occur simultaneously and we must weigh each against the other. Analysis and prediction in these kinds of problems must be firmly based in both social and physical-biological sciences.

THE GEOGRAPHY OF AIR POLLUTION AND INADVERTENT WEATHER MODIFICATION

In this discussion we will deal with both air pollution and weather modification. The term "air pollution" refers to natural or man-made substances which are put into the air as a result of man's activities. These substances singly or in combination may produce adverse aesthetic, economic, or biological effects in the environment. Common air pollutants are such things as sulphur dioxide (SO_2), carbon monoxide (CO), oxides of nitrogen, carbon dioxide (CO_2), dust, lead, asbestos, mercury, hydrocarbons, and other particles of various compositions. Weather modification, on the other hand, refers to a change in one of the elements we use to define weather. These factors are such things as temperature, precipitation, or solar radiation. Quite often air pollutants are thought to be causal factors in weather modification. Thus our division is to a certain extent artificial. Nevertheless it is important to keep in mind that air pollutants often have a direct effect on the environment without modifying the weather.

The concepts of site and situation are basic to our understanding the geography of air pollution. Surface configuration, or topography, is the most important site feature. When a place is level and at an equal or greater elevation than the surrounding area, light winds are able to remove air pollutants easily. Places such as valleys, mountain basins, and other depressions in the surface of the earth often help bring about an accumulation of air contaminants. It is possible for such site conditions to cause major disasters, euphemistically called "episodes."

Site characteristics caused two of the major air pollution disasters experienced by mankind. In 1930 air pollution in the Meuse River Valley of France killed at least sixty people. In 1948 in the Monongahela Valley at Donora, Pennsylvania, seventeen people were killed and 40 percent of the population made ill. Both cases resulted from air pollutants being trapped in the river valley by a low-lying temperature inversion.

Studies of the situation factor in air pollution indicate that distance is often the most important variable. Distance can be measured in the traditional ways of linear standards or in time. In some studies of air pollution an adequate measure of distance from sources of pollutants is the level of pollutant concentration observable at a given place. Consider pollution coming from a single source and whose dispersion is not affected by anything other than distance. George Woodwell irradiated an oak and pine forest with a single radioactive source. Within six months five concentric zones in the vegetation were established. Each zone had a particular type of vegetation, depending on the strength of the radiation. The vegetation ranged from only moss and lichens close to the source to an almost undisturbed forest in zone five.[1] It can be argued that air pollutants which have adverse effects on life would show the same patterns if the distance from the source were the only variable. Obviously the pattern follows the distance-decay model discussed in the first chapter of this book.

However, the situation of most places is more complicated than the simple distance-decay model. Because wind currents are the primary vehicle for the dispersion of air pollutants, we should expect the same distance-decay pattern to occur only if winds of equal strength were to blow from all directions with equal frequency. This is a very unusual situation. Rather, we expect some type of asymmetrical pattern based on the dominance of a certain wind direction and speed.

The concept of spatial interaction can also be used in examining problems of air pollutions. For example, the mean net flow of air across the United States is from west to east. Thus air entering the country along the West Coast is relatively free from pollutants. However, our West Coast cities, notably Los Angeles, add substances to the air. Part of this burden is removed as the air crosses the mountains. Minor yet substantial amounts of pollutants are added by Las Vegas, Salt Lake City, and Denver. East of Denver pollution levels again subside until the wastes of Kansas City and St. Louis are added. Thereafter, Great Lakes and East Coast industrial centers add their contributions. Pollutants from these centers produce the highest average, as well as the highest peak concentrations, of pollution in the nation. This mass of dirty air then moves out over the Atlantic. Its effects are visible several hundred miles out to sea.

This is an example of being located downwind from major pollution sources on a continental scale. We can, however, work at even a larger scale. Recent investigations have shown that the North Atlantic Ocean is rapidly becoming "dirty." There has been a large increase in particulate concentrations over the ocean. This pollution originates in North American cities. In a similar manner Greenland experiences unusually high concentrations of airborne precipitated lead. It seems very likely that the source of this lead is North America (leaded

[1] G. M. Woodwell, "Effects of Pollution on the Structure and Physiology of Ecosystems," *Science*, vol. 168, pp. 429-433, 1970.

gasolines?). Apparently the great low-pressure cells that cause much of the weather in North America concentrate our effluent over the North Atlantic and the northern islands.

It is clear that the level of air pollution, or pollution of any kind, in any given place is basically dependent upon its proximity to sources of pollution. It is becoming very difficult to find any places marginally located with regard to the nodes of pollution.

Naturally the location of place is time-specific; that is to say, its situation varies from time to time. In discussions of circulation systems geographers often refer to "periodized activity," that is, activity concentrated at a certain time. This notion helps us understand why more people are not killed in air pollution disasters. We have seen that most of the problems are created when persistent temperature inversions trap air pollutants beneath them. Fortunately these phenomena are not very common, and they eventually break up; that is, they are periodized. However, we cannot take comfort in the rarity of persistent inversions. Inversions occur on many mornings, although they often disappear within a few hours. The inversion is often created by dense cold air draining toward the bottom of a valley at night. This produces a situation where cold air lies beneath warm air. Although these frequent but short-lived inversions do not lead to major disasters, they do contribute to levels of pollutants which may have adverse long-term effects.

The scale at which a geographer looks at air pollution and weather modification determines the questions he asks and the answers he finds. As the relevant data are aggregated into larger and larger groups, the desirable facts and questions about the processes change. We can look at air pollution at three different scales: micro, meso, and macro or global.

MICROSCALE

Individual air pollutants and their combinations are of primary concern at the microscale. At this scale we ask questions about the type of pollutant an individual encounters as he moves through various environments. While the number of possible contaminants one could encounter is almost limitless, the following examples are the most important.

Water vapor is perhaps the most commonly seen air "pollutant" in urban areas. Often the great billowing masses of vapor seen rising from industrial plants contain nothing more than water. Although visibility may be reduced in some places, such releases of water vapor have no known adverse effects on health.

Carbon monoxide (CO) is one of the most common by-products of the incomplete combustion in automobiles. Carbon monoxide is quite toxic to animals because it has an affinity for oxygen and because it will reduce the oxygen carrying capacity of blood if it is inhaled. As is the case with most air pollutants, carbon monoxide is most dangerous to those suffering from chronic heart and lung disease. Prolonged contact with nonlethal doses of carbon monoxide is more of a problem. Drivers in central cities, traffic control policemen, and tunnel workers frequently complain of a reduced reaction speed and timing, as well as low-grade nausea and chronic headaches.

While the burning of coal and petroleum fuels are the most common sources of sulfur dioxide (SO_2), space heating, electric power generation, and solid waste incineration cause most of the SO_2 pollution. In moist atmospheric conditions the SO_2 and H_2O combine to produce sulfuric acid (H_2SO_4). The combination of sulfur and sulfuric acid can seriously affect life and property. In human beings SO_2 increases the airway resistance, while H_2SO_4 mist attaches to airborne particles and penetrates deep into lung tissue. Difficulty in breathing, chronic bronchitis, and other lung diseases are common nonfatal results of SO_2 pollution. It has been estimated that deaths in Chicago could be reduced by 800 per year if SO_2 pollution could be reduced to one-fifth of its present quantity.

High temperatures, such as those occurring in automobiles, often force a combination of nitrogen and oxygen. The various nitrogen oxides begin an intense and complicated series of photochemical reactions which account for many pollutants. Nitrogen dioxide (NO_2) absorbs ultraviolet light and begins a series of reactions which result in four major pollutants: (1) nitric acid, which has many of the same effects as sulfuric acid; (2) perooxyacetl/nitrate (PAN), which can have adverse effects on the young leaves of many plants and can irritate the eyes; (3) ozone (O_3), a toxic gas which in low concentrations decreases breathing capacity, injures leaves, weakens fabrics, and attacks rubber, and which at high concentrations may induce pulmonary edema and hemorrhage, drastically reducing the gas exchange capacity of the lungs; and (4) aerosols, which reduce visibility and act as catalysts to form other exotic pollutants.

Lead is another airborne contaminant. In sufficient quantity it can interfere with growth of red blood cells, damage the liver and kidneys, cause mental retardation, and contribute to abnormalities of fertility and pregnancy. Not a great deal is known about the effects of airborne lead. However, the possible effects are so severe that utmost caution is required.

The most common air pollutants are particles. They are caused by volcanoes, agricultural practices, thermal electric generating plants, fertilizer manufacturing plants, steel mills, cement plants, refineries, automobiles, and several other activities that put dust into the atmosphere. The size of the particles varies greatly and is most dependent upon the kind of generating process and the air pollution control devices used. No control device removes 100 percent of the particles produced. The particles remain in the atmosphere from a few minutes to up to two or three weeks.

The effects of particulate pollution at the microscale level range from annoying to dangerous. Suspended particles can and do substantially reduce visibility. As they settle out, particles soil objects causing increased cleaning costs. Particles can absorb relatively large amounts of hydrocarbons and acid, some of which have been found to cause cancer in laboratory experiments on rats. Finally, particulate pollution contributes to the discomfort of people with respiratory diseases. In addition, it is likely that particulates are a major contributing agent to lung ailments.

Such is the variety of dangers a person may encounter in his own living space. The degree to which an individual experiences air pollution depends on the location of his personal space, its site and situation. There is a great difference between a personal circulation system centered in a slum downwind from a steel mill and one centered in the far upwind suburbs of the same city.

MESOSCALE

Urban areas are the clearest example of inadvertent weather modification as well as the prime source area of air contaminants. In cities, concentrations of man, his activities, and his interactions produce waste products and cause alterations of the earth's surface. As a result, the entire range of atmospheric alterations is often found in every city. Table 12-1 summarizes the known climatic alteration made by urban areas. Clearly, substantial changes can occur, and the changes in temperature and precipitation warrant close study.

The central part of the city often experiences temperatures somewhat higher than those in the surrounding rural area. The maximum difference usually occurs at night and in early morning. The degree of difference depends upon several factors of site and situation, the most important of which are wind speed, atmospheric stability, cloud cover, the size of the city, and the season of the

Table 12-1 Climate Alterations in Cities*

CLIMATIC ELEMENT	COMPARISON WITH RURAL AREA
Clouds	5 to 10% more
Fog, winter	100% more
Fog, summer	30% more
Precipitation, total	5 to 10% more
Precipitation, days with less than 0.2 in.	10% more
Temperature	0 to 15°F warmer, especially at night

*After Landsberg.

year. Under extreme conditions the difference in temperature can amount to 15 to 20° F.

The two primary causes of urban-rural temperature differences, or heat islands, are seasonal. During the summer the city's geometry and thermal capacity contribute to the heat island. When the sun is high in the sky, solar radiation penetrates into the canyonlike city streets. There it is absorbed by the surface of the streets and the building walls. Man-made structures generally have low heat capacities, and heat diffuses through them rapidly. As a result heat is stored in the city. This heat is then released as rapidly as it was stored, and thus air temperatures rise. In addition, energy stored at the surface of the earth is usually converted into sensible heat, or latent heat, by evaporating water. Because a city is dry, most of the energy arriving at street level is converted into sensible heat. This of course contributes to the heat island.

Heat generated by human activity is the primary source of energy for the heat island during the winter. The quantity of heat generated by all the activities of the city ranges from an amount equal from one-sixth to one-third of the incoming solar radiation. By the turn of the century human activity in New York is expected to produce an amount of heat equal to one-half the energy coming from the winter sun![2]

Several other factors add to the formation of the heat island. Pollution tends to lie like a blanket over cities and concentrate near the city center. This mixture of particulates and aerosols readily absorbs energy radiated by the surface and then re-radiates it back to the earth. At the surface it is again transformed into sensible heat. To make matters worse, the frictional drag on air movements tends to be greater in urban areas. This decreases wind speed which reduces the ventilation of the city, thus inhibiting the movement of cool rural air into the central part of the city.

The heat island poses problems in our environment. During calm summer nights the heat island may exceed the temperature in the surrounding areas by 10°F, making an otherwise comfortable evening oppressive. In addition the heat island includes a circulation system that causes air to move upward over the city center out to the suburbs, then downward back along the surface toward the central city. Such a circulation system may significantly alter the distribution of pollutants and lead to a larger area of degraded air. Finally, the presence of several large hot spots on the surface of the earth may have an effect on the climate of the world—an effect which is, as yet, unknown.

The changes in the amounts and distribution of precipitation induced by cities are difficult to document because of very short and incomplete records. In

[2] R. T. Jaske, J. F. Fletcher, and K. R. Wise, "A National Estimate of Public and Industrial Heat Rejection Requirements by Decades through the Year 2000 A.D.," paper presented at the 67th National Meeting of the American Institute of Chemical Engineers, Atlanta, Ga., Feb. 17, 1970.

general we know that cities tend to have greater annual precipitation and more days of rain, thunderstorms, and hail. Cities may trigger excessive rain. Snowfall may be increased in small- and moderate-sized cities but decreased in large ones.[3] Apparently as air pollution increases, weather modification takes place at an increasing rate and poses problems of great concern.

MACROSCALE

Pollution in the form of the increasing CO_2 concentration in the atmosphere is probably the most discussed aspect of inadvertent weather modification on the global scale. CO_2 forms only a minute fraction of the atmosphere, about 0.03 percent by volume. Furthermore there are substantial time and space variations in the concentration. CO_2 is a very effective absorber of radiation from the earth's surface and thus plays a fundamental role in determining the temperature of the earth. The temperature should rise as the CO_2 concentration increases and fall as the concentration decreases. In the past few decades the CO_2 concentration has increased by some 15 percent.

Atmospheric CO_2 increase has been held responsible for the rise in the mean earth temperature of some 0.5°C from 1850 to 1940. There is some doubt as to the sources of this increase. Many people point to the burning of fossil fuels as the main source, while others believe that the oxidation of peat bogs and soil humus, as well as the clearing of land for farms, are most important. Whatever the cause, CO_2 is increasing, and the increase is likely to have an effect on the world's climate.

The temperature increase on a global basis gave considerable support to the theories of climatic change based on variations in CO_2 concentrations. However, since 1940 and especially since 1950, the global average temperature has fallen by about 0.2°C. What then of our concern about CO_2 pollution? Are theories of environmental alteration involving carbon dioxide incorrect? Are other factors intervening? Unfortunately there are no clear answers to these questions, although there is plenty of speculation. We cannot assume, however, that the lack of knowledge about the effect of CO_2 means that we can ignore it. Pollution whose effects are unknown must be considered most dangerous.

Atmospheric pollution by particles is often cited as a counterbalance to CO_2 pollution. Several scientists argue that the increased opaqueness of the atmosphere caused by an increase in the amount of particulate pollution can very effectively reverse any trend due to CO_2 concentration. It has been argued that a worldwide increase in turbidity of only 3 to 4 percent would have the same effect as the 15 percent increase in CO_2. It is possible that increased particle

---

[3] S. A. Changnon, Jr., "Recent Studies of Urban Effects on Precipitation in the United States," *Bulletin*, American Meteorological Society, vol. 50, pp. 411-427, 1969.

pollution can result in atmospheric warming if the particles absorb more energy than they reflect back out of the atmosphere to space.

The geographical concept of scale is fundamental to studies of air pollution. We must always try to have all spatial elements of the problem in mind when attempting to find solutions. Using defined areas for pollution abatement based on physical or political boundaries has been successful in many instances, particularly in watershed management. However, the atmosphere is notably inattentive to the regions we construct, especially the small region known as the "airshed," or a place's immediate source of atmosphere. The worldwide distribution of DDT and lead is prime evidence for questioning the regional approach to air pollution abatement.

It may not seem strange that DDT residues are widely dispersed because DDT is used all over the world, and it is notably persistent as well as toxic. However, there is evidence indicating long-distance transport of DDT by the atmosphere. For example, DDT concentrations of 170 parts per trillion have been observed over the British Isles. This is obviously a small amount, but two things must be kept in mind. First, the location of the British Isles provides some circumstantial evidence for long-distance transport from North America. Second, 170 parts per trillion is equivalent to one ton per inch of rain, or an average for the British Isles of 40 tons of DDT falling per year.

Observations made in the Barbados indicate the presence of North African dust. The DDT residue on this dust provides strong evidence for long-distance transport. Thus the atmosphere can transport pollutants and agents of macroscopic weather modification great distances. Therefore the airshed or other small area may be an ineffective basic unit for pollution control. We must consider what kinds and amounts of pollutants others dump into our common atmospheric circulation system. We must know our location in the world.

We have seen how the concepts of geography can be applied to the problem of air pollution and weather modification. Obviously there is a great deal of detail about these problems that we have not considered. However, a place's location, its site and situation, as well as the scale at which we examine the problems, are of overriding importance.

ENVIRONMENTAL PERCEPTION AND ENVIRONMENTAL QUALITY

Important as these concepts of geography are to studies of air pollution and inadvertent weather modification, all studies are premised on man's perception of and attitudes toward his environment. The importance of environmental perception in the cultural landscape has been discussed elsewhere. It is equally significant in the consideration of problems relating to the physical environment. Air pollution must be perceived by humans before it becomes a problem. The mere sensory experience of pollutants does not mean a problem has been recognized. The sensory experience must be interpreted according to one's perception of the environment and his relation to it.

Most contemporary discussions about air pollution as well as other environmental problems involve two opposing philosophies which in turn condition attitudes toward the environment and environmental problems. For simplicity, we can label one of these "man as master of nature" and the other "man as part of nature."

The origins in Western culture of the man-as-master-of-nature theme are obscure. It is, however, implied in Biblical accounts of the creation and the fall of man. Biblical admonitions to master and use the earth may have been used by some as a rationale for greatly altering the face of the earth. Nevertheless, the Bible contains several admonitions and pieces of advice such as love your neighbor, do not kill, and forgive your enemies, all of which have been consistently ignored. Therefore it is difficult to see why the man-as-master-of-nature theme could have been carried out with such singular success. It is more likely, however, that the pervasiveness of this idea stems from man's intense self-interest. This combination has resulted in the term "natural resource": that is, any part of the earth's crust deemed useful to man. Associated with these beliefs are individual freedom, free will, capitalism, social mobility, and the consideration of water and air as free goods.

The second theme, that of man as a dependent segment of nature, as only one of many species and life forms, is pleasing to those of us who have forgotten the hardships of searching for our daily sustenance. We remember only good times. However, being a part of nature means acting in accordance with nature's rule. It is hardly fashionable today to regard nature as a brutish, bloody, and complex contest for survival in which no individual can win. Instead, we read of a self-regulating, symbiotic concert consisting of beautiful cycles. Yet in the midst of this harmony, many plants manufacture substances toxic to others of their own species. Irritating if not deadly defense mechanisms exist. Well-developed territorial and social taboos abound. Evidence of free will is difficult to find in nature.

The state of being human implies a disassociation from nature. The very acts of using fire and manufacturing clothing and conscious cultural adaption to different environmental settings set man apart from other biotic populations in any given ecosystem, if only because of his disproportionate ability to alter an ecosystem. Most of us, nevertheless, find it pleasurable to view environments which manifest harmonious, symbiotic cooperation between man and nature. In any case, although man seems to be unique in nature, one should not conclude that man does not need nature, nor should one assume that man can adapt quickly enough to survive the threats to mind and body that are inherent in the environments he has created.

Our perception of the environment, then, dictates the kinds of concerns we have about it. For example, in natural hazard research, nature is viewed as a source of threats to the very life and welfare of mankind. Drought and floods, extreme heat and cold, all can destroy life and livelihood. Man tries to anticipate, confront, and even eliminate these dangers. Much time and money is spent predicting if, when, and how much rain will fall. Our most rapid communications are used to warn populations of tornadoes. River channels are deepened, widened, lined with concrete, and diverted to spare us the scourge of flood. Many of us fondly look forward to the day when earthquakes, tornadoes, and hurricanes will fall to the intellect and technology of man. Still others dream of protecting man from nature in great domed cities.

ENVIRONMENTAL PERCEPTION AND ECOLOGICAL THEORY

Many people regard man as a hazard to nature and consider his activities in the context of general ecological theory. At present the limited body of ecological theory consists of only two general statements: the theory of diversity and the theory of dominance. According to the theory of diversity, ecosystems, communities, and other functional organizations are most successful in perpetuating themselves and withstanding foreseeable and unforeseeable stresses and disasters when they are made up of a wide variety of species, that is, when they are diverse. Conversely, a simple ecosystem with a relatively small number of species and environmental niches is much more likely to be seriously disrupted by stress even if comparatively minor.

In ecological theory, dominance takes two forms: those dominants which are limited to specific environmental niches and those which can flourish in a variety of niches. Dominance implies the appropriation of niches by a particular species and the exclusion of other species. When this happens, ecosystems are simplified. Man is a general dominant. He is the only species that is able to occupy the full range of environmental situations. In many cases the "natural" mix of species, including dominants, have been replaced by man and his works, for example in urban areas and the agricultural regions of the world. The result has been a great simplification of ecosystems. Thus the natural ecosystems have become more fragile and susceptible to natural or man-induced stress.

In addition to species which are able to occupy exclusively one or more niches over a considerable area, there are some essential species. These are not dominant in the usual sense, but perform tasks that are necessary to the well-being of other species. Specialized bacteria and other microflora and microfauna are prime examples of these species. Man as a dominant species must be aware of these essential species and ensure their survival.

CONCLUSION

Even though people view the world and their relation to it in different frameworks, we all must understand the effect we have both as individuals and as groups on the environment. Part of this necessary understanding can be attained by directing the questions of geography at elements and processes in the environment. Obviously other questions must be asked to get a complete picture. In the final analysis, questions of air pollution, inadvertent weather modification, environmental quality, and man's place in the environment are very personal. After examining the potential effects man's actions can have on the earth, each person must decide his own philosophy, man as a part of nature or man as master of nature.

PART FIVE

FUTURE SPACE: THE INFLUENCE OF COMMUNICATIONS

The geography of communications is a field of study which has been little explored, but offers important insights into the spatial organization of our society. Scholars have noted the paradox that mankind seems to be becoming more homogeneous in life-style and cultural traits (perhaps most frequently exemplified by the ubiquitous Coca-Cola sign or the use of Americanisms such as "drive-in" or "parking lot" in foreign languages), and yet at the same time it treasures cultural differences. Thus, for example, while the Midwestern dialect of English becomes spread through the United States by way of television, there are at the same time increasing demands for the study of the history and characteristics of ethnic subcultures in our colleges and universities. The following essay, "Monoculture or Miniculture: The Impact of Communications Media on Culture in Space," deals with the complex spatial aspects of this dual trend and achieves a piercing analysis of the effect not only of the mass media, but also of what the author refers to as "minicommunications."

The essay differs from those in previous sections, for it concerns "space" measured not in miles, but rather in information or intensity of communication. The distance metric is neither effort nor time, but the understanding and willingness, or propensity, to exchange ideas.

The essay is important not only for the perspective it gives us on current conflicts concerning cultural unity or diversity, but also for the implications its message contains on our whole concept of space. As you read this essay, see if you can arrive at an answer to the author's question: more unity or more diversity?

CHAPTER THIRTEEN

MONOCULTURE OR MINICULTURE?*

The Impact of
Communications
Media on Culture in Space

RONALD F. ABLER

The paradox of our time is that humanity is becoming simultaneously more unified and more fragmented.

Zbigniew Brzezinski

Communications media are the most potent space-adjusting techniques that man commands, and their increasingly intensive use will inevitably affect human spatial behavior and the behavioral regions (culture and subculture realms) with which cultural geographers concern themselves. We normally assume that communications promote cultural and spatial homogenization. But careful examination of ongoing and probable future developments in communications suggests that media innovations may promote cultural diversity and spatial differentiation.

Isolation from other groups in geographical space is the strongest force promoting cultural diversity. The absence of interaction with different peoples reinforces and preserves culture traits. The isolation of the Georgia and South Carolina Sea Islands, for example, has preserved the continuity of the Senegambian and Congo-Angolan culture of the blacks who were brought there as slaves almost three hundred years ago.[1] If a cultural or subcultural group can avoid

---

[1] John F. Szwed, "Africa Lies Just Off Georgia," *Africa Report*, October 1970, pp. 29-31.

contact with dissimilar peoples, it can remain distinct or become even more unique. Closed information pools produce cultural differences.

We would expect that a process of spatial interaction like communication would reduce differences among groups because it can destroy the isolation upon which cultural diversities depend. Indeed, the global communication patterns which developed with European expansion have reduced the amount of cultural diversity in the world. Languages, religions, and even peoples have disappeared with the direct and indirect effects of Western global control and the elimination of isolation by Western communication and transportation technology. A prominent political strategist speaks of the "global city."[2] A popular social commentator describes "The Demise of Geography," assuming that "place . . . is no longer a primary source of diversity."[3]

Yet despite tremendous increases in information flows, cultural differences among peoples and places are not dissolving as fast as we might expect. There are even indications that groups are becoming more unlike. We encounter new self-consciousness and militance among formerly docile groups, while new groups form along regional, ethnic, age, and other lines. Brzezinski writes of the global city, but is worried about global ghettos.[4] Toffler thinks we are experiencing nothing less than an explosion in the number of "subcults."[5]

Such contradictory evidence and continued evidence of differentiation amid homogenization make it clear that the effects of communications technology on cultures and their spatial arrangements are more complicated than we thought. To get some idea of what the spatial pattern of cultures will be like in the future we must examine the effects of different communications media more carefully than we have in the past.

COMMUNICATIONS MEDIA AND CULTURE

Communications media can be cross-classified into mass and interpersonal media, and into formal and informal categories of each (Fig. 13-1). Formal mass media usually require prepared channels and are essentially one-way information delivery systems. Few people act as senders in the mass media; most people can only receive what the few transmit.

Until recently, there were no informal mass media. Now facsimile technology permits everyone to be his own publisher, and the success of the underground press, theater, and cinema in the last decade indicates that democratization of those media is underway.

Interpersonal media allow two-way communications. The average person can be a sender as well as a receiver of information. The informal interpersonal

[2] Zbigniew Brzezinski, *Between Two Ages: America's Role in the Technetronic Era*, Viking, New York, 1970, p. 19.
[3] Alvin Toffler, *Future Shock*, Random House, New York, 1970, p. 84.
[4] Brzezinski, op. cit., p. 35.
[5] Toffler, op. cit., p. 252.

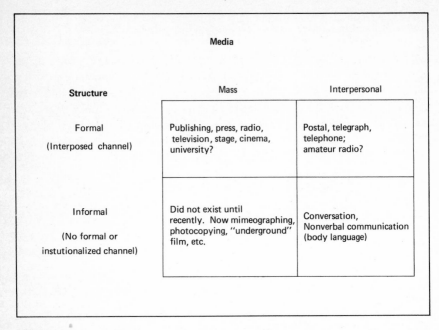

Figure 13-1   Cross-classification of communications media. Means of communication can be classified by two criteria: *media*, either mass or interpersonal, and *structure*, either formal or informal. Therefore, telephones are interpersonal and formal, while photocopy publication is mass and informal.

media are the most ubiquitous of the lot, whereas the formal interpersonal media are for the most part used only in economically advanced nations.

Mass media, especially formal mass media, promote homogenization. Messages flow from the few to the many, making receivers more like the senders. Interpersonal media promote differentiation. Messages can flow from many to many, and because people tend to address interpersonal messages to other people like themselves, interpersonal channels reinforce differences.

Contemporary mass media seem to make homogenization inevitable. Regional dialects disappear as "correct" speech patterns are learned from the mass media.[6] Exposure on national network programs makes slang phrases instantly ubiquitous, and national advertising promotes uniform tastes and patterns of consumption. Media coverage of events such as the Apollo moon landings can knit much of the world into a single audience:

[6] "Talking Like A Native," *Newsweek*, Mar. 9, 1970.

Global circulation of cultural styles and artifacts, through new forms of communication and distribution, has engendered shared attitudes and experiences in their use. Interpenetrating and diffusing through locally diverse cultures, these common elements form part of a transnational (that is planetary) culture.[7]

National and planetary cultures, however, may be transitory. It is becoming apparent that the mass media have peaked in importance. Innovations in communications technology indicate the development of sophisticated interpersonal media that Gumpert calls "mini-comm."[8] The costs of acquiring or using mass media channels are dropping rapidly at the same time that capacity is expanding and costs are dropping in the formal interpersonal media. As a result, smaller and smaller audiences with increasingly more specialized tastes can be reached with mini-media.

The evolution of mini-comm is most easily seen in printing, where individualization has been evident for decades. There now exist tens of thousands of specialized periodicals devoted to almost every conceivable interest and topic. In addition to local newspapers and regional editions of magazines, the "underground" press now includes some two hundred papers with an estimated six million readers and its own wire service. Even books are now custom-made. Publishers will produce a book if as few as one hundred sales are guaranteed, and the day of the complete do-it-yourself book in which each individual book's contents can be prescribed or chosen is not far distant.[9]

The broadcast media are also becoming more flexible. Whereas there were 32 black-oriented radio stations in the United States in 1956, there were 130 in 1970.[10] The American Broadcasting Company now offers advertisers four demographically distinct networks, claiming that "any resemblance to traditional radio networks is purely coincidental."[11] The capacity of such media to reach small groups has been constrained by technical limitations in broadcasting and by high equipment costs. Existing and future innovations will greatly lower costs, bypass technical limitations, and thereby make *narrowcasting* possible.

Foremost among the innovations that will make small-group narrowcasting viable is Community Antenna Television (CATV). CATV originally served isolated places where television reception was impossible without centralized antenna facilities. Soon, however, CATV began to penetrate markets already served by one or more television stations, and the innovation has been diffusing up the

---

[7] John McHale, *The Future of the Future*, Braziller, New York, 1969, p. 270.

[8] Gary Gumpert, "The Rise of Mini-Comm," *Journal of Communications*, vol. 20, no. 3, pp. 280-290, September 1970.

[9] Billy Rojas, "The Textbook of the Future," *School and Society*, vol. 99, no. 2,334, pp. 315-317, Summer 1971.

[10] *Broadcasting Yearbook/Markets, 1956 and 1965: Spot Radio Rates and Data*, Oct. 1, 1970.

[11] *Newsweek*, Mar. 29, 1971, p. 91.

nation's urban hierarchy since 1949. By the early seventies, CATV was entering the largest metropolitan areas.[12]

CATV provides between thirty and sixty (depending on the kind of equipment used) television channels, as contrasted with the twelve available on the UHF broadcast band. With CATV, the cost of providing each channel drops enormously. Once the cable network is installed, the cost of each additional channel is simply the cost of another television camera. CATV thus permits programming flexibility which is impossible in broadcast television.

Whereas a local broadcaster may not be able to justify programming aimed just at ballet enthusiasts, or the local Negro community, or aficionados of sports cars, a regional or even a national cable network might be developed which could enhance its appeal significantly through such specialized programming.[13]

CATV systems are starting to narrowcast high school football and basketball games, city council meetings, and numerous other events which cannot be broadcast because they appeal only to small, often highly localized groups.[14] Soon we can expect two-way transmission capability and switching capacity to be available in local, regional, and even national CATV networks, making it possible for anyone to be his own television producer for an audience of any size, just as facsimile technology makes it possible for anyone to be his own publisher.

The evolution of such specialized media is not wholly unprecedented. Foreign-language newspapers and ethnic radio programming were once commonplace elements of American mass communications. But the ability to reach *very small* groups at low cost and, even more importantly, the ability of *anyone* to act as a sender of information will be unprecedented. Such capabilities are eliminating meaningful distinctions between mass and interpersonal media, and formal and informal channels.

People normally prefer to communicate with people like themselves. Interpersonal and informal mass media have helped differentiate people into distinct groups by reinforcing their respective attitudes and information sets. Because media innovations make the traditional mass media more like interpersonal media, we can expect them to promote cultural differentiation. Besides facilitating the intensification of age, life-style, income, ethnic, and other groupings, communications media also make it increasingly difficult to achieve national political consensus by promoting a politics of confrontation among such groups.[15]

[12] E. Stratford Smith, "The Emergence of CATV: A Look at the Evolution of a Revolution," *Proceedings of the I.E.E.E.*, vol. 58, no. 7, pp. 967-982, July 1970.
[13] Nicholas Johnson, *How to Talk Back to Your Television Set*, Bantam, New York, 1970, p. 144.
[14] Ibid., p. 145.
[15] Herbert E. Alexander, "Communications and Politics: The Media and the Message," *Law and Contemporary Problems*, vol. 34, no. 2, pp. 276-277, Spring 1969.

The new media themselves, then, contain an important bias of communication which will probably promote greater cultural and subcultural diversity in the future. The democratization of communications is the revolutionary change which may make communications a differentiating rather than a homogenizing force. The effect of minicommunication and improved interpersonal communication will be to make society more individualized in its interests and tastes.[16]

SPATIAL POSSIBILITIES AND PROBABILITIES

How this increasing cultural diversity will be organized in space remains unclear. The same advances in communications that enhance diversity also eliminate the necessity for groups to agglomerate in space to maintain cohesion and distinct identity. Whether increased cultural diversity necessarily implies increased spatial diversity remains to be seen.

Without distinct territories cultures usually perish quickly. Even homeless groups like the Jews survived only in the pseudohomelands provided by the urban and rural ghettos they occupied between the Diaspora and 1949. The inability of cultural or subcultural groups to survive without a distinct territory leads us to equate the two. We think cultures have to have territories and that regions must have distinct cultures. Traditionally, spatial proximity has been the only settlement pattern that permitted the intense contact needed to preserve cultural distinctness.

McLuhan feels that the media have created a tribal world and that the United States will "break up into a series of regional and racial ministates."[17] Tribal existence is predicated on a land base.[18] Geographers and interpreters of current events have recently noted strident demands for "government by turf" in urban areas. Many North American cities are divided into distinct tribal turfs, more or less immune from control by central government.[19] Ethnic, racial, and other groups are now moving to provide social and educational services for themselves. At the same time, they demand greater control over those services provided by governments in their turfs. There is evidence, then, that increased cultural diversity implies greater spatial diversity.

Alternatively, many small groups now forming and reinforcing their respective differences are nonplace communities. "Swinging Singles" can plug into likeminded groups equally well in Miami, San Francisco, St. Paul, or Chicago. Similarly, the interests of a Harlem black militant and a Watts black militant in

---

[16]Ithiel de Sola Pool, "Social Trends," *Science and Technology*, vol. 76, pp. 87-101, April 1968.
[17]Gumpert, op. cit., pp. 284-285.
[18]Vine Deloria, Jr., *Custer Died for Your Sins: An Indian Manifesto*, Avon, New York, 1969, p. 230.
[19]James E. Vance, Jr., "Land Assignment in the Precapitalist, Capitalist and Post Capitalist City," *Economic Geography*, vol. 42, no. 2, April 1971, p. 119; Stewart Alsop, "It Would Not Be Fun," *Newsweek*, May 17, 1971, p. 116.

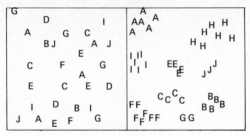

Figure 13-2   Future spatio-cultural alternatives. Entropic Homogeneity Differentiation, spatial entropy (no clear region) as opposed to a high organized space with many regions. Communications media can promote an entropic spatial homogeneity as they can promote spatial differentiation. A, B, C, etc., represent members of different cultural or subcultural groups. Minicommunications media enable them to live in nonplace communities as easily as they could live in place-based communities.

advancing the cause of black people everywhere may be more important than their residence in two different ghettos. Melvin Webber noted the possibility of community without propinquity by way of communications, and the resulting existence of two kinds of communities: one kind is firmly rooted in place and neighborhood, while nonplace communities are independent of location, neighborhood, region, or even nation.[20] Mobility and electronic communications create nonplace communities composed of affluent, well-educated, specialized people who can afford high costs of mobility and communications. Place-based communities are organized around informal interpersonal communications and are composed of less affluent, less educated residents of inner-city neighborhoods (Fig. 13-2).

The scrambling of traditional media categories and the development of nonplace communities combine to make the spatio-cultural future cloudy. We observe increased local and regional sensitivity at the same time that we note the development of supraterritorial groups whose shared interests and values override the locations of individual members.[21] Advanced communications technology can keep members of nonplace communities in close touch with each other regardless of location.

The "wired city" model of the future illustrates the spatial ambiguity inherent in advanced minicommunications. It will soon be possible for residents of

[20]Melvin M. Webber and Carolyn C. Webber, "Culture, Territoriality and the Elastic Mile," in H. Wentworth Eldredge (ed.) V.I., *Taming Megalopolis,* Doubleday, New York, 1967, pp. 35-53.
[21]Eugene Jennings, "Mobicentric Man," *Psychology Today*, vol. 4, no. 2, July 1970, pp. 34-36.

a metropolis to receive and transmit all communications through a coaxial cable network. The increased ability to form nonplace communities of narrow interest will be counterbalanced by increased local and neighborhood programming. Reston, Virginia, for example, has already begun local programming over its CATV system.[22] Proposals have arisen to provide neighborhood and special-interest programming by way of CATV in metropolitan areas.[23] Truly flexible media can promote regional diversity just as easily as they can promote mixed homogeneity.

Moreover, the two are not mutually exclusive. Minicommunications can simultaneously promote nonplace interest communities and place-based residential communities composed of people with diverse interests. Individual geographers often develop both regional and systematic specialities and seem to derive no schizophrenia therefrom; there is no reason not to expect others to divide their attention between narrow topical specialities and local affairs. Indeed, a combination of global, nonplace interests and local, place-based concerns would be the best of all possible worlds.

Whether the spatio-cultural future is an entropic homogeneity, a bewildering diversity of place-based groups, or a pleasing and judicious combination of the two, minicommunications will be necessary conditions of each alternative. But minicommunications are not in themselves sufficient conditions for any of the alternatives. The bias of minicommunications seems to make the non-place-based model more probable, but the ultimate effects of such media depend on the uses to which societies *choose* to put them. If we choose to promote spatial diversity, we can do so, and conversely, if we choose to promote non-place-based interest groups, we shall no doubt see them develop even more rapidly than they are now. To refuse to govern these technologies by making self-conscious policy decisions about the spatio-cultural future we want is to choose by default the continuation of current trends.

SOME CAVEATS, SPATIAL AND OTHER

Communications media are powerful and thus potentially dangerous tools. One of the hazards inherent in minicommunications media is the complete disappearance of a broader cultural and political consensus.

There is a growing ease of creating groups having access to distinctly differing models of reality, without overlap. . . . Imagine a world in which there is a sufficient number of TV channels to keep each group, and in particular the less literate and tolerant members of the groups, wholly occupied. Will members of such groups ever again be able to talk meaningfully to one another? Will they

[22] Thomas Grubisich, "Reston to Begin Cable TV," *Washington Post*, June 18, 1970.
[23] "O.E.O. Rejects Cable TV Pleas for Kansas City, Mo.," *Telephony*, June 6, 1970, p. 59.

ever obtain at least some information through the same filters so that their images of reality will overlap to some degree?[24]

Small groups or even individuals could withdraw from all human contact except that which can be achieved through electonic media. Bradbury's *Fahrenheit 451* is a chilling fictional description of such a society.[25] It would be particularly ironic if *communications* media become the technology that creates a haunting, hollow isolation of tiny groups of individuals.

It should also be obvious that increased cultural diversity, whether place-based or not, carries with it an enormous potential for conflict. Human beings will apparently discriminate against one another over almost any perceived difference, no matter how artificial.[26] People are currently killing one another over race, language, religion, politics, economics, and often, it seems, out of sheer human cussedness. Increased differentiation will enrich the world immensely, but it will also create new distinctions that a species with our casual attitude toward fratricide might seize upon to make life miserable for every disparate group.

There exists a regrettable tendency to view communications as panacea. If only conflicting groups will communicate with each other, many say, they will surely resolve their differences. Such a view is naïve at best, and is more likely absolutely disastrous. We must confront the largely unexplored, but very real possibility that information flows among groups promote as much hatred as understanding. Communications are powerful social, political, and cultural forces, and it is wishful to think that they will not cause great local, regional, national, and international tensions.

Thus, others might profit from the experience of American cities. According to the Kerner Commission, "the communications media, ironically, have failed to communicate," leading to fractionalization of the urban polity and to civil strife.[27] And to the extent that the metropolis itself is a specialized communications medium,[28] it too has failed to generate the information flows necessary to create viable metropolitan communities. The failures of the media and the American metropolis have serious global implications. Metropolitan communications systems are good spatial analogs of national and international conditions some

[24] Paul Baran, "On the Impact of the New Communications Media upon Social Values," *Law and Contemporary Problems*, vol. 34, no. 2, p. 249, Spring 1969.

[25] Ray Bradbury, *Fahrenheit 451*, Ballantine, New York, 1953.

[26] Henri Tajfel, "Experiments in Intergroup Discrimination," *Scientific American*, pp. 96-102, November 1970.

[27] *Report of the National Advisory Commission on Civil Disorder*, Bantam, New York, 1968, p. 383.

[28] Richard L. Meier, *A Communications Theory of Urban Growth*, M.I.T., Cambridge, Mass., 1962.

decades later.[29] If the American metropolis is a good spatial model of the future, we face serious problems. We can expect Brzezinski's global city to be composed of many antagonistic global ghettos created by minicommunications.

[29] Ronald Abler, "The Geography of Intercommunications Systems: The Post Office and Telephone Systems in the United States," unpublished Ph.D. thesis, University of Minnesota, 1968.

PROSPECT

Location has many obvious effects on man's behavior, and it has been generally observed that the farther away a place is, the less likely one is to consider it a part of his world or "action space." We must decide on which measurements of separation are most appropriate in determining location: the simplest measurement is that of standard earth space, be it 100 miles or 10 feet. However, we have seen that the values or perceptions of the interval which separate persons or places is often more important than absolute physical distance. In addition, one is often more interested in the amount of effort necessary to overcome a separation than in the phsyical distance itself; thus, we live 30 minutes from downtown or $1500 from Kenya. One can also be located in another dimension: if one locates himself in a landscape of love and hate, one is closer to loved ones hundreds of miles away than to the despised neighbor next door.

In recent years, geographers have been faced with the question of defining the meaning of distance as it affects spatial decision making. It is obvious that interaction is much more seriously affected by the time-distance (how many minutes or hours separating individuals) than by the absolute linear distance (how many miles "as the crow flies"). But even time distance has been modified by electronic communications. How "far" are two persons from one another when they are talking on the telephone? We are faced with the challenge of placing persons in a space no longer measured in miles, hours, or dollars, and the traditional location theory must be modified to come to grips with the possibilities that communications may be substituted for transportation.

Developments in telecommunications technology have important implications. If total environmental and societal costs are not prohibitive, and if interpersonal communication can be immediate, inexpensive, and so "lifelike" that face-to-face contact is no longer necessary, the effects of absolute earth distance can be to a large extent negated. Although a great deal of speculation is possible, it is interesting to consider at least two of the possible effects of telecommunications technology on urban life.

First, we are probably all familiar with the principles by which the optimal site is selected for a manufacturing plant or a store. Essentially the objective of the Economic Man is to choose the site which minimizes transportation costs and maximizes profits. Further, we are aware of the increasingly important role of "quaternary economic activities," those economic activities based on the creation, transmission, and marketing of information, such as advertising, education, research, and data processing. Until recently, such activities have continued to be located in or near the central business district or near outlying places close to freeways, to facilitate the face-to-face exchanges which these activities seem to demand. It is quite apparent, however, that if telecommunications can be substituted for face-to-face meetings, the necessity for concentration would be much eliminated, and the quarternary activities could be dispersed to locations such as the mountains or the desert, as one prefers. Furthermore, there would be little necessity for workers to commute to any central office; business could be conducted through telecommunications from home. The effects of the streetcar on urban structure and the concentration of business in the central business district have been well documented. The effects of the automobile in decentralizing the city, weakening the dominance of the central business district, and encouraging freeway-oriented business and industry have also been much discussed. What will be the effects of telecommunications media on employment in the growing tertiary and quaternary sectors of the economy? The answer to this question has important implications on urban planning and development.

A second effect of our increasing dependence on telecommunications has been the expansion of "life space" for a large proportion of Americans. Not only are we aware of our home and immediate neighbors, but through rapid transportation, many of us have traveled widely in our state, nation, or even the world, and furthermore have experienced many different environments through television and other media. For a substantial and growing proportion of the population, our "community" has changed in its meaning. The concept of "community," formerly applied to those persons who lived near us and who also shared in our way of life, is now used to represent not only the local area but also those persons, regardless of place of residence, who share similar beliefs, goals, and activities, and who communicate directly or indirectly with one another. Our "community" is thus not merely our next-door neighbors; it is also a large population who have interests and beliefs in common, but who are scattered over a wide area. In the same sense, cities are no longer areas bounded by particular political limits, but include persons who live at great distances and who commute perhaps 100 miles or more to work, or who are merely attached to the city through the newspaper, televisions media, and attendance at special events such as professional football games or the opening of an art exhibit. Our communities are as wide as our interests and our contacts. In this context questions such as metropolitan-wide taxation and the meaning of the "neighborhood school" become relevant in a new sense. If the city extends to include all those in its "urban realm," then who indeed should support city parks, police, fire protection, and street improvements? Is not everyone within the urban realm the beneficiary of such services and thus responsible for their financial support? In the controversies over the neighborhood school we must again ask what is the "neighborhood" or "community." Is our neighborhood or community only those who live near us? Viewed another way, are those who live near us actually a part of our community or interest? Does not our neighborhood encompass the entire metropolitan area, or even a wider realm? Surely such questions must be investigated with the new as well as the old space metric.

The changing nature of distance and connectivity has serious implications for urban and national policy. Lags in adjustments to shrinking time distances due to improvements in transportation technology and the largely eliminated time and effort distances with developments in telecommunications media are apparent. Such industries as advertising agencies, which are highly dependent on exchange of information, maintain locations in the central city, and furthermore remain concentrated on a national scale in New York and to a lesser extent in Chicago. In addition, there are lags in the ways we think about urban problems, apparent in controversies over who will pay for which city services and which children are actually a part of particular school districts. These lags in adjustment should be indications of arenas where change is probable, and their recognition should have useful implications for policy implementation.

Finally, the importance of the environment is also undergoing some transformation. A traditional geographical concept that in Western thought was said to unify the discipline of geography was the concern with "areal differentiation," or the study of variations in the occurrence and combination of phenomena on the earth's surface. Although this tradition has been subjected to reformulation and modification in the past twenty years of American geography, a concern with the diversity of man's surroundings has remained central to geographic study. As the effects of physical space on "optimal" locational behavior decline, the quality of environment looms more and more important in explaining residential and economic localization. Thus, with rapid and nearly ubiquitous transportation available, location within the metropolitan area becomes far less important than the particular site for a house or business. With instantaneous communications, and further refinements in the "lifelike" quality of image reception, the importance of the quality of the site, or local environment, can only increase in its localizing effects.

The variety of ways in which man inhabits the earth, the extent and pattern of areal differentiation itself, has also been undergoing important modifications. Dual trends are apparent: we observe both an increasing divergence and an increasing convergence in man's economic and cultural behavior. Instant telecommunications make it possible for most of the world to be aware of a particular event or to be exposed to an innovation. However, an increasing divergence in cultural practices has been noted, often accompanied by pleas for ethnic unity, national or racial pride, and political power. It is therefore quite reasonable that eminent geographers have viewed the course of man's cultural development as following both paths of differentiation and convergence, and have viewed this development with both hopefulness and alarm:

The passing of the colonial era, while signifying political withdrawal, has not stopped the spread of Occidental culture. Quite to the contrary, the newly independent peoples need to develop their technology, economic organization, and social structure if they want to move forward. This means more, not less, Westernization. However, each country must fit the alien ideas, institutions, and gadgets into its own culture pattern. In doing this, the independent country has more freedom in choosing what to accept and what to reject than was possible under a colonial administration. Moreover, it is not even desirable that Western Culture, like a bulldozer, flatten out all that came before. The philosopher Alfred N. Whitehead puts it this way: "Diversification among human communities is essential for the provision of the incentive, and material for the Odyssey of the Human Spirit." *Other nations of different habits are not enemies: they are godsends. Men require of their neighbors something sufficiently akin to be understood, something sufficiently different to provoke attention, and something great enough to command admiration.*

Broek and Webb, *A Geography of Mankind*,
1968, pp. 498-499

Mankind went through a long series of eras during which biologic and cultural divergence took place to the end that mankind became a veritable congeries of differing societies practicing increasingly differing systems of culture. Most of human time on the earth fell within that broad trend of divergence: 1,999,500 years out of 2,000,000 years. Only for the last 500 years, in round terms, has mankind been on the other trend of convergence, and our heritage still is too clearly with us. It may take a while for mankind to come to terms with its own past and the problems of its future. Meanwhile the problems grow more urgent, and they must be solved in revolutionary steps, if man is to continue in the mastery of the Earth. Man now faces the responsibility of living up to the culture-creating creature he has become.

The sheer diversity of mankind is one of the major problems facing man today. In the twentieth century man must work at the procedures needed to bring his kind back toward the types of groupings that can live on the one earth which man has recognized the planet to be. . . .

Spencer and Thomas, *Cultural Geography*, 1969, p. 565

Increasing specialization or divergence and increasing opportunities for homogenization or convergence are alternatives available to modern man. Whether we will become more isolated in the face of ever-increasing technical opportunities for interpersonal contact, or whether we will make use of the communications media available to us to bring mankind closer together are questions which we must come to grips with.

INDEX

Page references in *italic* indicate figure or table; in **boldface**, indicate map.